FOREWORD

This report summarizes the efforts of twenty-four researchers on service efforts and accomplishments (SEA) reporting in twelve significant program areas of state and local government. After exploring the state of the art in SEA reporting in each program area, the researchers recommend specific indicators for external reporting. Those recommendations are intended to serve as a starting point for the continued development of SEA reporting.

This is the second report in the GASB's series of Research Reports on SEA reporting. The first, issued in November 1989, was a detailed report on elementary and secondary education. Within the next six months, the GASB expects to issue detailed reports on most of the eleven other areas covered in this Overview: colleges and universities, economic development programs, fire department programs, hospitals, mass transit, police department programs, public assistance programs, public health, road maintenance, sanitation collection and disposal, and water and wastewater treatment.

The GASB believes that SEA reporting will become a major element of governmental financial reporting, assisting in fulfilling government's duty to be publicly accountable and in enabling citizens, elected officials, and other users of financial reports to assess that accountability. The Board recognizes that more work is needed before objective, generally accepted, cost-beneficial SEA indicators can be established. Widespread experimentation, which the Board encourages, is essential in laying the foundation for standards of SEA reporting.

The reader will note that the researchers identify four types of SEA indicators (input, output, outcomes, and efficiency), but they tend to emphasize the more complex ones: outcomes and efficiency. This is because the outcomes and efficiency indicators—relating efforts to accomplishments—are useful not only in accounting for the past, but also in planning for the future. They help answer some of the fundamental questions of state and local government: How much better off might the citizenry be as a result of a specific increase in resources for a particular activity? What are the trade-offs (in terms of likely outcomes) from applying an expected decline in resources to one activity as compared with another?

The Board appreciates the work of all the researchers on this extensive project, as well as the members of the SEA Advisory Committee who provided broad guidance and commented on the drafts prepared by the researchers. The Board also appreciates the help of the numerous individuals throughout the country who were interviewed by and provided documents to the researchers.

Norwalk, Connecticut
September 1990

Martin Ives
Director of Research

GASB Resolution on Service Efforts and Accomplishments Reporting

July 1989

In establishing objectives of financial reporting, the GASB stated that governmental financial reporting should "provide information to assist users in (a) assessing accountability and (b) making economic, social, and political decisions." The Board gave considerable weight to the concept of accountability: of "being obliged to explain one's actions, to justify what one does"; of being required "to answer to the citizenry—to justify the raising of public resources and the purposes for which they are used." In linking financial reporting to accountability, the Board recognized that the use of a broad concept of accountability for financial reporting has the potential to extend financial reporting beyond current practice.*

One objective established by the Board was that "financial reporting should provide information to assist users in assessing the service efforts, costs, and accomplishments of the governmental entity."† Information about service efforts and accomplishments (SEA) is an essential element of accountability. SEA information is needed for setting goals and objectives, planning program activities to accomplish these goals and objectives, allocating resources to these programs, monitoring and evaluating the results to determine if they are making progress in achieving the established goals and objectives, and modifying program plans to enhance performance. SEA information is therefore useful to management, elected officials, and the citizenry in making resource allocation decisions and in assessing the government's performance.

Realizing that the state of the art in SEA measurement and reporting is still in its formative stages, the Board undertook a research project to gather information on the practice of measuring and reporting SEA indicators. This research, which followed a 1985 GASB resolution on in-

---

*GASB Concepts Statement No. 1, *Objectives of Financial Reporting* (Stamford, CT: GASB, 1987), passim.

†Ibid., para. 77c.

frastructure and service efforts reporting, resulted in a Research Report that found that SEA measurement and reporting is rapidly developing. That report recommends that governmental entities further experiment with SEA indicators.

The Board and its staff participated in the research and have carefully reviewed the findings and recommendations and the bases underlying them. The research found that SEA indicators are being widely used; have been shown to be of value to elected officials, citizens, and management; and have reached a level of development that indicates their increasing acceptance for monitoring certain aspects of governmental performance. Nevertheless, the Board recognizes the need for extensive experimentation with and analysis of SEA indicators before they may be considered for inclusion as part of the information required for financial reporting. In particular, the Board recognizes the need for further work on (a) developing valid, generally accepted SEA indicators, (b) gathering data required for the indicators, and (c) developing methods of presenting, explaining, and verifying the information.

THEREFORE, the Board strongly encourages state and local governmental entities to become familiar with SEA measurement and reporting and to undertake experiments in selecting SEA indicators, gathering SEA information, and reporting this information both internally and externally.

ACKNOWLEDGMENTS

The editors are grateful for the diligence and dedication of the authors, who spent so much time performing the research and preparing the reports on the twelve service areas covered by this Research Report. We are also most appreciative of the time and effort the authors were required to spend in responding to the multitude of suggestions and review comments made by the editors, advisory committee, and others who were asked to review parts of this document.

In addition, the editors received considerable support and assistance from the members of the GASB Advisory Committee on Service Efforts and Accomplishments Reporting; GASB Chairman James Antonio; GASB Vice-Chairman and Director of Research Martin Ives; and GASB Board Members Elmer Staats, Philip Defliese, and W. Gary Harmer. Their assistance has made a significant contribution to the quality of this Research Report.

We also appreciate the many hours spent by Joanne Camas and GASB staff members Ellen Falk, Lynn Fallon Lewis, and Patti Sanchioni in diligently editing, verifying footnotes and quotes, and typing the many drafts of this Research Report as it was readied for publication. Finally, thanks go to the staff of the Financial Accounting Foundation's Production Department, who spent many hours working on this report.

Harry P. Hatry, James R. Fountain, Jr.,
Jonathan M. Sullivan, and
Lorraine Kremer

Copyright © 1990 by Governmental Accounting Standards Board
Library of Congress Catalog Card Number: 90-80879
ISBN 0-910065-35-7

RESEARCH REPORT

Service Efforts and Accomplishments Reporting: Its Time Has Come

An Overview

Editors

Harry P. Hatry
James R. Fountain, Jr.
Jonathan M. Sullivan
Lorraine Kremer

Contributors

Marita Alexander
Joan A. Allen
Marguerite Brannon
Richard E. Brown
Priscilla A. Burnaby
Vivian L. Carpenter
Don Chamberlain
Allan Drebin
Mark Fall
James R. Fountain, Jr.
Harry P. Hatry
Susan H. Herhold

William A. Hyman
Robert W. Parry, Jr.
Marc A. Rubin
Linda Ruchala
Florence C. Sharp
Jonathan M. Sullivan
James B. Tinnin
Relmond P. Van Daniker
Jannet Vreeland
Sharon Wagner
Wanda A. Wallace
John B. Waller, Jr.

GOVERNMENTAL ACCOUNTING STANDARDS BOARD
OF THE FINANCIAL ACCOUNTING FOUNDATION
401 MERRITT 7, P.O. BOX 5116, NORWALK, CONNECTICUT 06856-5116

RESEARCH REPORT

An Overview

CONTENTS

	Page
Foreword	iii
GASB Resolution on Service Efforts and Accomplishments Reporting	v
Acknowledgments	vii
Chapter 1. Overview *Harry P. Hatry, James R. Fountain, Jr., and Jonathan M. Sullivan*	1
Chapter 2. Colleges and Universities *Don Chamberlain and Relmond P. Van Daniker*	51
Chapter 3. Economic Development Programs *Mark Fall*	71
Chapter 4. Elementary and Secondary Education *Harry P. Hatry, Marita Alexander, and James R. Fountain, Jr.*	97
Chapter 5. Fire Department Programs *Robert W. Parry, Jr., Florence C. Sharp, Jannet Vreeland, and Wanda A. Wallace*	119
Chapter 6. Hospitals *Richard E. Brown*	141
Chapter 7. Mass Transit *Wanda A. Wallace*	157

Page

Chapter 8. Police Department Programs
Allan Drebin and Marguerite Brannon 187

Chapter 9. Public Assistance Programs
*Sharon Wagner, Richard E. Brown, and
James B. Tinnin* 207

Chapter 10. Public Health
*Vivian L. Carpenter, John B. Waller, Jr., and
Linda Ruchala* 223

Chapter 11. Road Maintenance
William A. Hyman and Joan A. Allen 247

Chapter 12. Sanitation Collection and Disposal
Marc A. Rubin 263

Chapter 13. Water and Wastewater Treatment
Priscilla A. Burnaby and Susan H. Herhold 287

LIST OF EXHIBITS

		Page
1-1	SEA Advisory Committee	6
1-2	Services Researched and Researchers	8
1-3	Issues Examined	9
1-4	Categories of Service Efforts and Accomplishments Indicators	12
1-5	Department of Sanitation: Street Cleanliness	22
1-6	Issues Examined and Recommendations	42
1-7	Example of Presentation Format: Elementary and Secondary Education SEA Indicators	46
2-1	Recommended SEA Indicators for Colleges and Universities	60
3-1	Recommended SEA Indicators for Economic Development: Business Attraction/Marketing Programs	80
3-2	Recommended SEA Indicators for Economic Development: Financial Assistance Programs	86
3-3	Recommended SEA Indicators for Economic Development: Export Programs	92
4-1	Commonly Found Goals and Objectives of Elementary and Secondary Education	101
4-2	Recommended SEA Indicators for Elementary and Secondary Education	106
4-3	Illustration of the Coverage of a Survey Requesting Students, or Ex-Students, to Rate Various Aspects of Their School's Contribution to Noncognitive Outcomes	110
4-4	An Example of a Comparison Display	114
4-5	Candidate Explanatory Factors	116
5-1	Recommended SEA Indicators for Fire Departments: Overall Performance	122
5-2	Recommended SEA Indicators for Fire Departments: Fire Suppression	124
5-3	Recommended SEA Indicators for Fire Departments: Fire Prevention	126

Page

6-1	Recommended SEA Indicators for Hospitals	150
7-1	Recommended SEA Indicators for Mass Transit	164
7-2	Communication of Information by the Straphangers	176
7-3	Eliciting Information on Customer Satisfaction	178
7-4	Collecting Information on Both Riders and Nonriders	180
8-1	Recommended SEA Indicators for Police Departments	192
9-1	Recommended SEA Indicators for AFDC and GA Programs	216
9-2	County of San Diego, Proposed Budget, 1989–90	218
10-1	Recommended SEA Indicators for Chronic Disease	228
10-2	Recommended SEA Indicators for Sexually Transmitted Diseases	232
10-3	Recommended SEA Indicators for Sexually Transmitted Diseases—AIDS	236
10-4	Recommended SEA Indicators for Maternal and Child Health (MCH) Care	238
10-5	Recommended SEA Indicators for Control of Stress and Violent Behavior	242
11-1	Recommended SEA Indicators for Road Maintenance	258
12-1	Recommended SEA Indicators for Solid-Waste Collection	268
12-2	Recommended SEA Indicators for Solid-Waste Disposal: Landfills	274
	Recommended SEA Indicators for Solid-Waste Disposal: Waste-to-Energy	276
	Recommended SEA Indicators for Solid-Waste Disposal: Recycling	278
12-3	Recommended SEA Indicators for Street Sweeping	282
13-1	Recommended SEA Indicators for Drinking Water	294
13-2	Recommended SEA Indicators for Wastewater Treatment	298
13-3	Recommended SEA Indicators for Storm Drainage	302

1. Overview

Harry P. Hatry, The Urban Institute

James R. Fountain, Jr., and Jonathan M. Sullivan, Governmental Accounting Standards Board

	Page
Introduction	2
Objectives of Research	4
Scope of Research	6
Methodology	7
Indicator Types	10
Overall Findings	11
Issue 1. Candidate Indicators	11
Input Indicators	14
Output Indicators	14
Outcome Indicators	15
Indicators That Compare Service Outputs and Outcomes to Inputs	16
Overall Findings on SEA Indicators	16
Issue 2. Disaggregation	20
Issue 3. Comparisons of Indicators	24
Issue 4. Explanatory Data	26
Issue 5. Verifiability of Indicators	28
Issue 6. Communication and Display of Indicators	29
Issue 7. Costs and Feasibility of Reporting	31
Issue 8. Uses for and Users of SEA Data	32
Recommendations	35
Final Observations	44

INTRODUCTION

This Research Report on service efforts and accomplishments (SEA) measurement and reporting is one of a series of reports to be published as part of the Governmental Accounting Standards Board's (GASB) research on the external reporting of SEA indicators. When completed, the set of reports will include this overview of the research with recommendations and summaries of the findings for each of twelve services,[1] and a separate report for each service. The service chapters in this report are excerpts from the individual full-length GASB Research Reports.

In 1987 the GASB—after completing and issuing its Concepts Statement No. 1, *Objectives of Financial Reporting* (May 1987)—initiated research into ways to improve the ability of public entity financial reports to present information useful in monitoring and assessing the "results of operations" of governmental entities. The GASB directed that the research seek ways to provide information useful in assessing not only *how much and on what* an entity spends its resources but also *what its citizens are getting* for the use of public funds and *how efficiently and effectively* these funds are being used.

This research on reporting SEA indicators responds to the GASB financial reporting objectives to "assist in fulfilling government's duty to be publicly accountable and . . . enable users to assess that accountability," and to "provide information to assist users in assessing the service efforts, costs, and accomplishments of the governmental entity."[2] This research also responds to concern—voiced by many managers, legislators, and citizens—that financial reports of governmental entities do not provide complete information to management, elected officials, and the public about the "results of operations" of the entity or its programs. Users, therefore, are not able to fully assess the adequacy of the governmental entity's performance or hold it accountable

---

[1]The services are colleges and universities, economic development, elementary and secondary education, fire, hospitals, mass transit, police, public assistance, public health, road maintenance, sanitation, and water and wastewater.

[2]GASB Concepts Statement 1, para. 77.

for the management of taxpayer and other resources.[3] Similarly, the governmental entity (its management and elected officials) is not able to communicate to resource providers information about goods and services provided or the entity's efficiency and effectiveness.

Several previous research projects on reporting SEA indicators have been performed, including a Financial Accounting Standards Board (FASB)-sponsored study by Peat, Marwick, Mitchell & Co. on the extent to which nonbusiness organizations report information about service efforts and accomplishments.[4] The Urban Institute has completed several research projects highlighting the measurement of efficiency and effectiveness by state and local governments.[5] Also, the General Accounting Office (GAO) of the U.S. government has recently released the 1988 revision of *Government Auditing Standards,* which includes standards for field work and reporting for performance audits.[6]

State and local governments are increasingly devoting part of their audit resources to performance auditing.[7] The Canadian Institute of Chartered Accountants recently issued an audit guide, *Value-for-Money Auditing Standards,* to assist Canadian chartered accountants being

---

[3]For governmental entities the goals are to provide goods and services efficiently and effectively rather than to generate profits. Present financial reports do not provide accountability information about the efficient and effective use of resources.

[4]FASB Research Report, *Reporting of Service Efforts and Accomplishments,* by Paul K. Brace et al. (Stamford, CT: FASB, 1980).

[5]See, for example, *How Effective Are Your Community Services? Procedures for Monitoring the Effectiveness of Municipal Services,* 1977; *Performance Measurement: A Guide for Local Elected Officials,* 1980; *Efficiency Measurement for Local Government Services: Some Initial Suggestions,* 1979 (all The Urban Institute Press: Washington, DC). Also see "Monitoring the Quality of Local Government Services," MIS Report (vol. 19, no. 2) (Washington, DC: International City Management Association, February 1987).

[6]U.S. General Accounting Office, *Government Auditing Standards* (Washington, DC: U.S. Government Printing Office, 1988 revision).

[7]Audit reports from the states of Tennessee, Kansas, and New York; cities of Dallas, Texas, and New York; and King County, Washington, provide examples of performance audit work being done. Performance auditing has been defined as a systematic process of objectively obtaining and evaluating evidence regarding the performance of an organization, program, function, or activity.

requested to perform value-for-money audits in the public sector,[8] and the Canadian Comprehensive Auditing Foundation has published a book on effectiveness reporting and auditing.[9]

In May 1987, the GASB initiated a preliminary study to examine whether the state of the art in measuring and reporting SEA information was sufficiently developed to warrant a full research project. The research, performed with the assistance of The Urban Institute, indicated that considerable experimentation with SEA measurement had already been undertaken in many public services, and that significant progress was being made in measuring SEA for many public services. Formal reporting of SEA data appeared to be "taking off" in many areas.

That report recommended proceeding with the full research project and identified eight primary issues associated with SEA reporting to be addressed. The GASB approved the full research project with a principal focus on gauging the state of SEA reporting practices covering the major activities of a number of public services. This report is the result of that research and presents the overall findings and recommendations, summarizing these for the twelve services researched. Full Research Reports for most of the public services are now being prepared for publication as separate reports. The report on elementary and secondary education was published in November 1989.

OBJECTIVES OF RESEARCH

The primary objective of this research was to determine whether the state of the art in SEA measurement is sufficiently developed to warrant the GASB, state and local governments, and public interest groups encouraging governmental entities to present SEA indicators as part of their financial reporting. If so, the GASB asked that the researchers provide suggestions as to the structure and method of reporting, such as which SEA indicators to include and how they should be reported.

GASB Concepts Statement 1 identifies accountability as the cornerstone of all financial reporting in government and defines it as "being obliged to explain one's actions, to justify what one does." The objectives of financial reporting include the presentation of SEA information

---

[8]Canadian Institute of Chartered Accountants, *Value-for-Money Auditing Standards* (CICA, 1988).

[9]Canadian Comprehensive Auditing Foundation, *Effectiveness Reporting and Auditing in the Public Sector* (Ottawa: CCAF, 1987).

in the financial report to help users "assess the economy, efficiency, and effectiveness of government."[10] The U.S. GAO's *Government Auditing Standards* also highlights the need for program evaluation information. In *Management: Tasks, Responsibilities, Practices,*[11] Peter F. Drucker clearly articulated the need to hold service institutions, including government, accountable for their use of public resources through SEA information. However, previous efforts to build SEA measurement into the reporting structure of governments have proven difficult. They have been hampered by difficulty in developing objective indicators that adequately measure the results of programs or activities. Often there is a lack of verifiable data about the outcomes and efficiency of programs or activities. Management and elected officials have, at times, resisted the prospect of being required to report the results of operations, especially if that reporting is to include data on outputs and outcomes. This often has occurred because of a lack of agreement on what needs to be measured and how accurate and valid that information would be. This research explores these and associated issues, and provides recommendations on the direction that future SEA reporting might take. It also recommends SEA indicators for each service.

This research was based on the belief that it is the desire and responsibility of elected officials and managers of governmental entities to use the resources provided them in as efficient and effective a way as possible, to strive continuously to provide the highest quality services at a reasonable cost, and to be accountable by giving information that will assist the public in assessing the results of operations for the entity. To meet this accountability objective, management and elected officials need to have access to timely SEA information. Through the measurement, analysis, and evaluation of SEA data, public officials can identify ways to maintain or improve the efficiency and effectiveness of activities and provide the public with objective information on their results.

---

[10]GASB Concepts Statement 1, para. 77c.

[11]Peter F. Drucker, *Management: Tasks, Responsibilities, Practices* (New York: Harper & Row, 1974).

SCOPE OF RESEARCH

This research was completed under the guidance of the GASB and an advisory committee of experts on SEA measurement (Exhibit 1-1). The research was directed by a project team led by Harry P. Hatry, director of the state and local government research program of The Urban Institute, and James R. Fountain, Jr., assistant director of research of the GASB.

The project team, working with the advisory committee, chose twelve services (Exhibit 1-2) to be researched. These services were selected based on the proportion of state and local resources allocated to them and their perceived importance to elected officials and citizens. Eleven of the services are among the first fifteen in magnitude of total state and local government expenditure; the other, economic development, has received much attention because of questions about program effectiveness and its major implications for state and local

---

Exhibit 1-1
SEA Advisory Committee

Gordon Crabtree
Director of Finance
State of Utah

Robert G. Cronson
Auditor General
State of Illinois

Thomas W. Finnie
City Manager
Springfield, Missouri

James Flanagan
City Auditor
Phoenix, Arizona

Ronald D. Picur
Associate Professor of Accounting
University of Illinois at Chicago

James B. Pyers
Director of Finance
Wooster, Ohio

Ronell Raaum
Assistant Director, Accounting and Financial Management Division
U.S. General Accounting Office

Glen E. Robinson
President and Director of Research
Educational Research Service

Harold Steinberg
Partner
KPMG Peat Marwick

revenues. The research was performed by teams from the GASB staff, Urban Institute staff, academia, and experts in the specific services (Exhibit 1-2). Each research team sought to include only those activities that represent the most significant product(s) or service(s) being provided. For example, the elementary and secondary education research addresses regular instructional activities but excludes special education, vocational education, and adult education.

The GASB decided that the study would focus on both state and local (city and county) governments; public school systems; public universities and colleges; public hospitals; and quasi-public organizations such as transportation, and water and wastewater authorities.

METHODOLOGY

The research teams first prepared preliminary reports based on their research, which were reviewed by the GASB and Urban Institute project staffs. The authors subsequently revised their reports, which were then reviewed by selected experts in each of the specific services and by members of the advisory committee.

The research teams used a variety of sources in developing their reports. These included literature searches, examination of reports provided by state and local agencies, interviews with practitioners and other public officials, and, in some cases, mail surveys of public officials.[12]

Each research team was asked to address the eight issues listed in Exhibit 1-3. That list was developed in the first phase of the project to ensure that certain critical issues were addressed for each service.

A basic assumption made for each service was that the service is essential and should be provided. The researchers concentrated their attention on SEA indicators that would measure the inputs, outputs, outcomes, and efficiency of the program. The issue of whether a service should be provided at all would require a different type of analysis and, therefore, is beyond the scope of this research.

---

[12]As an example, the researchers preparing the report on fire services surveyed over 200 U.S. cities that had experimented with reporting SEA data or had received other distinctions such as the Government Finance Officers Association "Certificate of Achievement for Excellence in Financial Reporting" or "Award for Distinguished Budget Presentation."

Exhibit 1-2
Services Researched and Researchers

Service Area	Researcher	Affiliation
Colleges and Universities	Don Chamberlain	Murray State Univ.
	Relmond P. Van Daniker	Univ. of Kentucky
Economic Development	Mark Fall	Urban Institute
Elementary and Secondary Education	Harry P. Hatry	Urban Institute
	James R. Fountain, Jr.	GASB
	Marita Alexander	Urban Institute
Fire	Robert W. Parry, Jr.	Indiana Univ.
	Florence C. Sharp	Ohio Univ.
	Jannet Vreeland	Texas A&M Univ.
	Wanda A. Wallace	Texas A&M Univ.
Hospitals	Richard E. Brown	Kent State Univ.
Mass Transit	Wanda A. Wallace	Texas A&M Univ.
Police	Allan Drebin	Northwestern
	Marguerite Brannon	Chicago Tribune Charities
Public Assistance	Sharon Wagner	Kent State Univ.
	Richard E. Brown	Kent State Univ.
	James B. Tinnin	Kent State Univ.
Public Health	Vivian L. Carpenter	Wayne State Univ.
	John B. Waller, Jr.	Wayne State Univ.
	Linda Ruchala	Indiana Univ.
Road Maintenance	William A. Hyman	Urban Institute
	Joan A. Allen	Urban Institute
Sanitation Collection and Disposal	Marc A. Rubin	Miami Univ.
Water and Wastewater Treatment	Priscilla A. Burnaby	Bentley College
	Susan H. Herhold	Univ. of New Hampshire

In preparing these Research Reports, we recognize that accounting and financial reporting objectives are primarily concerned with collecting, classifying, and reporting information about an entity's acquisition and use of financial resources, and the results of operations. Accordingly, these Research Reports are directed toward issues concerned with the uses of SEA data, and how to measure SEA and communicate these measures, especially to elected officials and the public. *The very important issues of determining what goals and objectives to establish, performance levels to expect, targets to set for performance, and methods to use to improve the results of governmental services are the domain of professionals in the specific service and elected and appointed officials. They are, therefore, outside the scope of these reports.*

Exhibit 1-3
Issues Examined

1. What types of SEA indicators should be considered? What SEA indicators should be candidates for reporting? To what extent are these indicators measurable, valid, and comprehensive?
2. How, and to what extent, should individual SEA indicators be disaggregated?
3. What comparisons should be reported for the various SEA indicators?
4. What explanatory data should be included with SEA indicators, and how should these data be presented?
5. To what extent are these SEA indicators verifiable?
6. How should SEA information be communicated and displayed? In what types of documents should the SEA indicators be reported?
7. What are the likely added costs and the feasibility of obtaining and reporting SEA indicators?
8. What are the uses for, and who are the users of, SEA data?

INDICATOR TYPES

A preliminary question for this research was which categories of financial and nonfinancial indicators should be included under the term *service efforts and accomplishments.* The categories of SEA indicators established by the project team are listed in Exhibit 1-4. These SEA categories are as follows:

1. *Input indicators.* These are designed to report the amount of resources, either financial or other (especially personnel), that have been used for a specific service or program. Input indicators are ordinarily presented in budget submissions and sometimes external management reports.
2. *Output indicators.* These report units produced or services provided by a service or program.
3. *Outcome indicators.* These are designed to report the results (including quality) of the service. Examples of outcome indicators are the change in students' test scores, the percentage of hypertensives treated who now have controlled blood pressure, and the value of property lost due to crime.
4. *Efficiency (and cost-effectiveness) indicators.*[13] These are defined as indicators that measure the cost (whether in dollars or employee-hours) per unit of output or outcome. Examples are cost per million gallons of drinking water delivered to consumers, or cost per thousand gallons of effluent treated to a certain level of quality.
5. *Explanatory information.* This includes a variety of information about the environment and other factors that might affect an organization's performance on SEA indicators. Examples would be weather conditions for road maintenance, percentage of students with English as a second language for education, or quality of source water for water service.

---

[13]The term *efficiency* as used in this report encompasses the measurement of both cost per unit of output and cost per unit of outcome. In the FASB Research Report on reporting of service efforts and accomplishments, by Paul K. Brace et al., efficiency was used to identify cost per unit of output, and effectiveness to identify cost per unit of outcome (p. 8).

OVERALL FINDINGS

In this section we present the overall findings on each of the issues identified in Exhibit 1-3. Additional findings for each service, especially on Issues 1 through 4, are presented in the individual service chapters in this report.

Based on the findings of the research teams, we believe that *the state of the art in SEA measurement has developed sufficiently to warrant widespread experimentation with the use of SEA indicators in external reports.* The annual financial report is the primary accountability document made available to the public by governmental entities; as such, it is a logical place for SEA information to be reported, even if it also appears in another report. We believe that SEA information, where reported, has been of significant value to elected officials and citizens in assessing the results of governmental programs, leading to improvements in efficiency and effectiveness in accomplishing program goals and objectives. The following findings on each of the issues support this conclusion.

ISSUE 1. What SEA indicators should be candidates for reporting? To what extent are these indicators measurable, valid, and comprehensive?

The research teams found a number of major developments in recent years in the collection and reporting of performance indicators. A list of the indicators that each research team believes warrant consideration for external reporting is presented in the individual service chapters in this report. Some of these developments strike us as remarkable. They include:

- Major experimentation by institutions of *higher education* in measuring student achievement from entry to graduation, and even after graduation in certain cases.
- The explosion of reporting of *elementary and secondary school* outcomes, with major impetus from state departments of education.
- The recent production by the U.S. Health Care Finance Administration (HCFA) of mortality statistics on an individual *hospital* basis and by category of illness.

Exhibit 1-4
Categories of Service Efforts and Accomplishments Indicators

A. **Indicators of Service Efforts**

1. Inputs—Dollar costs of the service during the period.
   a. In "current" dollars.
   b. In "constant" dollars, that is, adjusted for price level changes.
   c. Per household or per capita, and in either current or constant dollars.
2. Inputs—Amounts of *non*monetary resources expended, especially the amount of work time expended during the period (for the service). These might be expressed in such units as full-time-equivalent years or employee-hours.

B. **Indicators of Service Accomplishments**

1. Outputs—Amount of workload accomplished.
2. Outcomes—A numeric indicator of program results. This category includes indicators of service quality (such as timeliness), effectiveness, and amount or proportion of "need" that is (or is not) being served.

C. **Indicators That Relate Service Efforts to Service Accomplishments**
(These can also be labeled efficiency indicators,[a] which for the purposes of this report include both input/output and input/outcome indicators.)

1. Amount of input related to (divided by) amount of *output*. "Input" can be any of the variations included under Section A, and "output" refers to B.1, not B.2.
2. Amount of input related to (divided by) amount of *outcomes or results*. Again, "input" can be any of the variations noted in Section A. "Outcome" refers only to B.2, not B.1.

---

[a]The term *productivity indicator* is sometimes used instead of *efficiency indicator.* Productivity is usually defined in the productivity literature as "output divided by input," the reciprocal of "input divided by output."

Exhibit 1-4 (continued)

3. Productivity (or efficiency) *indexes.* These traditionally have been used in reporting national productivity trends. Indexes are calculated by relating the ratio of productivity in the current year to that of a preselected base year. These indexes have the advantage that the productivity ratios for different activities for a service, or across services, can be combined by weighting each ratio by the amount of input for each activity.

D. Explanatory Information

This is a term used to cover a variety of information relevant to a service that helps users understand the performance on the SEA indicators and factors affecting an organization's performance. The explanatory information should be grouped into two categories:

1. Elements substantially outside the control of the public agency, such as demographic characteristics.
2. Elements over which the agency has significant control, such as staffing patterns.

- Recent experiments in assessing *state economic development programs* aimed at better identifying program outcomes such as export-trade and business-attraction programs.
- The increasingly widespread collection of data on road condition by *transportation* agencies.
- Emerging professional-interest group activity for both *hospitals and public health* in establishing service quality indicators.

Nevertheless, even with such developments it appears that the great majority of state and local agencies rarely report any SEA indicators externally, and only a few even seem to regularly report many SEA indicators internally. Indeed, some grass-roots citizens' organizations have been formed to collect and disseminate SEA information in the absence of public disclosures.

Although individual steps have been taken toward the development and reporting of SEA indicators, a sharing of this process and a coordinated attempt to disseminate the procedures and encourage development and reporting is warranted. We suggest a set of SEA indicators for each service and recommend that each entity use these as a basis for developing an appropriate set of SEA indicators designed specifically for their jurisdiction and service. The findings on the various categories of SEA measures listed in Exhibit 1-4 are summarized below.

Input Indicators

These are the indicators traditionally reported in budget documents and financial and other reports. They provide the user with information about the expenditure of resources and the types or mix of resources being used. They also show the level of resources applied to a service. These measures, although reasonably widespread in use, have been criticized for focusing the attention of resource providers only on the narrow concern of *how much* is being expended and not *what* is being accomplished or produced with the resources.

Input indicators have generally been divided into the measurement of financial resources (money) and other resources such as employee-hours, acres of land, capacity of landfills, or square feet of building. In addition to the traditional indicators of dollars and employee-hours expended, we found some use of indicators that attempt to "normalize" (that is, relate) these units to some indicator of the potential workload, but not the product (output) of the service. Some examples include number of students per teacher, dollars spent per pupil, dollars spent per capita on police or fire service, and the number of police per 100,000 people.

The researchers did not attempt to assess the data-collection procedures used or the validity of input indicators. Yet these are concerns that need to be considered by any entity developing and reporting SEA indicators. For example, the costs of general governmental services do not normally include a measure of the cost of use for capital assets. In addition, support services such as central personnel and purchasing, and even the cost of employee benefits, are often not allocated to specific services or programs. This results in inconsistent cost information for many services, which can lead to inaccurate comparisons over time or between entities.

Output Indicators

Output indicators are designed to report the quantity or units of service or product that are being provided to the service population. The research teams identified numerous indicators of service output.

Examples of output indicators found include the amount of potable or wastewater treated, number of student-days, number of persons screened, number of passenger trips provided by public transit vehicles, and the tons of solid waste processed.

Output indicators occasionally were found in external reports, but more often in budget documents, especially if the jurisdiction used a program budget format. These indicators were used, infrequently, as the basis for efficiency measures that compared output to input indicators (dollars or employee-hours).

Outcome Indicators

Indicators of outcomes of public programs were a major focus of all the research teams' efforts. These indicators show the results (outcomes and quality) being received from the service. They are perhaps the most significant measure of results of operation for governmental programs.

The research teams did not find external reporting of outcomes in most instances, yet there are a number of important exceptions, and the collection and use of outcome indicators appears to be growing. Examples of external reporting include the reporting of scores of students on achievement tests, number of bus or train trips off schedule, crime rates and crime "clearance" rates, bed-disability days per treated client, quality of water after treatment, mortality rate at a hospital for patients with a certain illness, amount of toxic material deposited in the landfill, response time of police and fire departments to calls, and percentage of fires that do not spread beyond a prescribed amount after arrival of the firefighters.

Outcome indicators can also provide a basis for developing efficiency (cost-effectiveness) indicators when compared with inputs. *Relating outcomes, rather than outputs, to resources used can provide important additional information to elected officials and the public about the cost of the results of program activities, thereby enabling them to consider the value of the service relative to its resource requirements.*

Many of the researchers identified outcome indicators that require special data-collection procedures, such as the use of client surveys, "trained observer" ratings by independent observers (usually to rate a physical condition that the agency is attempting to improve or maintain), or the use of some form of technological device, such as water-quality measuring instruments. These introduce "new technology" into service accomplishments measurement. The current use of each procedure and outcome indicator, however, is still quite sparse. Only a few governments, for example, regularly report indicators derived from feedback from service clients. These special collection procedures are sufficiently developed to be used, as long as they are applied correctly by the agency.

The research teams found prevention services to be a particularly difficult area for identifying meaningful outcome indicators. For example, police, fire, and public health services each have a major prevention function (prevention of crimes, fires, and various illnesses). Unfortunately, obtaining valid data for outcome indicators, such as numbers of crimes/fires/illnesses that were prevented, is not feasible. The closest practical approximation appears to be outcome indicators that measure the number of incidents *not* prevented.

Indicators That Compare Service Outputs and Outcomes to Inputs

The research teams found that indicators of efficiency were reported only rarely. Indicators of cost per unit of physical output were found to be in widespread use in water supply and treatment (cost per gallon treated), schools (cost per student-day), road maintenance (cost per repair), and public transit (cost per trip-mile).

Some of the research teams suggested efficiency (or cost-effectiveness) indicators using *outcome* indicators instead of physical units of output as the denominator. For example, for elementary and secondary education, the research team suggested an efficiency indicator be used that reports cost per student who achieved a prespecified test score gain. Similarly, for road maintenance, the research team introduced the indicator of cost per mile of road maintained at some satisfactory level or condition, or that had achieved a certain minimum improvement in condition. The public health team included indicators that report cost per client who achieved a certain measurable improvement, such as reduction in blood pressure. Such indicators, while potentially representing a major improvement in measuring service efficiency, are largely untested and should be considered experimental.

Overall Findings on SEA Indicators

1. Generally, current reporting by public entities, even internally, has not included outcome or efficiency indicators, though some of the services we examined have begun to experiment with outcome and efficiency indicators. The advent of readily available and inexpensive

data-processing equipment and more sophisticated technical tools, such as samples and surveys, has opened the door to many of these trials and provides considerable potential for improved reporting.

2. Much of the SEA data being collected are primarily reported internally for use by management. This is, of course, appropriate since these are the people who use such data on a regular, ongoing basis for operational decisions.

3. Reporting outside the operating agency is becoming more widespread, especially in certain services such as elementary and secondary education. This increase in external reporting appears to have been due to events such as:

- The tightening of public resources, which has caused increased attention to be focused on waste, abuse, and inefficiency in government, and greater pressure to be exerted on officials to be accountable for the use of public resources. This has led to the need for information on service performance to support requests for additional funding or to maintain the current level of funding.
- A much greater focus on accountability for overall performance, which began in the late 1970s, has emerged particularly since Proposition 13 in California and the numerous other fiscal containment efforts in the 1980s. These have resulted in both elected officials and the public asking more penetrating questions about the value they are getting for their money.
- Data-processing breakthroughs, which have greatly increased the ability of governmental entities to process, organize, and report large amounts of data.
- The trend toward both elected officials and the public providing more aggressive input into public policy choices. This probably resulted in part from the increasing election to state and local legislative bodies of officials who have more education and professional training, and who are activists, willing to ask more difficult questions of their operating agencies.
- The influence of managerial and elected state and local officials whose academic training has given them increased exposure to new concepts in public administration, such as program evaluation and policy analysis. This has also contributed to operating agencies' increased acceptance and use of SEA data.

- The considerable federal government effort, since 1980, to place increased fiscal responsibility on state and local governments by reducing federal mandates and grants, and transferring responsibility for programs to state or local government.

4. It is clear that there is no set of SEA indicators that is "perfect." However, for any service or program, the research found that there are generally accepted indicators for many aspects of performance and other, currently less used, indicators with considerable potential usefulness. Accordingly, we can recommend (at least for experimentation purposes) the reporting of selected SEA indicators for each service to elected officials and the public.

5. What also seems clear is that the state of the art in SEA reporting presents an opportunity for major improvement. Current external reporting of SEA indicators usually provides only a very sparse perspective to elected and appointed officials and the public on the efficiency and outcomes of governmental products and services.

It appears, however, that experimentation with SEA indicators is already beginning for many services, and substantial improvements are possible in the near future if the development and reporting of SEA indicators is encouraged and broadened to include more governmental entities and services.

6. As indicated in this report and the separate reports for each service, the researchers identified numerous outcome and some efficiency indicators that deserve careful consideration. These indicators, or others like them, if reported in a consistent and appropriate fashion, would give public officials and the public a reasonable (though partial) perspective on SEA and form a sound basis for future development of SEA reporting. The addition of outcome and efficiency indicators based on client feedback and trained-observer procedures provides a major possibility for improvement.

7. *The extent to which public agencies can affect or control the outcome and efficiency of the service being measured is of continuing concern to public officials.* As with financial performance, SEA reporting does not indicate *why* the results are what they are, or *what or who* has caused or contributed to those results. These questions can be answered only, if at all, through in-depth evaluation and investigation. Fortunately, for public disclosure of SEA information, as with financial information, it is accepted that the information presented should be ap-

propriate and accurate in measuring the results. This information is not expected to indicate clearly who or what caused the reported performance to be at the levels it is.

For SEA reporting to provide valid information on governmental performance, the public agency should be able, through its actions, to affect the results for each outcome and efficiency indicator that is reported, at least to some reasonable extent. This has been of particular concern for certain outcome indicators, such as crime rates, fire rates, incidence of various types of illnesses, and jobs created—examples of common outcome indicators used for police, fire, public health, and economic development programs, respectively. Clearly, the governmental agency plays only a partial role in reducing crime, preventing fires or illnesses, and creating jobs. Nevertheless, such indicators provide an important part of the picture relating to these agencies' results, and each is at least partially affected by public agency action. As the reports on the individual services indicate, *the researchers recommend that such indicators be presented, despite their limitations, because this information is needed by governmental officials and the public in order to give them a comprehensive perspective on results.*

8. None of the research teams recommended, or even identified, instances of composite SEA indicators that combine data from two or more indicators into one index for a service. The closest to this are composite efficiency indexes (sometimes called "productivity" indexes) such as those recommended for road maintenance. In this instance, numerous unit-cost indicators, each covering one of many road maintenance activities, are combined to provide an overall composite index (as is done by the U.S. government in deriving national productivity indexes). For mass transit, multidimensional indicators have been recommended in past research, although such indicators were not observed in practice.

9. Finally, and perhaps most importantly, the individual service reports of the research teams are unanimous in recommending that indicators of SEA be reported both internally and externally. Internally reported SEA indicators may be needed in more detail and at greater levels of disaggregation than what is necessary for external reporting if they are to be of value to management. Recognizing this possible difference in reporting requirements, the researchers all concluded that the state of the art in measuring SEA was sufficiently developed in the programs researched to warrant the use of indicators in management of the program and presentation to elected officials and the public as part of the entity's annual reporting system.

It is not, of course, the purpose of this research to recommend a definitive set of indicators. Each research team, however, has recommended a set of indicators for consideration. These can and should serve as a starting point for discussion by state and local agencies in developing a set of indicators that meet their reporting needs.

ISSUE 2. How, and to what extent, should individual SEA indicators be disaggregated?

Reporting disaggregated SEA data for individual indicators is likely to be much more useful than presenting only jurisdiction-wide data. Overall averages can conceal considerable information that is potentially useful to governmental officials and the public, as well as to the managers themselves. In addition, information is often needed for users to be able to identify results for specific geographic areas of the entity or for certain segments of the population. This is an important consideration as part of equity and distributional issues between the various geographic areas and population groups within the jurisdiction.

Currently, regular reporting of disaggregations of data is not common. There are, however, some important exceptions. For example, crime data are often reported in major cities by geographical area of the community. (Fire incidence data are rarely reported in this way.) As the sanitation Research Report notes, New York City's annual "Mayor's Management Report" presents a map showing street cleanliness ratings by area throughout its five boroughs (Exhibit 1-5). The elementary and secondary education report notes that many school systems report test-score data broken down by individual school and by ethnicity.

Economic development agencies sometimes break out some indicators such as new employment by size of firm, product category, minority status of the firm, and geographical location. The U.S. Health Care Finance Administration (HCFA) has begun to report mortality rates by individual hospital and also provides information for each hospital broken out by major category of illness. Public health agencies often prepare public reports on incidence of certain health problems by age, sex, race/ethnicity, and geographical area of the community.

Some agencies collect and internally report data by *geographical area* within their jurisdiction. For example, in addition to the street cleanliness and public health examples given above, the road maintenance report notes that some states, such as Pennsylvania, track unit-cost (efficiency) information and road quality by road maintenance district. Many transportation agencies map road conditions for segments of their road system.

Another form of disaggregation results in SEA data being reported by degree of *difficulty* of the incoming workload. The researchers found this form of disaggregation to be rare. However, HCFA's public reporting of mortality rates disaggregates these rates for different groups of patients based on such client-difficulty characteristics as patient age and severity of the patient's condition at initial contact. Another important example occurs in elementary and secondary education, where many school systems are beginning to disaggregate test scores, and occasionally other indicators such as dropouts, and report them for various disadvantaged groups. Public transit agencies report transit indicators separately for peak and off-peak periods to help distinguish the context of these SEA indicators.

The researchers pointed out a number of other opportunities for disaggregation in the various services. For example, road maintenance agencies could report on road condition indicators for groups of roads classified by amount of traffic, amount of truck traffic (trucks can add a considerable burden to maintaining roads), and soil and other terrain characteristics that affect road conditions. The fire research team recommended disaggregation of fire incidence by type of fire and age or type of building. Another example is crime investigation; case clearances (solutions) can be differentiated for cases that have come to the investigations unit with considerable evidence collected at the crime scene (relatively easy to solve) as distinct from cases with little evidence (where the likelihood of solving the crime is considerably lower).

Members of the advisory committee expressed concern that disaggregation could be carried too far, swamping users of the SEA reports with too much information as well as adding cost and verifiability problems. The predominant current practice, however, is not to provide disaggregations in reports. More disaggregation seems desirable and likely to be useful for many governmental program and policy issues, but selectivity is needed to provide only major disaggregations in basic reports and more detail, where needed, in special backup reports.

Exhibit 1-5
Department of Sanitation:
Street Cleanliness

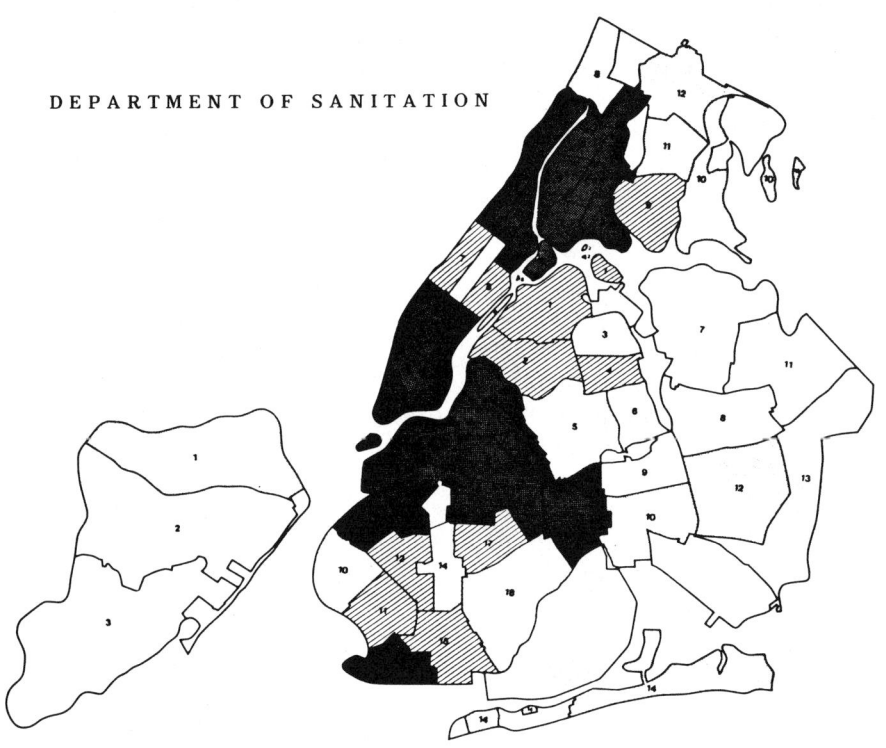

NEW YORK CITY FY 1980
CHANGE IN LEVELS OF CLEANLINESS FOR THE 59 SANITATION DISTRICTS

No. of Districts FY '80*		Cleanliness Level	
28	■	0 - 33	Percent of Streets Rated Acceptably Clean.
10	▨	34 - 50	
13	▢	51 - 67	
8	▢	68 - 100%	

Source: Mayor Edward I. Koch, "The Mayor's Management Report" (New York, September 15, 1988), p. 231.

Exhibit 1-5 (continued)

NEW YORK CITY FY 1988

CHANGE IN LEVELS OF CLEANLINESS FOR THE 59 SANITATION DISTRICTS

Number of Districts		Cleanliness Level		Number of Districts	Degree of Change - FY '87 - '88
FY '88*	FY '87*				
0	0	▓ 0 - 33.0	Percent of Streets Rated Acceptably Clean.	4 ▲	Significant Improvement in Cleanliness of +5.0% or More.
3	1	▨ 33.1 - 50.0			
33	37	░ 50.1 - 67.0		3 ■	Significant Decline in Cleanliness of -5.0% or More.
23	21	☐ 67.1 - 100%			

Source: Mayor Edward I. Koch, "The Mayor's Management Report" (New York, September 17, 1986), p. 96.

23

ISSUE 3. What comparisons should be reported for the various SEA indicators?

A key question in SEA reporting for managers, elected officials, and the public is whether the level of service accomplishment reported is "good" or "bad," how good or bad, and whether it is improving, worsening, or staying about the same. Inevitably, users of SEA data will seek to compare current performance with other numbers to obtain a perspective on the adequacy of the current level of performance. How can this be done meaningfully?

The researchers identified six major types of comparison:

1. *Comparison of current SEA information with previous years' performance.* This is a well-accepted form of comparison that is often expanded to include data from several past years to enable the report user to develop an indication of trends in the data.
2. *Comparisons with similar jurisdictions.* Some researchers placed considerable stress on this type of comparison, such as for public transit, elementary and secondary education, and public hospitals, where data are commonly available. This also applies to crime rates, crime clearance rates, fire incidents, amount of fire loss, and some public health data. This type of comparison is also common in state governments' reports on school systems within their own borders. For example, the states of California and South Carolina report test-score data for individual school systems grouped with other school systems that have similar demographic characteristics. HCFA has recently begun publishing data on hospital mortality rates, providing for direct comparisons with facilities in other jurisdictions.

    All researchers reported concern over comparability of data from different jurisdictions. Clearly, the usefulness of this type of comparison depends on the availability of information on other jurisdictions believed to have similar key characteristics. A number of researchers noted that for certain services comparisons with other jurisdictions are laden with problems. This is especially true where the services being provided differ substantially; where there are differences in the service population, in climatic conditions, or terrain; or where the objectives of the service are different.

    In many cases where interjurisdictional comparisons are used, federal reporting has facilitated their use. For example, the FBI Uniform Crime Reports provide various crime data by location and population size; the Urban Mass Transportation Administration presents various public transit data by size of the operation; the HCFA reports hospital mortality rates across states; and the U.S. Department of Commerce regularly reports on a variety of economic development indicators, such as jobs and export sales, reporting these for each state, broken out by size of firm and product category.

In addition, comparative data on inputs—such as dollars of expenditure and employee-hours—are often available nationally for many, if not most, services through either the federal government or a national professional association. For example, figures on expenditures, numbers of staff, student-teacher ratios, and the like are reported annually by such organizations as the U.S. Department of Education and the Educational Research Service.

3. *Comparison with technically developed standards or norms.* Probably the classic example here is school system cognitive testing, where the performances of individual schools and school systems are compared with national or state-developed norms (based on scores for a national or state sample of students when the test was developed). Efficiency indicators, such as unit costs for road maintenance activities, are sometimes compared by state or local agencies (such as the State of Pennsylvania) to work standards developed by industrial engineering techniques. Otherwise, however, the researchers did not find evidence of systematic comparisons to norms or standards. Some comparisons labeled as comparisons to standards are actually comparisons to other jurisdictions, not with technically developed standards or norms.

4. *Comparisons of actual SEA with targets or goals set by the agency at the beginning of the year.* The researchers found this approach was used only rarely. Budget documents that present nonfinancial data typically present projections (targets) of certain SEA measures for the forthcoming budget year and actual data for previous years. But very seldom did budgets present both actual and projected data for the same year.

None of the researchers reported finding targets linked to a specific plan of action in public reports (and linking projected SEA to dollars or staff requested for the forthcoming year). However, they did identify a few instances of *internal* use of this procedure, usually linked to some form of management by objectives (MBO) process.

5. *Comparison among geographical areas or client groups within the same jurisdiction.* Under Issue 2, we indicated that disaggregating SEA indicators by individual region, precinct, or district of a jurisdic-

tion (whether local or state), though not commonly reported in most of the services examined, can be used to identify geographical areas with particular problems. Such disaggregations can also be used to compare SEA in one area with SEA in another area, or with an average of all areas within the jurisdiction. For example, as previously noted, New York City's annual "Mayor's Management Report" includes a map showing street cleanliness levels to permit readers to compare various parts of the city. Similarly, to the extent that an agency has different operating units (such as police, fire, sanitation districts), voting districts, or facilities (such as more than one school or public health office), elected officials and operating management could compare SEA information to see how each area facility or group is performing against the others, or to the jurisdiction-wide average. The researchers found few examples of such comparisons, however, in most services.

6. *Comparison of public-sector costs and results with similar private organizations.* This type of comparison appears to be only in limited use in public reports at present. This is understandable, because many government services are not comparable with private-sector activities. Exceptions include public hospitals, public transit, schools, and water and wastewater systems. The HCFA mortality data are provided for both private and public hospitals (for all hospitals that receive Medicare funds), and school performance has been compared for public and private institutions. Many ad hoc studies have compared public and private delivery of services, such as sanitation, but such data have usually not been made part of ordinary public reporting.

ISSUE 4. What explanatory data should be included with SEA indicators, and how should these data be presented?

A major concern, if not *the* major concern, of operating managers and elected and appointed officials about reporting SEA information is the possibility of misinterpretation and misuse of the data. They fear they will be blamed unfairly for findings that are beyond their control (for example, results caused by external circumstances). This concern, reported by many of the research teams, is likely to be a principal obstacle to regular reporting of SEA data.

One approach to alleviating some of this concern is to include explanatory data with the SEA data in public reports.[14] This can be done by (1) providing *ad hoc* information giving explanations and rationales for particular problems highlighted by the SEA data, (2) *regularly reporting* on selected explanatory factors that are identified as likely to have a substantial effect on SEA performance, or (3) *doing both.* The value of selecting a set of explanatory factors and presenting them each year is that this avoids the tendency of agencies to alter the explanatory data each year in order to report on only those factors the agency believes to be in its self-interest to report.

In a few instances the researchers found public agencies including explanatory information with performance data. One example is the inclusion in some state reports on school system performance of explanatory data regarding each school system's demographic characteristics—particularly characteristics indicating the number and percentage of disadvantaged students and the relative wealth of the community in which the school system operates.

On occasion, persons writing about external factors distinguished those factors over which the agency had little control from those factors over which it had significant control.

All researchers identified a number of items, usually quantitative, that might be provided, along with SEA information, to help users of the reports gain a better perspective on the performance figures. For example, for state economic programs, a variety of *national* economic indicators are relevant in interpreting job growth and employment rates for individual state or local jurisdictions, and the magnitude of a state's export trade is affected by foreign exchange rates. For mass transit, knowledge about the types and ages of equipment in use provides information for assessing equipment operating and maintenance costs. Road maintenance officials suggested that information on weather conditions during the year (and, for state agencies, relative weather conditions in various parts of the state) is relevant when interpreting data on road conditions and unit costs of maintenance. (Rain, ice, and certain temperatures can affect road surfaces, resulting in both poor quality and higher maintenance costs to keep the roads up to standards.)

---

[14] Explanatory data include information that helps to give the reason for, support, or explain why an SEA indicator is at the level it is. These can include such diverse information as percentage of population below the poverty level, climatic condition, volume and type of vehicles using a segment of highway, condition of incoming water before treatment, or percentage of school population with English as a second language.

An important question is how many explanatory factors to include in reports. Because there are a great number of explanatory factors applicable to any service, and their relationships to the SEA indicator may not be clear, care should be taken not to overload users with too much information. It is also important to explain the relationships between these factors and SEA indicators.

An additional question is where and how explanatory data should be presented. These explanatory data sets could be included as part of the same tables that present SEA indicator information, or they could be presented in a separate table. Another option is to provide explanatory data in notes after the SEA data; this seems more appropriate for identifying unusual circumstances that occurred during the year than for providing a regular set of explanatory data.

ISSUE 5. To what extent are these SEA indicators verifiable?

Verifiability varies considerably depending on the particular SEA indicator and how the data for that indicator have been obtained. The research teams indicated that most, if not all, SEA indicators recommended as candidates for regular reporting are verifiable. Some of these indicators come from basic government records and thus are subject to the same kind of verification that is undertaken by auditors of public financial information.

Nonfinancial SEA data appear to be only infrequently verified. Data collected by the federal government, particularly mandatory data, are subject to occasional, probably quite intermittent, ad hoc review or audit by federal offices. An example is the review procedure to which filings by mass transit agencies are subjected. Verification of SEA data is likely to occur primarily when a governmental audit or evaluation unit examines particular programs, but reviews of any particular service generally occur infrequently. For example, in recent years it has become common for state legislatures to call for reviews of the performance of economic development agencies, but only once every several years.

Some of the SEA indicators recommended by the research teams present special verification problems. For example, a number of the research teams suggested the use of surveys of agency clients for obtaining service outcome data. Verifying data that a public agency has collected through surveys presents special problems. Nevertheless, this data-collection procedure can be at least partially verified by checking the specific survey procedures used by the agency (and any survey contractor), such as reviewing the methods used for sampling, examining the response rates to see if they are adequate for the claims made by the agency, comparing respondents to nonrespondents on demographic characteristics, and perhaps even verifying a percentage of the survey responses by re-calling a portion of those in the sample.

Similarly, procedures involving ratings by trained observers or by special technical equipment (such as of road condition) can be undertaken by reviewing the procedures used and rerating a sample for the conditions being rated. The verifiers might need to obtain the services of specialists or experts to undertake these special examinations (such as to rerate road structural conditions that had previously been assessed by an operating agency).

Some SEA indicators have other special verification problems. For example, the elementary and secondary education research team recommended an indicator of student physical fitness based on standard physical fitness tests. The researchers pointed out that as the tests are administered by people with a self-interest in the results, the indicators could be subject to manipulation. Post-testing a small representative sample of students could be done and would be a good verification method, but it would have to be done soon after the original testing, since fitness can change over time.

It is clear from the research that considerable work remains to be done in developing and implementing methods to verify SEA indicators in a cost-effective manner. Questions remain on the level of verification necessary, the specific audit procedures to be used, and who should perform the verification. Nevertheless, it appears that adequate verification technology exists for SEA indicators such as those recommended.

ISSUE 6. How should SEA information be communicated and displayed? In what types of documents should the SEA indicators be reported?

The project advisers encouraged the project team to emphasize clear, concise reporting. Some of the research teams' full reports include illustrations of a few of the more effective reporting formats they found. These include such formats as mapping individual service outcome indicators to indicate the outcomes for various geographical areas of the community (for example, New York City's mapping of street cleanliness conditions, Exhibit 1-5). Other formats include a variety of nontabular formats, such as charts and graphs. The majority of reporting that has been done is in tabular form. If the data are not packed too densely, such presentations may suffice.

An important option for reporting is to present tables displaying each type of SEA data (expenditures, employee-years, outputs, outcomes, and efficiency), perhaps along with selected explanatory data. This presentation provides readers with a comprehensive set of available information on SEA, particularly if data are presented for several past years. This is similar to the format already used by many local governments in their budgets, though these seldom present comprehensive coverage of SEA data.

The research teams found that the most prevalent document used by public agencies to report their SEA data was the jurisdiction's annual budget. Some budgets present no SEA indicators, others present a few, others report many—and this pattern held across all services. Annual department reports are another form of reporting. These generally focus on activity information and provide little outcome or efficiency data. Only a few of the research teams reported finding this type of document to be a significant form of current SEA reporting.

Annual financial reports are the primary accountability documents made available to the public, but they generally include little, if any, nonfinancial information. However, there has been a recent trend in modifying financial reports to make them more attractive and understandable to readers. For example, Charlotte, North Carolina and Dallas, Texas are now producing financial reports that also include considerable information on activities undertaken during the year. These reports, however, still do not include much SEA information. In general, financial reports have been criticized as falling short of providing much of the information needed by elected officials, citizens, and other users to assess the results of operations of the entity.

The inclusion of SEA indicators in the financial report could greatly enhance the report's utility as an accountability document and could lead to its more widespread use. This information, if made available to the public, could also help modify discussions or arguments about the adequacy of government programs and the need for revenues by focusing these discussions on issues of quality, efficiency, and results of government programs, and perhaps lead to exploration of ways to improve the provision of these services. Wider use of SEA information could even help to make citizens more knowledgeable about the governmental entity and the outcomes of its products and services.

Another type of document used for regular reporting is the special annual report, particularly those issued by local governments. Examples are New York City's "Mayor's Management Report" and Charlotte's "Objectives" reports. However, for these reports as well as for annual financial reports, the timeliness of the publication may pose a problem. For example, annual financial reports often are not completed and released until many months after the end of the fiscal year. More timely reporting is important if SEA indicators are to be of use in decisions regarding resource allocation and program objectives.

We believe that entities using SEA indicators would be well advised to consider carefully several different reporting methods, perhaps even obtaining feedback from citizens and other users as to the method they prefer. This could lead to the selection of methods that, while different for different entities, would reflect the needs of the potential users. Inclusion of SEA data in the comprehensive annual financial report is recommended, even if a separate SEA report is issued.

ISSUE 7. What are the likely added costs and the feasibility of obtaining and reporting SEA indicators?

The majority of SEA indicators presented for the individual services are derived from agency data likely to be available in most jurisdictions and are not likely to require significant additional cost. However, some of the disaggregations proposed in the reports are not currently generated, so many public agencies may need to undertake procedural revisions—probably minor—to provide the SEA indicator disaggregations.

Some of the SEA indicators, however, require data-collection procedures not commonly used by governments today. These are usually outcome indicators requiring procedures such as client surveys and trained-observer ratings. Many of the research teams identified surveys of clients as a potential important source of data on customer satisfaction with service results. Such surveys require special effort and possibly added cost for most governments. Fortunately, if proper sampling procedures are used, small samples can usually provide sufficient precision for most state and local agency purposes, so costs are not likely to be excessive. In some instances, if the public agencies have existing internal capability (such as larger school systems), these procedures (for example, surveys of students and parents to obtain feedback on the various aspects of their school experiences) are not likely to require significant additional cost.

We note, however, that while most of the SEA indicators identified by the research teams have been used by at least a few public agencies, most jurisdictions do not currently collect such data. For these jurisdictions, collecting the data will require extra effort and cost. For example, while many police and fire agencies report data on "time to respond to calls for help," others do not. If these data are not currently collected, or if provision is not made to break these figures out by emergency and nonemergency calls, then extra effort by the jurisdiction will be needed.

The public health research team noted that in many cases the resources made available to public health departments include funds for collection of data for SEA indicators. Therefore, the reporting of these indicators is already an ongoing function of these departments.

Another example is the rating of road conditions by both smoothness of ride and structural condition. Many state departments of transportation already undertake such measurement at least on portions of their road systems. For such jurisdictions, reporting (including providing disaggregations by location within the state) is not likely to be a large chore. For state or local governments without such procedures—or whose procedures do not cover major parts of the road system—increased costs, both to start up the system and to maintain it, will be required.

An additional cost to which governments are not accustomed is the cost of verification of the SEA indicators. If SEA data are reported externally and become an important part of accountability reporting or are used for major program and policy decisions, these data will need to become subject to verification by independent auditors. As far as the research teams have been able to find, SEA data are not now routinely verified. (One exception is mass transit agencies, which are required to submit review certifications by CPAs in support of necessary information underlying federal revenue allocation formulas.) Verification is usually done on particular indicators only periodically. For example, it may be requested when a legislative body schedules a performance audit or evaluation, or when some national organization, such as a federal agency, reviews agency data-collection procedures. But these reviews are not done routinely or annually. Thus, verification cost itself becomes a new ingredient to be considered.

ISSUE 8. What are the uses for, and who are the users of, SEA data?

The research focused on users external to operating agencies, such as elected officials, the public, private businesses, bond rating organizations, and the media. SEA indicators are, nevertheless, also of direct and major concern to internal operating-agency management. Internal management is a significant, if not the primary, user of the SEA data. Thus, clearly management interests and concerns need to be considered.

A number of the research teams surveyed potential users, both elected and operating officials, about their perceptions of the utility of various SEA indicators. By and large, these users reported that most of the proposed indicators would be very useful to them in developing positions and making decisions. This suggests that SEA data will be useful and should be encouraged. Such surveys, however, are not the same as testing the actual utility of the information. Nor were those surveyed asked how much funding they believed the jurisdiction should be willing to provide annually to obtain the data for the indicators.

The research teams collectively identified a number of potential uses for SEA data:

1. SEA indicators can provide much *greater accountability* of governmental entities in their use of funds, permitting consideration of not only whether the funds are being used legally and for the purposes for which they were intended, but also whether they are being used efficiently and with appropriate results. This use appears to underlie much of the current impetus for external reporting of SEA information.
2. SEA information can be used as a *major basis for motivating public employees* by providing incentives, rewards, and sanctions. The presence of SEA indicators provides public agencies with an opportunity to encourage managers and staff to set goals and targets for themselves for each indicator and, with periodic feedback on actual performance, to determine whether the targeted performance has been achieved. By providing a more systematic basis for evaluation of performance, rather than depending solely on the usual qualitative judgments, public agencies can have a performance appraisal process that is more objective and easier for public officials to administer.

   For example, as the detailed reports describe, in both higher education and elementary and secondary education, SEA indicators have sometimes been used to determine rewards (such as added funding for teacher bonuses) or sanctions (various penalties, including such extremes as school system takeover). In such cases, SEA indicators usually are not the only basis for determining specific rewards or sanctions. They are almost always complemented by other means, including on-site inspections.
3. The presence of SEA reporting to the public can *stimulate the public to take greater interest in governmental entities and provide more encouragement* to officials to provide quality services. For example, as noted in the full elementary and secondary education report, New

York State officials wrote: "Public review and debate about student achievement has proven to be one of the most effective ways to develop the concern of parents and the public and to bring about action."[15] This was reiterated by the State of Florida: "Public persuasion is a powerful tool for maintaining positive change."[16]

4. SEA data can help *determine and justify the need for government programs* and, thus, be used for *budgetary decisions.*
5. With SEA indicators available, public policy discussions may be more likely to *focus on issues concerned with program results and have a more factual basis.* In the past, those discussions often have been concerned with inputs and process issues and have relied heavily on personal perceptions and feelings.
6. Finally, a main purpose of SEA indicators is to *encourage improvement in government programs and policies.* Each of the previous five uses, indirectly if not directly, should encourage attention by public officials to both service quality and efficiency. And the results shown by the indicators should pinpoint elements of the service that need improvement and help direct the attention of public officials to them. The SEA indicators will help raise questions that lead the agency to search out reasons for problems and to identify corrective actions. The improvement in the level of street cleanliness depicted in Exhibit 1-5 provides a clear indication of the possible results of reporting appropriate SEA indicators.

A problem not directly addressed in this series of Research Reports is that many public officials are not familiar with the use of SEA indicators, particularly those relating to service outcomes and efficiency. Public officials have not been accustomed to requiring SEA information from operating agencies. As discussed earlier, the surveys of users undertaken by the research teams usually revealed considerable interest in the indicators, but user experience with many of these indicators apparently is quite sparse. Experience with, and perhaps even some training about, SEA indicators and their uses is likely to be needed before SEA information can be used effectively.

---

[15]New York State Education Department, Division of Educational Testing, "Guide to Comprehensive Assessment Report, 1986 Edition" (Albany, 1986), p. 1.

[16]Florida State Department of Education, "The Use of Performance Reporting to Inform and Encourage School Improvement." Unpublished report to the U.S. Department of Education (OERI, 1987), pp. 9–10.

As noted earlier, public managers and elected officials have expressed considerable concern over the potential for misunderstanding and misuse of SEA data. Information from public reporting will inevitably be used on occasion by interest groups and the media to criticize the agency and public officials. Considering such inevitable criticism, the question must be raised: Do the advantages of public reporting of information on service outcomes outweigh the potential problems that may arise?

The concerns raised clearly point to *the need for additional research into the effect of external reporting of SEA indicators on the governmental entity and the services being measured.* This research is a natural part of the experimentation with SEA indicators being recommended as the next phase of this project.

RECOMMENDATIONS

As the decade of the 1990s begins, governmental entities appear ready to expand experiments with external reporting of SEA indicators on a regular basis. Although SEA indicator reporting is not currently widespread, elected officials, the media, and the public seem eager for information on the SEA of programs to determine what they are getting for the money being spent. Governor John Ashcoft of Missouri highlighted this need in his Foreword to the Governors' Report on Education: "We need better indicators of educational progress. We need to know what our students know, what they should know, and what kinds of programs will help them learn what they need to know."[17]

The summary chapters in this report and the separate full reports provide detailed recommendations for each of the twelve services. Each research team suggested a set of SEA indicators for external reporting. For each service, a number of indicators are almost universally accepted (such as crime rates, number of fire incidents, student standardized test results, and frequency of missed schedules by public transit vehicles). However, each service also has aspects of service quality and efficiency for which better SEA indicators are needed.

We make the following recommendations based on the collective findings of the research teams. Exhibit 1-6 (p. 42) briefly summarizes these recommendations relative to each of the eight issues examined.

---

[17] National Governors' Association, *The Governors' 1991 Report on Education, Results in Education: 1988* (Washington, DC, 1988), p. vi.

1. *We recommend that state and local governments begin external reporting of a comprehensive set of SEA indicators.* These organizations should also encourage departments and agencies to undertake such reporting for their particular programs and activities. One precedent for this has been state departments of education requiring school systems to undertake specified SEA reporting.

   Similarly, we encourage the professional associations for each service to be part of the effort to develop sets of SEA indicators that governmental agencies would be encouraged to report. The SEA indicator reporting process should be designed to encourage self-improvement by internal operating personnel. External accountability, though vital, should not be the only process design criterion. This means that internal personnel should play a major role in developing the specific SEA indicators and data-collection procedures. Internal managers may want to obtain more detailed indicators (such as more disaggregations of the indicators and more workload indicators) and need feedback more frequently (such as quarterly).

   The SEA indicators used should relate to the goals and objectives of the service, thereby providing a means of assessing results and directing efforts to improve performance in accomplishing these goals and objectives.

   Although we recommend that SEA data be reported in the comprehensive annual financial report, reporting should also be encouraged in such documents as a separate SEA report, the annual budget document, and various special reports issued by the jurisdiction.

2. *More emphasis should be placed on outcome measurement in the set of SEA data reported* and not only on input or output indicators. Outcome indicators are likely to be of particular importance, interest, and value to elected officials and the public in assessing service and program results. Reporting only the number of physical units of outputs or the resources being provided (the more common form of nonfinancial reporting) seems of limited use. Providing data on many of the outcome indicators will require agencies to implement some new, and perhaps nontraditional, data-collection procedures including the use of citizen surveys. However, the benefits of having information that will assist users in assessing the quality and results of services are likely to far exceed the cost of obtaining that information.

3. *Governmental entities should undertake experimentation to develop and test indicators that relate cost* (dollars and/or employee-hours) *to measures of service results,* especially indicators that consider

the quality and outcomes of the service. Assessment of efficiency (including cost-effectiveness) is a generally undeveloped area of SEA measurement for most services. Most current measurements relate costs to physical units of output, but do not consider the quality or effectiveness of that physical output.

The research teams have identified a number of opportunities such as cost per crime solved (cleared), cost per unit of student gain (for example, on test scores and in self-esteem), cost per mile of road whose condition has been maintained or improved to acceptable standards, cost per client who after treatment achieved controlled blood pressure, and cost per business that both reported increased employment and attributed it at least in part to state economic development program assistance.

4. *When SEA indicators are reported, certain commonsense disclosure requirements should be followed.* When SEA indicators are presented externally to elected officials and the public, it seems incumbent that the users be able to depend on these indicators being directly related to the goals and objectives of the organization and being reasonably accurate and valid representations of the performance being measured. Thus, when SEA data are presented in official documents, we recommend that they have the following characteristics (similar to those required in reporting financial data):

   a. *The indicators should be thoroughly defined* so that readers of the report will be able to understand what the indicator measures. We note that many of the indicators identified by the research teams as candidates for reporting could be ambiguous, unclear, and misleading if careful definitions were not provided. For example, the definitions of school "dropouts," transit system "on-time rates," police "clearance rates," and so forth, need to be carefully defined in the report, perhaps in footnotes. The definition should also clearly specify which time period the data cover.
   b. Similarly, *each indicator should be understandable and not overly technical.* Even if a definition is included in the footnote, an indicator should not be too complex for readers to understand.
   c. *The indicators should be relevant* to the service for which they are being reported. They should be valid indicators of performance, and the agency should be able, at least partially, to affect the performance being measured by the indicator.

d. *The indicators should be reported in a timely manner.* The data should be recent, so as to be useful for elected officials' decision making and so the public can hold officials accountable.
e. *The indicators should be consistent and comparable over time.* We are concerned that agencies, particularly if under stress, might redefine their SEA indicators or data-collection procedures from one year to the next to give a more favorable picture of the agency's performance. Frequent major changes from year to year, for any reason, will tend to undermine the comparability and utility of the information and the confidence of its users. There will be occasions when changes in SEA reporting are required. When the definition of the indicator or the data-collection procedures change significantly, this should be clearly noted in the report, and to the extent possible, the effects of these changes on the value of the indicator should be estimated.
f. *The data shown should be verifiable.* This concern is discussed further in Recommendation 9.

5. *We recommend that governmental entities provide their SEA indicators in a comprehensive format* such as that shown in Exhibit 1-7. That is, we believe the presentation should include key SEA indicators for each major category of SEA indicator shown in Exhibit 1-4 and for each major goal and objective of the entity. We recommend that a set of explanatory data elements be included at the end of the table. An example of such reporting is found in New York City's "Mayor's Management Report" and the same city's annual reports of the Citizens' Budget Commission. This form of reporting can be quite useful in providing a comprehensive perspective that enables readers to examine trends in cost, service quality, and efficiency together. It also enables readers to examine trends in the explanatory factors, providing possible explanations for performance.

6. We urge governmental entities to *tabulate and report major disaggregations of SEA indicators,* as discussed under Issue 2. Disaggregations of service results by geographical area, facility, and level of difficulty of incoming workload appear particularly useful for most services. For services directed to individual clients, disaggregations by various key demographic characteristics (such as income, ethnicity, household composition, or age group) are likely to be appropriate. The disaggregations of most value will depend on the particular

service. Disaggregations increase the information that needs to be reported; such information will probably need to be provided in separate tables to avoid overcrowding tabular report displays.

7. *The reports should enable readers to compare current results with benchmarks.* The comparisons discussed earlier (under Issue 3) should be very helpful to users of these reports, both elected officials and the public. Comparisons that appear appropriate for most, if not all, services include comparisons with (a) SEA indicators in previous years, (b) SEA targets identified in budget or other documents, (c) other comparable jurisdictions that collect comparable data, and (d) established norms or standards that reflect what is considered to be an acceptable level of performance, and comparisons of (e) SEA of individual facilities or individual locations, with other locations or with the jurisdiction-wide average for SEA indicators. We suggest that agencies be encouraged to establish specific quantitative goals and targets for each SEA indicator and report comparisons of actual performance against targeted performance. This latter type of comparison is likely to be of considerable interest to agency management and to elected officials, especially as part of the budget process.

8. *Explanatory factors need to be included with the SEA indicators, and program managers should be the first public officials to review the SEA indicators.* These steps can help alleviate the concern held by both agency people and elected officials about reporting "bad news." Both operating agency managers and elected officials are concerned—legitimately so—that the indicators may be misinterpreted and misused to their detriment. They worry, for example, that the data will get to the press before these officials themselves have had adequate time to examine the information. To reduce anxiety over this problem, we recommend that the operating agency receive the information first, even if it is collected by some central office. The operating agency should have the opportunity to review the information and provide explanations for unusual performance, whether good or bad. Explanatory information is essential in communicating the reasons for variations in performance and in helping report users understand the environment within which the organization is operating and how it may differ from that of other organizations providing similar services.

More difficult is the problem of misinterpretation by outsiders after the SEA indicators are reported. To help address this problem, we recommend the inclusion of explanatory data (as discussed under Issue 4). The explanatory data presented should include a basic set of explanatory elements that are regularly reported. These should be grouped into two categories: (a) elements substantially outside the control of the public agency, such as demographic characteristics, and (b) elements over which the agency has significant control, such as staffing patterns.

The agency should also be able to include ad hoc narrative explanations for performance that varies significantly from expectations. This practice, of course, is not unusual and is common in private company annual reports to stockholders. It is possible, of course, that the explanations will sometimes be no more than rationalizations and excuses, but nevertheless the operating agency should have the opportunity to provide what it believes to be an appropriate explanation. The overall process, we believe, should not inhibit the disclosure of bad news as it occurs, but at the same time it should permit explanations to be provided.

9. *Governmental entities need to consider the extent to which SEA indicators reported externally must be verified through some type of formal review or audit process.* Currently, verification is seldom undertaken for nonfinancial indicators. The dilemma is illustrated by a 1988 U.S. GAO report that examined a federal agency's reporting on actual performance versus agency targets. The report stated, "We noted that data used to report actual target accomplishments are not routinely verified or checked for accuracy."[18]

Verification costs money, but as SEA indicators become a part of public disclosures, the public has the right to expect that the data will be based on sound data-collection practices, just as financial data should reflect sound accounting principles and practices. However, requiring verification may discourage some public agencies from disclosing and reporting SEA indicators, at least in formal reports. This is another reason why legislative requirements and the support of professional organizations are likely to be needed to encourage officials to disclose SEA information in a comprehensive and accurate manner. However, government officials need to keep in mind that, even when used for internal management purposes, SEA data are of more value if subjected to the level of verification necessary for management use.

---

[18]U.S. General Accounting Office, "Forest Service: Evaluation of 'End-Results' Budgeting Test," GAO-AFMD-88-45 (Washington, DC, March 1988), p. 10.

The discussion under Issue 5 provides more specific suggestions on such verifications. This type of verification is not as costly as that necessary for financial information being presented in the financial statements.

We recommend that verification to the level necessary for management use be performed for all indicators. For example, for internal management purposes, the verification could be performed by an organizational unit within the entity but independent of the unit responsible for the particular service. For external reporting, however, the verification should be done by an organization independent of the executive branch of this entity. The level of verification of SEA data should also increase when SEA indicator information is used for performance evaluation or for resource allocation decisions.

10. We recommend that *collection* of nonfinancial data for SEA indicators be the responsibility of the particular operating agency. *Verification* of the data (where needed) should be the responsibility of an agency independent of the operating agency being reported on. *Compilation, production,* and *dissemination* of the SEA indicators probably should be the responsibility of a central staff office reporting to the chief executive or chief administrative officer. This could be a financial office or another analytical staff office. The external report of SEA indicators can be provided as a "new, separate" report or other, existing report. Even if reported in another report, we recommend that a comprehensive set of SEA indicators be included as part of the entity's comprehensive annual financial report.

Exhibit 1-6
Issues Examined and Recommendations

1. **What SEA indicators should be candidates for reporting?**
   For each service researched, the researchers recommend a set of SEA indicators as a beginning point for developing a comprehensive set to be experimented with in external reporting. This report and the separate reports for each service contain details. The recommended types of indicators are input, output, outcome, and efficiency (including cost-effectiveness). We also recommend that more emphasis be placed on outcome and efficiency measurement in the set of SEA indicators reported.

2. **How, and to what extent, should individual SEA indicators be disaggregated?**
   We recommend the reporting of major disaggregations of SEA indicators. Consideration should be given to disaggregations by geographical area, facility, and demographic characteristics of clients, especially those that reflect the "difficulty" of the agency's workload.

3. **What comparisons should be reported for the various SEA indicators?**
   The SEA report should enable readers to compare current results with benchmarks. Comparisons that appear appropriate include comparisons with (a) SEA indicators in previous years, (b) SEA targets identified in budget or other documents, (c) other comparable jurisdictions that collect comparable data, (d) established norms or standards that reflect what is considered an acceptable level of performance, and (e) SEA of individual facilities or individual locations with other locations or with the jurisdiction-wide average.

4. **What explanatory data should be included with SEA indicators, and how should these data be presented?**
   Explanatory factors that help report users to understand the environment within which the service is delivered and the factors that may affect the results of that service should be included with the SEA indicators. These explanatory factors will differ from service to service and between jurisdictions. These factors should be classified as to the extent to which the agency can affect the explanatory factor.

Exhibit 1-6 (continued)

5. To what extent are these SEA indicators verifiable?

All indicators recommended seem to be verifiable, but questions remain regarding the cost of this verification and the degree of verification necessary. We recommend that verification to the level necessary for management use be performed for indicators and that as the technical capabilities of auditors increase in performing this type of verification, the level of verification increase, especially for indicators used for performance evaluation or for major resource allocation decisions. Verification should be the responsibility of an agency independent of the operating agency reported on.

6. How should SEA information be communicated and displayed?

We recommend that SEA data be reported in the comprehensive annual financial report, with reporting also encouraged in separate SEA reports, the annual budget document, and various special reports issued by the jurisdiction.

7. What are the likely added costs and the feasibility of obtaining and reporting SEA indicators?

Many SEA indicators presented for the individual services are derived from agency data likely to be available in most jurisdictions and should not require significant additional cost. However, some recommended SEA indicators will require data collection not currently performed, some of which may result in added cost for most entities. Therefore, the entities should use care in choosing which SEA indicators to report, considering the benefits from the additional information as well as the data-collection and reporting costs.

8. What are the uses for, and who are the users of, SEA data?

The research teams identified several potential uses for SEA data including:

a. To provide greater accountability by governmental entities for their use of resources,
b. To motivate personnel, such as by encouraging managers to set goals and targets and providing periodic feedback on actual performance,
c. To stimulate the public to take greater interest in the provision of quality services,

Exhibit 1-6 (continued)

    d. To help explain the need for and value of government programs and provide a basis for budgetary decisions,
    e. To help focus public policy discussion on issues concerned with program results, and
    f. To encourage improvement in government programs and policies.

Users of SEA indicators include program managers, top management, elected officials, citizens, taxpayer groups, and other governmental organizations (oversight bodies, and so forth).

FINAL OBSERVATIONS

As the title of this Research Report series indicates, the findings of the research teams strongly suggest that the time has come for major experimentation in implementing service efforts and accomplishments measurement and reporting SEA indicators to elected officials and the public. The project team believes *it is now important for governmental entities to experiment widely with external reporting of SEA indicators.* These experiments could start with the sets of indicators recommended for the twelve services researched and presented in this report. But it is important that the SEA indicators not be limited to those being recommended, or even necessarily include all of the recommended SEA indicators. Experimenters should seek to identify and develop SEA indicators that will best report the results of operations for the program being considered, especially as they relate to accomplishing the goals and objectives established for that program. Several possible methods should be considered for external reporting of SEA indicators, including publication as part of governmental financial reports in their several forms and of various other reports such as budget documents, popular reports, and even special performance reports on SEA with the indicators presented in both graphic and tabular form.

We recognize that some may criticize the recommended SEA indicators as being too comprehensive, others as not being comprehensive enough. Some may believe the recommended indicators are not fully valid measures of performance. However, we believe the recommended indicators provide an excellent point to begin the development of a comprehensive set of SEA indicators and that, if used for expanded experimentation with the external reporting of SEA data, they can help focus and advance efforts aimed at improving the means of reporting accountability information to be used in monitoring the performance of governmental entities.

Exhibit 1-7
Example of Presentation Format:
Elementary and Secondary Education SEA Indicators

Indicator	Next Previous Fiscal Year	Previous Fiscal Year	Current Fiscal Year	Percentage Change from Previous Fiscal Year	Target for Current Fiscal Year	Average of Comparison Jurisdictions[e]
Inputs:						
Expenditures[a] (in millions) (may be broken out by type of activity)						
Current dollars	$63.5	$68.5	$73.7	8%	$72.5	$75.5
Constant dollars	$55.7	$58.0	$60.6	4%	$59.6	$62.0
Total number of personnel (may be reported by type of activity)	1,062	1,074	1,080	1%	1,075	1,100
Outputs:						
Number of student-days (thousands)	2,583	2,543	2,452	−4%	2,535	2,842
Number of students promoted/ graduated	12,700	12,400	11,900	−4%	12,400	13,900
Carnegie units as percentage of required[b] (Carnegie units required may be reported by major subject area)	100.0%	102.5%	105.0%	2%	107.5%	105.0%
Absenteeism rate	5.4%	3.4%	5.1%	50%	3.0%	4.1%
Dropout rate (annual)	4.2%	3.9%	5.9%	51%	3.8%	4.2%

Outcomes:

Test score results—*for each major subject area*						
Average percentile on standardized tests	48.6%	49.5%	50.2%	1%	60.0%	52.1%
Percentage of students above the 50th percentile[c]	45.6%	45.9%	47.4%	3%	56.0%	49.0%
Percentage of students reaching their grade level of proficiency or higher	72.3%	74.3%	73.5%	−1%	77.0%	76.5%
Percentage of students achieving grade-level gain on achievement test[d] (may be presented for major subject areas as well as overall)	78.0%	77.0%	73.0%	−5%	83.0%	88.0%
Percentage of students scoring higher than prespecified level of self-esteem	61.0%	65.0%	58.0%	−11%	68.0%	64.0%
Percentage of students achieving specified physical fitness test standards	67.2%	70.1%	68.2%	−3%	75.0%	67.8%

[a] A clear description of which expenditures are included or excluded should be provided.

[b] One Carnegie unit equals five hours per week of instructional class time on a subject for an entire school year.

[c] The 50th percentile is the point that one-half of the students who were used to develop the test norm scored at or above and one-half scored below.

[d] A grade-level gain is the measure of a student's progress by school year, as assessed by a test score, for example, from the 6.1 grade level to the 7.1 grade level.

[e] Comparison jurisdictions should be chosen based on demographic and other factors that have been shown to affect educational achievement. California, for example, has developed one method of selecting comparison jurisdictions that appears promising.

Exhibit 1-7 (continued)

Indicator	Next Previous Fiscal Year	Previous Fiscal Year	Current Fiscal Year	Percentage Change from Previous Fiscal Year	Target for Current Fiscal Year	Average of Comparison Jurisdictions
Outcomes (continued):						
Percentage of graduates gainfully employed or continuing education two years after graduation	76.8%	77.9%	79.2%	2%	81.0%	81.6%
Percentage of students rating as good, excellent, or improved—their own:						
Work and study skills	85.4%	87.2%	83.5%	−4%	90.0%	88.5%
Self-discipline	72.8%	68.7%	75.4%	10%	90.0%	77.0%
Interpersonal skills	65.7%	72.3%	71.0%	−2%	90.0%	74.8%
Knowledge gained	61.3%	68.2%	70.3%	3%	75.0%	73.6%
Percentage of parents rating their children as good, excellent, or improved in:						
Work and study skills	55.6%	59.0%	63.2%	7%	85.0%	74.5%
Self-discipline	65.0%	63.2%	67.6%	7%	85.0%	76.0%
Interpersonal skills	78.0%	76.9%	73.9%	−4%	85.0%	81.2%
Knowledge gained	57.8%	63.2%	61.8%	−2%	75.0%	72.5%

Efficiency:						
Cost per output						
Per student-day	$25	$27	$30	11%	$29	$27
Per student promoted/graduated	$5,000	$5,524	$6,193	12%	$5,847	$5,432
Cost per outcome						
Per student achieving grade-level score gain	$5,815	$6,570	$7,620	16%	$6,519	$5,644
Explanatory Data:						
Controllable						
Average number of hours per student in oversized classes (per day)	1.4	1.6	1.3	−19%	N/A	0.98
Not controllable						
Average daily attendance	13,244	13,041	12,574	−4%	12,998	14,577
Percentage of minority students	26.7%	27.5%	27.8%	1%	N/A	24.8%
Percentage of students participating in subsidized lunch or other public welfare program	16.4%	15.9%	16.3%	3%	N/A	13.5%
Percentage of students needing special remedial programs	14.2%	13.9%	14.7%	6%	N/A	11.9%
Student mobility rate[f]	5.0%	5.0%	9.0%	80%	N/A	4.0%
Percentage of students with English as second language	8.0%	9.5%	10.5%	11%	N/A	7.5%
Student enrollments	14,000	13,500	13,250	−2%	13,400	15,200

[f] One definition for this is: Percentage of school's beginning enrollment entering, or departing, after the start of the school year.

2. Colleges and Universities

Don Chamberlain, Murray State University

Relmond P. Van Daniker, University of Kentucky

	Page
Introduction	52
Objectives of Higher Education	52
Methodology	53
Scope	53
Growing Interest in Higher Education Performance Assessment and Accountability	54
Recommendations	57
Higher Education Environment	58
SEA Indicators	58
Input Measures	59
Output Measures	59
Outcomes Measures	59
Efficiency Measures	65
Disaggregation	67
Comparison Information	67
Explanatory Information	68
Conclusions	69

INTRODUCTION

Higher education enjoyed tremendous growth in enrollments and resources during the 1960s and 1970s. Expansion occurred at all levels of higher education. New programs were developed and new facilities were constructed. More recent years, however, have been characterized by declining or stable enrollments, retrenchment of programs, and, not surprisingly, greater emphasis on efficiency and effectiveness.

This chapter describes this emerging phenomenon, especially the widespread attention to outcomes assessment, and recommends service efforts and accomplishments (SEA) indicators for public reporting. Readers with a specific interest in SEA reporting in higher education are encouraged to review the full-length report available soon from the GASB.

OBJECTIVES OF HIGHER EDUCATION

Educators have debated the role of higher education in society for many years. The Carnegie Commission on Higher Education suggested the purposes of higher education might be:

1. The provision of opportunities for the intellectual, aesthetic, ethical, and skill development of individual students, and the provision of campus environments which can constructively assist students in their more general developmental growth
2. The advancement of human capability in society at large
3. The enlargement of educational justice for the postsecondary age group
4. The transmission and advancement of learning and wisdom
5. The critical evaluation of society—through individual thought and persuasion—for the sake of society's self-renewal.[1]

---

[1] Carnegie Commission on Higher Education, *The Purposes and the Performance of Higher Education in the United States: Approaching the Year 2000* (New York: McGraw-Hill, 1973), p. 1.

The report noted that individual institutions would relate to some of these purposes more than others, depending on their respective missions. It is this variety of missions that makes assessing SEA and accountability difficult.

METHODOLOGY

More than 150 higher education institutions were contacted and asked to forward their annual reports, statistical profiles, fact books, institutional research reports, budget documents, and any special reports they believed might contain examples of SEA data. More than 300 documents from some 85 institutions were received and reviewed.

In addition, telephone interviews were conducted with more than 40 individuals, ranging from recognized authorities in the performance reporting arena, to accreditation personnel, to institutional representatives responsible for preparing the reports reviewed. Their insights have greatly influenced the comments and recommendations included in the following pages.

Finally, accounting and higher education literature was reviewed. The wealth of information on outcomes assessment, while at times overwhelming, was invaluable in gaining a perspective on both the difficulties and opportunities that lie ahead in this area.

SCOPE

Higher education's primary functions include instruction, research, and public service. In addition, support functions like student services, libraries, operation and maintenance of plant, auxiliary services, and others greatly influence the intellectual and personal development of students.

This chapter focuses on regular, undergraduate instruction to the extent a single program can be studied separately. Clearly the measures discussed here are affected to varying degrees by these other activities that are an inherent part of the delivery of "higher" education.

GROWING INTEREST IN HIGHER EDUCATION PERFORMANCE ASSESSMENT AND ACCOUNTABILITY

Higher education has not escaped the nation's growing demand for greater accountability on the part of its public entities. In fact, higher education officials themselves are examining operations more closely, in response to tighter budgets as well as calls for evidence of effectiveness. While attention has traditionally focused on input and output measures, more recently the focus has been on outcomes.

Halpern perhaps best characterizes the new emphasis on "outcomes assessment":

> Usually we recognize superior universities by their research reputations and by the size and cost of their physical plants. By these criteria, only the large research institutions will be judged excellent, while small colleges and universities, especially those with major commitments to teaching undergraduates, are doomed to mediocre standing at best. Assessment of learning outcomes is one solution to this lopsided notion of educational quality. Instead of documenting excellence by variables unrelated to learning, like research reputation and size, or inferring quality by examining opinion surveys, number of volumes in the library, and retention rates, we can assess educational quality more directly by examining what and how much students actually learn.[2]

In short, the interest in outcomes assessment reflects a growing recognition by policy makers and educators that higher education can no longer use inputs (amount of resources expended, number of faculty, number of volumes in the library, etc.) as the only means to measure effectiveness. Now, student scores on national and locally developed exams, their perceptions of the quality of instruction and services, the opinions of graduates and employers, the accomplishments of students and faculty, and similar "results-oriented" data are increasingly being used for assessing how well institutions are meeting their goals and objectives.

---

[2]Diane F. Halpern, "Student Outcomes Assessment: Introduction and Overview," in Diane F. Halpern (ed.), *Student Outcomes Assessment: What Institutions Stand to Gain,* New Directions for Higher Education, no. 59 (San Francisco: Jossey-Bass, Inc., 1987).

Several excellent models of assessment have emerged. Northeast Missouri State University has approached assessment using a "value-added" perspective, measuring the general education levels of students when they enter college and again at the end of their sophomore year. In addition, major field exams are administered to graduating seniors. These tests, coupled with attitudinal surveys of enrolled students, alumni, and employers, form the basis for assessing the institution's effectiveness. The data derived are used to identify and correct weaknesses in curricula, teaching methods, facilities, and other aspects of the instructional environment.

Alverno College, a private liberal arts women's college in Wisconsin, has taken a slightly different approach. While both general education and discipline-specific learning are measured through testing, Alverno places a very high priority on noncognitive outcomes. Some eight critical abilities, each with six levels of performance, must be demonstrated by all students.[3] Their Assessment Center is responsible for coordinating the program, and external evaluators from industry, government, business, and other potential employer groups are heavily utilized.

The University of Tennessee at Knoxville (UTK) has also initiated a major assessment effort, partially in response to a decision by the Tennessee Higher Education Commission to allocate a portion of the state's higher education appropriation on the basis of performance. Like the above programs, UTK's effort measures both cognitive (knowledge) and noncognitive (satisfaction, values, etc.) outcomes across several dimensions.

Other assessment efforts under way include those in New Jersey, Virginia, Florida, Georgia, California, South Dakota, and South Carolina, to name but a few. In total, nearly two-thirds of the states have begun some form of assessment and others are reviewing the desirability of such programs for their colleges and universities.[4]

New Jersey has undertaken perhaps the most ambitious statewide assessment program to date. In its College Outcomes Evaluation Program (COEP), the state has delineated some eight outcomes clusters/

---

[3]These eight areas include communications, analysis, problem solving, values in decision making, social interaction, taking responsibility for the environment, involvement in the contemporary world, and aesthetic response.

[4]Carol M. Boyer et al., "Assessment and Outcomes Measurement: A View from the States," in *ECS Working Papers,* PS-87-1 (Denver: Education Commission of the States, 1987), p. 2.

variables to be measured.[5] These range from general intellectual skills and learning in the major field, to student involvement and satisfaction with their educational experiences, to the research and scholarship endeavors of the faculty. Both statewide and locally defined outcomes will be measured, and plans call for periodic public reporting of most elements of the program.

The accrediting agencies in higher education have also joined the assessment movement. The Southern Association of Colleges and Schools (SACS), which accredits colleges and universities in the southern United States, has completely revised its accreditation standards into "criteria." In its criterion on institutional effectiveness, SACS notes:

> ... A comprehensive approach to accreditation, however, takes into account not only the resources and processes of education (such as faculty and student qualifications, physical plant, fiscal resources and other elements addressed in the *Criteria*) but also the evaluation of the results of education and plans for the improvement of the institution's programs.[6]

The U.S. Department of Education (DOE) stimulated accreditation agencies to add such requirements. The DOE recently adopted administrative regulations under which it will require accreditation agencies, as a condition for recognition, to include required assessment of student outcomes in their guidelines.[7] Further, many discipline-specific accreditation organizations, such as the American Assembly of Collegiate Schools of Business, have explored the desirability of incorporating outcomes assessment into their criteria.[8]

Not to be underestimated is the demand for evidence of effectiveness by public officials such as legislators, governors, state higher education officials, and others. They are now calling for evidence that students are leaving college with the requisite knowledge and skills that institutions are entrusted to provide. For example, the report of the

---

[5]Advisory Committee to the COEP, "Report to the New Jersey Board of Higher Education" (1987).

[6]SACS, *Criteria for Accreditation: Commission on Colleges* (Atlanta: SACS, 1987), p. 10.

[7]DOE, "Secretary's Procedures and Criteria for Recognition of Accrediting Agencies," *Federal Register,* vol. 53, no. 127 (Washington, DC, July 1988).

[8]American Assembly of Collegiate Schools of Business, *Outcome Measurement Project: Phase III Report* (St. Louis, 1987).

National Governors' Association, *Time for Results: The Governors' 1991 Report on Education,* made several recommendations regarding enhancement of quality and outcomes assessment. Two especially relevant suggestions include:

> Each college and university should implement systematic programs that use multiple measures to assess undergraduate student learning. The information gained from assessment should be used to evaluate institutional and program quality. Information about institutional and program quality also should be made available to the public.[9]

and

> The higher education accrediting community should require colleges and universities to collect and utilize information about undergraduate student outcomes. Demonstrated levels of student learning and performance should be a consideration in granting institutional accreditation.[10]

While higher education institutions are required to report extensively to many levels of authority, this reporting has focused principally on input, output, and process information. Consequently, these are the areas where some degree of standardization and public reporting has been effected. The future will hopefully bring much in the way of advancements in the reporting of outcomes, in response to both growing calls for accountability and the quest for improved program offerings.

RECOMMENDATIONS

SEA indicators are currently being reported by most institutions, although in varying degrees of comprehensiveness. The focus remains on inputs and outputs, but outcomes assessment initiatives are beginning to provide additional effectiveness measures. Before recommending specific indicators for reporting, however, a brief discussion of some contextual issues is appropriate.

---

[9]NGA, Center for Policy Research and Analysis, *Time for Results: The Governors' 1991 Report on Education* (Washington, DC, 1986), p. 161.
[10]Ibid., p. 163.

Higher Education Environment

The nation's higher education system is best characterized by its diversity. Large, small, public, private, land grant, open admissions, regional, comprehensive, teaching-oriented, and research-oriented are but a few of the terms describing the varying missions of our institutions. Such diversity makes the application of common "yardsticks" difficult at best. Sensitivity to these differences will be an important element of any proposed reporting framework.

Further, colleges and universities have traditionally enjoyed a high degree of autonomy. Even within states that exercise extensive financial control over their higher education institutions, the academic domain has largely remained independent. This autonomy has yielded the creative management so necessary in creative endeavors, and nurtured the diversity mentioned above.

Finally, and as discussed in the previous section, higher education institutions across the country are currently initiating efforts to assess their outcomes. Responding to pressures from within and outside, schools are seeking the information needed both to demonstrate accountability and to improve extant programs. Such efforts should be encouraged, and fears of punitive actions by regulatory agents based on assessment data should be alleviated.

These characteristics should not suggest that higher education be exempted from scrutiny. To the contrary, institutions themselves will be the first to advocate that high standards of accountability be established. Still, a sensitivity to the diversity and autonomy which characterize our colleges and universities, and to their emerging efforts to assess their results, will likely yield the best system of SEA reporting over the long run.

SEA Indicators

Exhibit 2-1 presents the SEA indicators recommended for public reporting, along with the rationale for including each measure. (As noted earlier, the list focuses on the instruction/learning domain and does not address research and public service activities.) A comprehensive set of measures should include input, output, outcomes, and efficiency indicators. Further, explanatory data necessary to provide users with a complete context for understanding and evaluating the indicators should be provided.

Input Measures

The number of faculty and the level of instructional expenditures are the input indicators recommended for public reporting. Since faculty compensation is generally the principal instructional cost component, changes (up or down) in the number of faculty warrant close scrutiny. Obviously, the qualitative and demographic characteristics of faculty are also important, and are recommended for inclusion as valuable explanatory information in a later section.

Instructional expenditures reflect the amount of resources being dedicated to the instruction effort. Reporting the level of expenditures in terms of both current and constant dollars will convey a more complete picture of available resources and the effects of inflation. Common indexes used include the Consumer Price Index (CPI) and the Higher Education Price Index (HEPI).

Output Measures

The recommended output measures are currently being reported to many internal and external agencies. The number of degrees and certificates awarded, student credit hours generated, and FTE (full-time equivalent) students generated are widely accepted output measures of the instructional effort. Variation exists in the calculation of FTE students, but an explanatory note can explain how the unit is being measured.

Outcomes Measures

Outcomes assessment is one of higher education's exciting new initiatives. Several universities already have programs in place and others are in the planning or implementation phases. (Readers are encouraged to familiarize themselves with the programs at Northeast Missouri State University, the University of Tennessee at Knoxville, and Alverno College, as well as the state of Tennessee's performance funding system and New Jersey's COEP initiative.) While the approaches to assessing outcomes are many and varied, some common themes are apparent. The outcomes measures recommended below appear frequently in the models observed.

Exhibit 2-1
Recommended SEA Indicators for Colleges and Universities*

Indicator	Rationale for Selecting Indicator
Input:	

Instructional Expenditures:
   Current dollars
   Constant dollars
	To provide a measure of the resources used to provide instruction

Number of Faculty:
   Full-time
   Total FTE
	To provide a measure of the number of faculty available to provide instruction

Output:	
Number of Degrees and Certificates Awarded	To provide a measure of students satisfactorily completing educational requirements

Number of Student Credit Hours (SCH) Generated:
   Unweighted
   Weighted
	To provide a measure of work load and productivity (Weighting can be used to equate differences among disciplines and course levels.)

Number of FTE Students (fall semester)	To provide a measure of work load and productivity; FTE students are derived from student credit hours
Outcomes:	

Academic Test Scores:
   General education
     National exams
       Average percentile score
       Percentage scoring above 50th percentile
     Local exams
       Average score
       Percentage scoring 70% or above
	To provide direct measures of student learning across the general education field, and comparisons with selected standards

Major field
  National exams
    Average percentile score
    Percentage scoring above 50th percentile
  Local exams
    Average score
    Percentage scoring 70% or above

⎫
⎬ To provide direct measures of students' learning in their chosen fields of study, and comparisons with selected standards
⎭

Student Ratings of Select Aspects of College,[†] e.g.:
  Help in reaching select goals
    Increasing knowledge in major field
    Learning life-enriching skills
    Improving self-image
    Improving leadership skills
  Adequacy of general education program in developing:
    Effective writing and speaking skills/habits
    Independent work skills/habits
    Understanding of different philosophies and cultures
    Ability to define, analyze, and solve problems
  Adequacy of academic major program in areas such as:
    Gaining knowledge of issues and trends pertinent to specialty
    Applying knowledge in defining and solving problems
    Identifying values and responding ethically
    Integrating career and personal goals

⎫
⎬ To provide student perceptions of the quality of instruction and guidance received; both cognitive and noncognitive dimensions are addressed
⎭

---

[*]The recommended indicators presented in this exhibit are illustrative. They are intended to serve as a starting point for use in the development of a comprehensive set of SEA indicators for external reporting of an entity's results of operation.

This exhibit does not provide illustrations of indicator disaggregation or of comparison data such as trends, targets, or other comparable entities. Both disaggregation and comparison data are important aspects of SEA reporting. They are discussed in the chapter and in the Overview.

[†]These sample criteria were taken or adapted from survey instruments used at Northeast Missouri State University.

Exhibit 2-1 (continued)

Indicator	Rationale for Selecting Indicator
Outcomes: (continued)	

Alumni Ratings of Select Aspects of Their Instruction Program,[†] such as:
  Overall impression of general education courses
  Overall impression of courses in major field
  Overall quality of instruction in major
  Overall quality of faculty academic advising
  Help in achieving occupational goals
	To provide alumni perceptions of the quality of instruction received (*Note:* Some institutions may also wish to obtain responses to some or all the questions asked of students per the above measure, providing a "second look" perspective.)

Licensure and Certification Exam Results
  Number Taking Exams
  Percentage Passing Exams
	To provide a measure of student success in meeting criteria established by professional groups; also, can suggest currentness and relevance of curricula

Retention/Graduation Rates, such as:
  Percentage of entering first-time, full-time freshmen still enrolled/graduated after
    4 years
    5 years
    6 years
	To provide a measure of success in retaining students until they complete their degree objective (*Note:* Similar measures can be developed for two-year and certificate programs.)

Employment and Graduate Study Rates, such as:
  After one year, percentage of graduates' indicating:
    They were currently employed full-time
    They were currently enrolled in a program of study
	To provide measures of student success in obtaining employment and student interest in further study as evidenced by enrollment in programs of study

Employers' Satisfaction† with Graduates:
  Knowledge/skills specific to the job
  Reading and writing skills
  Work attitudes
  General academic preparation
  Overall rating of the graduate

} To provide a measure of employer satisfaction with graduates

Efficiency Measures:

Instructional Expenditures/Student Credit Hour (SCH):
  Unweighted
  Weighted

} To provide a measure of the cost of generating a unit of output; measures one dimension of efficiency

FTE Students/FTE Faculty (fall semester):
  Unweighted
  Weighted

} To provide a measure of work load and productivity; measures one dimension of efficiency

Explanatory Data:

Role and Mission Statement
State Appropriations:
  Total
  Per FTE student
Average Class Size
Other:
  Faculty data
  Enrollment data
  Entering-student test scores
  Listing of degree programs
  Other explanatory data and notes as needed

} To provide information on factors that affect student learning and development, and the efficiency and effectiveness with which instructional services are delivered

63

a. *Results on academic tests.* Students' scores on tests of general education and major field examinations are the most direct method of determining how much students have learned. National and locally developed exams can and are being used. Test scores can be supplemented, if desired, with results from senior seminars, senior projects, interviews, etc.

   Testing does have its detractors, who argue that many of the national exams are biased or do not specifically focus on subject material deemed most important at a given school. Using locally developed instruments can alleviate these shortcomings, but considerable time and effort are required. The quantifiability of results makes testing a particularly attractive and common element of most existing assessment programs.

b. *Student and former student ratings.* The attitudes of students and former students can be especially enlightening. Both national and locally developed instruments are utilized. Present and former students can be polled regarding the institution's general education or major field programs, the extent to which their college experience helped them achieve certain goals or attain certain skills, etc. The specific content of the survey would likely vary from school to school, but the sample criteria shown in Exhibit 2-1 are appropriate for most institutions.

c. *Results on licensure and certification exams.* In many fields, students must pass a licensure or certification exam before they can enter the profession or function in certain capacities. Their performance on these exams is an indication of the extent to which students' preparation meets criteria established by the professional organizations. While institutions should not (and do not) let professional examination standards dictate the structure of their programs, such exams do serve as a helpful "litmus test." Insight regarding not only student performance but the relevance and currentness of curricula and classroom instruction can be gleaned from the results.

d. *Retention and graduation rates.* A general indicator of the extent to which an institution's instructional (and other) programs are meeting their desired goals is the retention/graduation rate of students. Retaining students until they complete their degrees is universally considered important. Faculty and others across the campus play an important role in stimulating students' interest in learning and guiding them through difficult situations. While some attrition is expected, efforts to retain students should be monitored. Students' reasons for leaving should be documented, analyzed, and used as a basis for improving retention.

e. *Employment and graduate study rates.* Higher education institutions endeavor to provide students with skills and knowledge that will serve them in all aspects of life. Few colleges or universities espouse job placement as a goal, but they, along with students, parents, government officials, and others, are quite sensitive to the ability of graduates to obtain jobs. The extent to which former students desire and actually enroll in further study also is deemed important.

Potential measures in these areas might focus on the proportion of students employed or enrolled in programs of further study after some specified period of time, say a year. Some colleges or universities may wish to learn more specific information, such as whether employment is related to the field of study, beginning salary levels, plans for further study, etc.

f. *Employers' satisfaction with graduates.* While job-related skills are but one dimension of the education process, many colleges and universities consider employers' satisfaction with their graduates to be important. Like academic tests and licensure and certification exams, the results of employer surveys can reveal the extent to which students have acquired important knowledge and/or skills. Employers can address both occupationally related knowledge and abilities and more general dimensions like writing and speaking ability, interpersonal skills, leadership, and motivation.

The above measures are recommended as core indicators; experimentation with other measures is also recommended. Where appropriate, explanatory notes should be used to comment on, or explain, points of interest or concern. Where tests and surveys are to be used, care in designing instruments and drawing samples is critical. SEA reporting will clearly entail additional costs, but careful planning and application of the information obtained to improve programs and services can help keep expenses within reasonable limits.

Efficiency Measures

Probably few other topics in higher education generate as much debate as the subject of efficiency. While most agree that the measurement of efficiency is important, few agree on how to measure true efficiency. Most of the efforts to date have focused on input/output as opposed to input/outcomes relationships, although the latter is more likely to convey the desired information.

Instructional expenditure per student credit hour (SCH) is a commonly reported and relatively easily understood measure. This indicator reveals the relative cost per unit when displayed at the discipline (subject field) level of disaggregation. However, problems with allocating costs among disciplines are common, often resulting in the use of only direct expenditures.

Also recommended for reporting is the ratio of FTE students to FTE faculty. A workload/productivity indicator, this measure is also often reported in the form of student credit hours per FTE faculty. (Student credit hours can be converted to FTE students by dividing hours by a conversion factor, typically 9 or 12 for graduate courses and 12, 15, or 16 for undergraduate instruction.) The method of calculation of FTE students (and FTE faculty) would need to be detailed.

In an effort to account for differences among disciplines, some institutions have utilized a system of "weighting," in which select fields of study or levels of instruction are recognized as requiring lower student/faculty ratios. As an example, a discipline that has generated 240 FTE students using 10 FTE faculty would have an unweighted ratio of 24:1. However, if that discipline has been determined to require a weighting factor of 1.5, then its "weighted" ratio would be 36:1 (24 multiplied by 1.5). Similarly, its weighted instruction cost/SCH would fall from, say, $48/SCH to $32/SCH. The weighted indicators would be roughly comparable across disciplines, with the weights being derived at some central administrative level (hopefully with input from the instructional departments).

Unfortunately, input/output relationships suggest little about the effectiveness of the outputs or outcomes. Hence, while changes in these indicators or variations from established norms warrant scrutiny, care must be exercised not to draw conclusions not substantiated by other information.

As progress is made in the area of outcomes assessment, institutions hopefully will develop input/outcomes indicators. For example, a ratio such as "percentage change in instruction cost/percentage gain in average test score" could convey the extent to which increased resources are yielding better results.

DISAGGREGATION

Most of the suggested indicators can be reported at three levels of specificity—university-wide, college or major division, and department or discipline level. Generally, the indicators are more useful at the lower (more specific) level, i.e., when reported by department or discipline.

Breakouts of the data by select categories also enhance its usefulness. These categories include gender, ethnicity, age, class level, whether resident or commuter, and discipline (major field).

Difficulties can arise when allocating inputs and outputs to the various departments within a college or division. Consequently, care should be taken when attempting to compare data for two or more institutions. Explanatory notes should describe the procedures used to compile potentially uncomparable data.

COMPARISON INFORMATION

Comparative information is essential to presenting a complete perspective for interpreting SEA information. Four types of comparisons are recommended for use by colleges and universities:

1. *Comparisons with prior periods.* Comparisons with prior periods are often the most valid and useful presentations available. Reporting SEA data for the most recent two, three, or even five years can help identify trends and detect potential problems early.
2. *Comparisons with other institutions, including "benchmark" institutions.* Many colleges and universities report comparisons with other institutions. Particularly useful are comparisons with "benchmarks" (colleges and universities of a similar size, program mix, and mission). Frequently, institutions have informal information exchange arrangements with other schools, making special efforts to ensure that compilation procedures are similar. These arrangements should be encouraged.
3. *Comparisons with national and local norms.* Comparisons with national and local norms are useful and should be utilized whenever possible. Normative data are available for most of the commercial exams and surveys being marketed. These norms are frequently available by institutional type, size, and geographic region and often can be restricted to include only selected institutions.

4. *Comparisons with established targets or goals.* Few colleges presently report comparisons with targets or goals, though it seems likely these targets do exist. As part of their outcomes assessment programs, institutions can establish measurable goals or targets against which results can be reported. Many colleges and universities already have detailed institutional planning initiatives that spell out goals and objectives, so these comparisons should not be difficult to report.

Reporting this information can be threatening to schools that do not compare favorably with their counterparts, or have failed to meet established targets or goals. This fear is heightened when a punitive action like reduction of funding is possible. Comparative analyses should focus on constructive courses of action, and footnotes for "explainable" shortcomings should be permitted. The inclusion of explanatory information, discussed in the next section, can also help mitigate institutions' concerns with comparison data.

EXPLANATORY INFORMATION

A major concern of college and university administrators is that SEA indicators will be misinterpreted or misused. Officials can help minimize these occurrences by including select explanatory data whenever SEA reports are prepared.

Factors that seem useful for explaining a broad range of possible issues and are therefore recommended for inclusion in public reports are:

- Role and mission statement
- State appropriations information
- Faculty data
- Enrollment data
- Test scores of entering students
- Listing of degree programs (by discipline)
- Other explanatory data and notes as needed.

Data on enrollments and faculty are easily compiled and reported, and tell much about the nature of the institution, its programs, and its operating environment. Breakouts of enrollments by gender, ethnicity, class level, field of study, and age are especially enlightening. Possible faculty disclosures include tenured versus nontenured status, number and percentage with doctorates, age, gender, rank, and level of compensation. Test scores of entering students provide a context within which to evaluate outcomes, such as subsequent test results and retention and graduation rates. Appropriations information indicates the level of support the state is providing and can be contrasted with other sources of revenue and the support provided to benchmark schools in other states.

The role and mission statement explicitly states why the institution exists, whom it is to serve, and how. These statements provide a framework from which to view SEA data. If formal planning objectives are prepared, those relevant to the SEA report should be included.

Other explanatory data and notes may be needed and should be included whenever necessary to avoid misinterpretations and/or misuse. For example, a particular program may reflect low enrollments and high per unit costs. An explanatory note advising users that the program is new and that enrollments are expected to increase over the next three years could eliminate needless discussion and concern.

Care should be exercised not to overload reports with explanatory information. An option is to include in an appendix information explaining dramatic changes in select indicators, deviations from norms or standards, and other similar results.

CONCLUSIONS

The incremental cost of reporting SEA information is difficult to estimate. Much of the input, output, efficiency, and explanatory information recommended is already collected (and often reported) by many institutions. While outcomes reporting may entail additional testing and surveying costs, careful planning and the use of sampling techniques and standardized instruments can help minimize expenditures. Growing demands for this information by accrediting agencies and its value to administrators further suggest the costs will not be prohibitive.

Some specific comments and conclusions are:

1. Colleges and universities are encouraged to experiment with SEA reporting.
2. While differing missions may dictate some differences among institutions, colleges and universities are encouraged to include the recommended "core" indicators in their reports.
3. Both the cognitive and noncognitive dimensions of student learning and development should be addressed.

4. Users should view SEA reporting as a basis for taking constructive corrective action. Punitive action will only discourage SEA reporting and promote efforts to disguise potentially unfavorable (but nonetheless important) findings.
5. Decision making based on SEA indicators should entail the use of multiple measures. Reliance on a single measure of an activity or program should be avoided.
6. To be cost-effective and worthwhile, SEA reporting should provide institutions with the information necessary for improving programs and services. Corrective initiatives should be designed and implemented.
7. Comparison information enhances the value of SEA data to users. Comparisons with prior years, other institutions, established norms, and targets or budgets are strongly encouraged.
8. Colleges and universities should endeavor to develop efficiency measures that relate inputs to outcomes. These measures will provide a more substantive view of efforts and results.
9. SEA reporting should be extended to include the research and service programs of colleges and universities. In addition, indicators of how well institutions meet selected goals in areas such as student recruitment, affirmative action policies, etc., should be developed and reported.

The collection and reporting of SEA information affords colleges and universities the opportunity to address both quality and accountability concerns. Governor John Ashcroft of Missouri, chairman of the National Governors' Task Force on College Quality, stated well the case for publicly reporting on the activities of colleges and universities:

> The public has the right to know what it is getting for its expenditure of tax resources; the public has a right to know and understand the quality of undergraduate education that young people receive from publicly funded colleges and universities. They have a right to know that their resources are being wisely invested and committed.[11]

SEA reporting is an important and necessary step toward providing the public with the information to which it is entitled.

---

[11]Ibid., p. 154.

3. Economic Development Programs

Mark Fall, The Urban Institute

                                                                                                                   Page

Introduction and Scope 72
    Overview 72
    Scope 73
        Business Attraction/Marketing Programs 73
        Financial Assistance Programs 74
        Export Development Programs 74
        Global Program Objectives 75
    Methodology 75

Recommendations 78
    Indicators Considered 78
    Disaggregation 89
    Comparison Information 90
    Explanatory Data 91

Conclusions 95

INTRODUCTION AND SCOPE

Overview

This chapter addresses the use of nonfinancial service efforts and accomplishments (SEA) indicators for economic development programs, particularly those at the state level, although most of this discussion applies to local economic development programs as well. The chapter discusses the current uses of these indicators and makes recommendations for improvements.

Economic development is an extremely broad topic; the term is often used to describe any government activity designed to have a positive impact on the economy. This chapter focuses on three program areas that seem to be typical of the types of programs that exist in most states and many larger local governments. These are (1) business attraction/marketing programs, (2) targeted financial assistance programs, and (3) export development programs. These are certainly not the only types of economic development programs, but for illustrative purposes will serve to cover a range of the issues associated with economic development SEA measurement. This chapter makes no judgments as to whether or not state and local governments should have these programs, but instead addresses ways to improve the SEA measures used to account for them. Improving the quality of SEA measures should help governments determine the effectiveness of their programs and make decisions as to the types of programs they should pursue to accomplish their objectives.

Other important economic development activities not included in this discussion are tourism programs, jobs and training programs, educational programs, and programs designed to provide information and technical assistance to start-up or existing businesses within a state. The issues and indicators that arise in other programs will have some application to these programs, too.

This chapter focuses on state economic development programs; however, most state programs are similar to the programs that exist at the local level, particularly within larger cities and counties, and similar indicators should apply to local government economic development programs.

The chapter will analyze the SEA indicators and different approaches used to develop these indicators for economic development programs. The characteristics of these approaches will be discussed, and recommendations made.

Scope

SEA measurement is examined in three economic development program areas:

1. Business attraction/marketing programs;
2. Targeted financial assistance programs; and
3. Export development programs.

Each program is defined below and its objectives explained.

Business Attraction/Marketing Programs

Business attraction/marketing programs are those designed to identify and attract new businesses interested in locating in a state or locality. The primary activity of these programs is to provide interested firms with information, including details on the state and local economic and social conditions, identification of particular sites suitable to the client's needs, details on local labor supply, and information about quality-of-life characteristics, such as the quality of local educational institutions and available housing. These programs also may offer firms financial and nonfinancial incentives to attract them to a state or locality. Incentives may include financial assistance programs as described below, tax inducements, or job training funds.

These programs often focus on attracting new manufacturing or high-technology companies, or other types of firms a jurisdiction feels are particularly valuable (because of their likelihood to increase rapidly in size and profitability, or because they match well with the resources available in the jurisdiction).

The objectives of these programs are to:

1. Increase the number and quality of jobs in a particular location through business attraction;
2. Increase the economic well-being of the jurisdiction by increasing growth (or decreasing losses) in related industries; and
3. Increase government revenues through taxes generated from new business and related growth in other industries.

Financial Assistance Programs

Financial assistance programs are usually designed to target particular social outcomes that are felt to be desirable, such as providing assistance to minority, small, or female-owned businesses, or to target economic development to specific locations. (Enterprise zones, for example, are a uniquely structured targeted financial assistance program, but are not specifically addressed here.) Financial assistance programs offer these firms two things: First, a market advantage—essentially an economic subsidy—such as below market-rate interest loans, loan guarantees, or other financial instruments to encourage their growth. Second, they fill a "capital gap" that exists for firms that traditionally have not been able to obtain financing from private sources because of their minority status, size, or female ownership. Usually these firms are required to demonstrate that they were unable to obtain adequate financing from private sources before they qualify for government assistance.

The objective of financial programs designed to target or encourage development in a particular location is to use these financial incentives to bring about development that would not otherwise have taken place, or would have taken place elsewhere. The objective is to provide these firms with an equal opportunity to compete (because traditionally they have greater difficulty obtaining financing from private sources) and to provide assistance at a lower rate than might be obtained from private sources. The objective for the second group is to use the financial inducement to encourage growth in an area the state or local government is targeting for development.

Export Development Programs

Export development programs are designed to help firms compete in non-U.S. markets. There is a considerable economic advantage to having products manufactured within a jurisdiction and then sold outside its borders, particularly if they are sold in other countries.

These export development programs usually involve a technical assistance component, which is addressed in this chapter, and sometimes a financial assistance component. Export development programs often include one-on-one counseling, seminars, and workshops to assist firms in developing their capacity to export and help in developing trade leads, such as through trade and catalog shows and trade missions. These programs are sometimes targeted at specific products whose cost makes them internationally competitive and therefore more likely to be successful.

The objective of export development programs is to increase export sales and thus improve the relative economic well-being of a jurisdiction. Exports bring in new dollars, rather than simply shifting or recycling money within the borders of a particular jurisdiction, and offer a major opportunity for growth. Increased exports lead to increased employment that is supported by sales that are not limited by local consumption tendencies. Exporting also leads to diversification within the economy. If the jurisdiction experiences an economic downturn, exporting firms may not suffer so severely, thus preserving important parts of the local economy.

Global Program Objectives

Departments of economic development also have overarching goals that include objectives of all three of these programs. These objectives are usually macroeconomic, or not related directly to program activities, although the programs may play a small but important role in affecting them. Global objectives include reducing unemployment, increasing growth in the economy, and increasing tax revenue. Traditionally, legislative and executive officials have paid great attention to global objectives.

Methodology

The information in this chapter is derived from a variety of sources. We examined budget documents from 43 states and selected local governments. These provided a partial picture of the current state of SEA measurement in economic development. In those instances where we found SEA indicators reported in the budget documents (23 states), we followed up to determine how information for the indicators was collected, how frequently it is reported, how the indicators are used by the departments, and so forth. We made contact with states we felt were likely to be using SEA indicators of some kind for their programs although they were not reporting them in their budget documents.

We also examined legislative audit reports from 16 state and local governments. These provided valuable information on the methodologies that had been used to assess and evaluate economic development programs. Although many audits shied away from attempting to determine the effectiveness of economic development programs, we did find a few outstanding reports. These were useful in either thoroughly analyzing the problems inherent in assessing economic development programs, or providing insights on methodological questions applicable for the development of SEA indicators.[1]

Research work by individuals who have explored the role of states in economic development was also reviewed.[2] On the whole, these works focus on the policy questions relating to economic development programs that states have been, or should be, addressing. These authors provide support for the notion that it is necessary to have some mechanism that permits the assessment of economic development programs.

In addition, we analyzed several "business climate surveys" from a variety of sources to assess the characteristics that they viewed as important in rating states, particularly as they related to the activities of state government in economic development. It is important to recognize that business climate surveys focus on the state's overall business climate and very little on areas (other than taxes) over which the

---

[1] State of Minnesota, Office of the Legislative Auditor, Program Evaluation Division, *Economic Development,* March 1985; State of Mississippi, Joint Legislative Committee on Performance Evaluation and Expenditure Review, *Management Review of the Mississippi Department of Economic Development,* December 1987; State of Tennessee, Department of Audit, *Limited Program Evaluation: Department of Economic and Community Development,* March 1984; State of Washington, Economic Development Program, Preliminary Report: "Program Profile & Evaluation Study," November 1986; and State of Oregon, Joint Legislative Committee on Trade & Economic Development, *Oregon Business Development Fund Program Evaluation,* June 1988.

[2] We recommend Marianne K. Clarke, *Revitalizing State Economies;* Committee for Economic Development, *Leadership for Dynamic State Economies;* Mt. Auburn Associates, *Factors Influencing the Performance of U.S. Economic Development Administration Sponsored Revolving Loan Funds;* David Osborne, *Economic Competitiveness: The States Take the Lead;* and Roger J. Vaughan et al., *The Wealth of States: Policies for a Dynamic Economy.*

state, much less a department of economic development, would have much control. In this regard, they provide little information for assessing the SEA of a state's economic development program.[3]

Since July 1987, The Urban Institute has been working with the states of Maryland and Minnesota to develop prototypical performance-monitoring procedures for their economic development programs, with particular emphasis on export development activities. This chapter draws heavily from that work. Previous work by the Institute set the stage for the current project.[4]

Maryland and Minnesota, in cooperation with The Urban Institute, have been addressing the problems of developing practical SEA indicators for state economic development programs to improve assessment of the performance of their programs. Under a grant from the Economic Development Administration of the U.S. Department of Commerce, the Institute has been developing and testing procedures for the regular monitoring of state economic development programs. This work is unique in that it involves the collection of information directly from businesses that have received assistance from the state programs to gauge program performance. These indicators provide a tool for assessing the performance of state programs.

---

[3]These business climate surveys differ in their approaches to analyzing the characteristics of a state that may make it attractive to firm locations. Grant Thornton publishes an annual study of general manufacturing climates in each state. The Grant Thornton approach focuses on a "least cost" assessment of states, meaning that low taxes, cheap nonunion labor, and inexpensive production costs will rank a state highly in comparison to others. This analysis does not assess the "benefits" that may exist in states with higher taxes and more-expensive labor and production costs. Typically, these states will have better public services of all kinds (state and local), educational systems, and access to markets, making them far more attractive to high-tech manufacturing businesses. The Grant Thornton analysis is certainly not the only one available to businesses interested in relocating or opening a new facility. The Corporation for Enterprise Development also produces a rating of states, as do *Inc.* magazine, Ameritrust Corporation, SRI International, and several others. Each has a different approach to assessment and focuses on different indicators of performance for the state's economy. Few focus on the activities of state departments of economic development as a factor in their analysis.

[4]Richard E. Winnie, Harry P. Hatry, and Virginia B. Wright, *Jobs and Earnings for State Citizens: Monitoring the Outcomes of State Economic Development and Employment and Training Programs,* September 1977; National Association of State Development Agencies, *Directory of Incentives for Business Investment and Development in the United States,* 2nd ed., 1986; and National Governors' Association, Committee on International Trade and Foreign Relations, *Foreign Direct Investment in the United States: A Governor's Guide,* July 1987.

RECOMMENDATIONS

Improved measurement and reporting of SEA indicators of economic development programs would facilitate the understanding of these programs by elected officials and the public.

Indicators Considered

Exhibits 3-1, 3-2, and 3-3 summarize the indicators we recommend be considered for each program discussed. We suggest that economic development programs do the following to improve SEA measurement of their programs:

1. *Place less emphasis on indicators of outputs, i.e., measures of program activities.* Economic development programs have relied heavily on output indicators for public reporting on performance. They are relatively easy to collect and measure. Because these counts of activities have limited value in determining the effects of the programs on client businesses, they are of use primarily to internal operating managers. However, a small number of activity measures will likely be of interest to elected officials and, as indicated in the exhibits, should be included in external reports. Counts of the activities of the program, holding the caseload input as constant, provide some indication of the relative productivity of the staff, given that the *quality* of the activities measured also is unchanged.

2. *Focus greatest attention on firms assisted by the economic development programs and the contribution of services to the outcomes these firms experience.* Indicators of the SEA of economic development programs should place their greatest emphasis on firms that have been clients of such programs. If, for example, a firm makes a decision to locate in a state and subsequently seeks assistance from that state's business attraction program in locating a specific site, it would not seem justifiable for the program to "take credit" for the jobs the new firm would bring. But if the firm felt that the state program's assistance had been significant in determining where within the state it would locate, the program should be able to report that it was able to influence the location decision of the firm, provided the state was able to convince the firm to locate in an area targeted by the state for development. Programs should consider as "successes" only clients that indicate that the program's services had contributed to the outcomes they experienced.

3. *Make use of client surveys and state unemployment insurance data for indicators.* There are two major ways that we suggest economic development programs collect information on assisted firms. The first is through the use of client surveys; the second is to use data available through state unemployment insurance programs.

Client surveys can be practically applied to economic development programs to produce regular SEA data on their activities. The Urban Institute, in conjunction with the states of Maryland and Minnesota, has been working to develop practical procedures so each state can monitor the performance of its programs. These procedures have included development of a data base of clients from whom performance information will be obtained; developing appropriate survey instruments that will yield valid and reliable data and receive an appropriate response rate; selecting the appropriate lag time from the point at which the client first received assistance to the time of the survey follow-up; and determining who will be responsible for the mailing, tabulation, and report generation of results from the data collected. Most of the programs in the two states are collecting quarterly information on their clients. One state does the mailing, tabulation, and report generation internally, while the other uses a contractor. The results demonstrate the feasibility of conducting regular surveys of clients to obtain SEA information. The feasibility of client surveys for local governments may depend on their size and the resources that can be utilized—we have estimated that it will take at least one full-time clerical/data-entry person to conduct regular client surveys. Additional expertise may be necessary for the tabulation and report generation.

Another useful source of information on the SEA of assisted firms is from a data base used for state unemployment insurance programs (sometimes referred to as the state unemployment insurance compensation data base, or ES-202 data). This data base contains firm-specific information on employment, location, and standard industrial classification (SIC) code for approximately 95 percent of the firms in a state. A state or local government economic development program with access to this data base would be able to track changes in employment for firms that received assistance from its programs. The data could also be used to examine changes in the economy for particular industries in certain areas. Programs seeking to utilize these data may face problems with access, and concerns about protecting the confidentiality of the data because of its proprietary nature may pose problems. If these hurdles can be overcome, economic development agencies may find ways to use this information to examine the performance of these programs.

Exhibit 3-1
Recommended SEA Indicators for Economic Development:
Business Attraction/Marketing Programs*

Indicator	Rationale for Selecting Indicator
Inputs:	
Dollars spent on the program's activities (current and constant dollars)	Provide information on the resources available to the program
Number of staff-hours expended by the program	
Outputs:	
Number and percentage of business prospects identified that may be interested in locating	Measure of the program's outreach function
Number of businesses from target industries identified that are interested in locating	Identifies success with targeted industries
Number of contacts made with firms interested in locating	Measure of program follow-up
Number of firms that received assistance from the program (by type of assistance)	Provides indication of the number of actual program clients
Percentage of leverage (nongovernmental) funds used to finance project	Estimate of amount of other funds leveraged by a project

Outcomes:

Intermediate outcomes:

Number of visits by interested businesses that received assistance	Measures important intermediate response by clients
Number and percentage of responses to advertising or direct mail solicitations	Provides information on number of potentially interested businesses

Longer-term outcomes:

Number and percentage of firms that received assistance and located elsewhere	Indication of program failures
Number and percentage of firms receiving assistance that located in jurisdiction and that felt that assistance contributed to their location decision	Major performance indicator for the program; measures the contribution of services to the observed outcomes
Number of actual jobs created by assistance 12 months/24 months after their initial contact with the program (and comparison with projected number of jobs to be created)	Major stated goal of business attraction programs
Average wage of jobs created by locating firms that receive assistance	Partial measure of job "quality"
Dollars of capital investment made by locating firms receiving assistance 12 months/ 24 months after the announcement of their location decision	Provides an indication of the local economic impact of the firm location

---

*The recommended indicators presented in this exhibit are illustrative. They are intended to serve as a starting point for use in the development of a comprehensive set of SEA indicators for external reporting of an entity's results of operation.

This exhibit does not provide illustrations of indicator disaggregation or of comparison data such as trends, targets, or other comparable entities. Both disaggregation and comparison data are important aspects of SEA reporting. They are discussed in the Economic Development Programs chapter and in the Overview.

Exhibit 3-1 (continued)

Indicator	Rationale for Selecting Indicator
Outcomes (continued):	
Amount of added tax revenues relating to assisted firms that located in the jurisdiction	Government return on investment in the program
Percentage of clients rating the *timeliness* of each service they received as excellent, good, fair, or poor	Service quality indicator
Percentage of clients rating the *helpfulness* of each service they received as excellent, good, fair, or poor	Service quality indicator
Percentage of clients locating elsewhere for reasons over which agency had some influence	Indicates potential problems within the program or agency
Estimated number of workers displaced by assisted firms that located	Measures a negative impact of business attraction programs
Efficiency:	
Program expenditures per actual job created at 12 months/24 months after receiving assistance	Measures program costs for each job created
Program expenditures per estimated tax dollar generated by client firms	Compares program expenditures with direct return through taxes

Agencies should also attempt to distinguish outcomes by the type and amount of services received by clients so they can identify the *firms for which the services had a significant impact on the outcomes subsequently realized.* This linkage is critical in defining the impact of the program on its clients. Other than to track the overall performance of the economy, measures of nonassisted firms, or all firms in a state or locality, should only be used as comparison data or as explanatory factors for the differential SEA of assisted firms, because the linkage between government services and outcomes in aggregate for all firms is extremely difficult to determine.

4. *Add a focus on intermediate outcome indicators.* In the instances where state economic development agencies have focused on outcomes at all, they have usually focused on longer-term outcomes such as the number of jobs created by locating firms and the increased export sales of firms. In some cases it may take many months, if not years, for these outcomes to occur. Paying attention only to long-term indicators misses many of the short-term successes of these programs that are relatively easy to measure, such as the number of visits made by firms interested in locating, and measures of increased interest in exporting resulting from publications or counseling. Some intermediate outcomes can be generated from well-kept program records. Because they are shorter-term outcomes, results can be seen more quickly, providing timely feedback to the programs.

5. *Improve longer-term outcome indicators.* Many important longer-term outcome indicators, such as jobs created and increased sales, have relied on questionable methodologies. For example, job creation has been the most heavily used outcome indicator by state economic development agencies, and is an important indicator of program SEA. The problem with this indicator is the way the information is typically collected and reported. In the case of business attraction/marketing programs, the job creation indicator reported by the program is usually derived from projections made by firms that have announced their intention to locate in a particular state. Occasionally, the state will ask firms to project their employment for a particular time period, or at the point at which the firm expects to be at full capacity. The questionable accuracy of these projections makes their use as SEA indicators unreliable and potentially subject to abuse if they are not labeled and reported accurately. In at least two states, newspapers have attempted to verify these projections and found them to be of questionable reliability, causing the programs public embarrassment. Alternative methods for collecting data that are of better quality exist.

Obtaining information directly from program clients through regular and systematic surveys is a valuable resource for SEA indicators and provides a distinctly better methodology for collecting information. The kinds of information that can be obtained from clients after they have received assistance are not available from other sources. The costs, complications, and feasibility of regular survey work are issues with which economic development agencies will have to wrestle. Work currently being conducted will shed some light on these areas and provide state agencies with specific estimates of the costs and feasibility of client survey systems. Several intermediate and longer-term outcome indicators can be derived from client surveys, such as their ratings of the services received and the contribution to their outcomes.

Investigating state unemployment insurance (UI) data as a source for SEA information may also provide an alternative to job creation projections obtained from firms. The costs and practicality of this data base are still undetermined, but it appears promising.

A third potential data source, state tax data, may serve as a source for SEA information. Although little seems to have been done to use tax data for SEA indicators, further examination appears to be warranted. There is interest in estimating the tax realized from firms receiving assistance as a way to justify the costs of programs. Questions about access and confidentiality of information must be resolved before more can be done.

6. *Add indicators of service quality.* Obtaining information directly from clients through systematic surveys also provides an opportunity to collect information about the quality of the services from the client's perspective. The characteristics for which ratings may be obtained include the timeliness of assistance, the knowledgeability of program staff, its appropriateness in relationship to the client's needs, and the overall helpfulness of the services. Indicators based on information from the recipients of services are important in judging quality of services and for suggesting areas needing improvement.

7. *Define and label indicators clearly and appropriately.* This is simply the appropriate way to present indicators and it is particularly important for job creation indicators. If an indicator is based on a projection from a firm, for example, then it should be labeled "Projected jobs to be created in x years." Failure to make these distinctions clear is misleading and may result in embarrassment for the program and department. Inadequate labels also make interpretation by other outside users very difficult. Ambiguity limits the value of the information presented, regardless of the quality of the method by which it was obtained.

8. *Investigate methods for determining the "quality" of jobs created by assisted firms.* This aspect of service outcomes has, by and large, been neglected. There seems to be no simple method for determining the quality of new jobs. Data on average wages from state unemployment insurance may be used as a proxy. Inclusion of a measure of job quality would help deflect some of the attention currently paid to job creation numbers and focus attention on the relative value of jobs created.

9. *Consider worker displacement.* More attention should be given to the problem of displacement of existing workers by workers in new businesses, particularly in firms that are receiving some financial assistance. There is little advantage to a program in providing assistance to locating firms that will be competing with existing firms in the same market. Economic development programs should attempt to limit any potential displacement by assessing the characteristics of a new firm's market *before* assistance is given, while any "actual" displacement caused by subsidized firms should be considered as an important SEA indicator for the program.

To assess potential displacement, programs should use UI data to determine the number of businesses and workers in a particular SIC and county. Assessment of the new firm's market can be made by examining the characteristics of the firm's product. If the firm is a retail or service establishment, it is unlikely that its market is outside the borders of the city or county in which it is located. If there are firms with the same SIC in that county that are serving that market, providing a new firm with a market advantage subsidy may adversely affect the existing firms. This could serve as an estimate of the potential displacement that might occur. Programs could use this methodology to examine the actual employment changes in all firms in the new firm's SIC and county at one- or two-year intervals. Employment of the assisted firms could be compared with any changes in employment of competing firms to determine if significant displacement has occurred.

10. *Experiment with improved efficiency measures, such as expenditures per job added by assisted firms that reported that assistance was significant in contributing to their outcomes.* Little emphasis has been placed in this chapter on efficiency indicators for SEA of these programs. This is not because we feel they are unimportant, but because their interpretation has limitations. For example, program expenditures per job created in firms rating assistance as significant to their location decision provides an indication of the return on the state's investment in these programs. One problem is that not all jobs are equally valuable. The wage rates, while important, provide only a partial

Exhibit 3-2
Recommended SEA Indicators for Economic Development: Financial Assistance Programs*

Indicator	Rationale for Selecting Indicator
Inputs:	
Dollars spent on the program's activities (current and constant dollars)	Provide information on the resources available to the program
Number of staff-hours expended by the program	
Outputs:	
Number of technical assistance seminars/workshops conducted	Measure of program activity; easily collected
Number of applications reviewed	Workload output measure
Number and percentage of applications approved	Information on the proportion of applications that are approved
Average length of time for review of an application	Service quality indicator
Number of loans (or loan guarantees) made	Workload output measure
Dollar value of loans (or loan guarantees) made	Provides information on total expenditures resulting from loans
Average loan (or loan guarantees) size	Provides information on average size of a project
Number of on-site monitoring visits conducted	Measure of program follow-up and monitoring
Outcomes:	
Intermediate outcomes:	
Number of loan applications processed and decided upon	Workload outcome measure for the program; easily collected

Total and average attendance at seminars/workshops	Measure of the success of program outreach
Longer-term outcomes:	
Number of jobs added by firms receiving loans 12 months/24 months after receipt of loan	Major outcome indicator for financial assistance programs
Number of jobs retained by firms 12 months/24 months after receipt of loan	Major outcome for business in jeopardy of losing employees
Total and average amount of private capital leveraged by loans (or guarantees)	Leverage indicates the amount of capital the program was able to activate
Loan default rate (percentage of loans made that are currently in default)	Offers information on the "riskiness" of loans made
Percentage of scheduled repayments made on time	Provides an indication of loans behind in payments, but not in default
Percentage of clients rating *information* on the program, including application instructions, as excellent, good, fair, or poor	
Percentage of clients rating the *length of time for processing* of their application as appropriate	Service quality indicators
Percentage of clients rating the *knowledge-ability of program staff* as excellent, good, fair, or poor	

*The recommended indicators presented in this exhibit are illustrative. They are intended to serve as a starting point for use in the development of a comprehensive set of SEA indicators for external reporting of an entity's results of operation.

This exhibit does not provide illustrations of indicator disaggregation or of comparison data such as trends, targets, or other comparable entities. Both disaggregation and comparison data are important aspects of SEA reporting. They are discussed in the Economic Development Programs chapter and in the Overview.

Exhibit 3-2 (continued)

Indicator	Rationale for Selecting Indicator
Outcomes (continued):	
Percentage of clients reporting that they would have had to (a) forgo, (b) delay substantially, or (c) cut back significantly the size of their new operations if state financing assistance had not been provided	Measure of the program's contribution to the identified outcomes
Percentage of clients who, after receiving financial assistance, were able to secure additional financing without assistance from the program (i.e., were able to become more self-sufficient)	Provides an indication of self-sufficiency
Efficiency:	
Program expenditures per actual job added or retained by assisted firms	Major measure of the cost per job for program
Loan (guarantee) dollars per actual job added by assisted firms	Measure of the loan amount per job added

picture. Jobs that tend to create other new jobs in support industries may be as valuable as or even more valuable than high-paying jobs with little indirect job creation potential. While efficiency indicators can provide some information on what the state is getting in return for its expenditures, calculating the benefits is difficult. Other similar efficiency measures suffer from the same limitations.

11. *Treat global indicators as comparison or explanatory data.* We believe that global indicators have limited value as SEA indicators for economic development programs, and are so frequently abused that they should not be the central focus of SEA measurement. For example, the impact of *any* government program on the unemployment rate would rarely be large enough to justify use of the unemployment rate as an outcome measure for the program. The unemployment rate is a measure of the performance of the economy, of which economic development programs represent a small amount monetarily. Because the department's managers, the legislature or city council, and the governor or mayor will be very interested in the unemployment rate, the data should be monitored by the department, but not treated as SEA data.

Disaggregation

Disaggregations can be very useful in providing information to elected officials and the public, as well as being of major importance to program managers. Selected disaggregations should make SEA data of greater value to outside users by offering more-detailed information on specific characteristics. Particularly, we recommend information be disaggregated by the following characteristics:

1. Location (e.g., region, county).
2. Size of firm.
3. Minority status.
4. SIC code.
5. Type, quantity, and quality of assistance received.

Locational disaggregations allow users to assess the differences in impact throughout a jurisdiction. Certain areas may be expanding rapidly in jobs or exporting firms while others are contracting. Unless data are disaggregated, the totals hide such differences. Disaggregation is especially important in assessing the performance of programs designed to impact particular regions, and can be used to help target development to distressed areas, or where firms seem to be having greater difficulty. Disaggregating information by region of origin will help business attraction/marketing programs to identify where their clients originate. Primary export country should be an important disaggregation for export development programs.

Similarly, disaggregation outcome data by business size will indicate whether a program is successfully serving various size firms. Outside users may have an interest in firms of a particular size, often small businesses. Disaggregation by the size of client firms is essential in determining the kinds of services that will be successful with different size firms.

A key element of some financial programs is the minority status of businesses that apply for assistance. These programs are designed to provide minority firms with assistance, because they traditionally have experienced greater difficulty in obtaining financial assistance from the private sector. The program should also be concerned about the extent to which it is reaching minority firms with information about assistance, as this may indicate a problem with dissemination of information.

The product line, or SIC, of firms provides a useful breakout of information. It helps identify how programs are serving firms in different product markets. If a program is intended to focus on manufacturing or high-tech firms, this disaggregation will help measure the program's success in targeting.

Knowing how much and what types of assistance a particular firm received may be important in explaining differences in outcomes experienced. Measurement of the quality of assistance as reported by firms could help explain their interest in pursuing certain outcomes.

Comparison Information

There are four basic comparisons that economic development programs should utilize. The first is to compare SEA over time. Once a program has a system for regularly reporting SEA information, the change over time in the SEA of programs should be tracked annually and quarterly, with annual totals compared with at least three previous years to help establish any pattern.

Comparison with other jurisdictions, particularly those that share similar characteristics, is the second important comparison. The difficulty with this is finding comparable data across jurisdictions. States may have to rely on federal sources, while local programs may be able to use UI data to compare their performance with other jurisdictions in the state.

Goals and objectives provide the third major comparison. If programs set targets for particular activities, these should be used for comparison purposes with actual performance. Care should be taken in setting targets so that they are not unrealistic or too easily fulfilled. Targets or goals should be based on staff and funds expected to be available to the program.

Finally, comparing firms that received assistance with firms that did not provides another valuable reference to gauge performance. Information for this comparison may come from UI data for all firms in a state, or from information collected directly through client surveys from nonassisted firms, just as information may be collected through surveys of assisted firms.

Explanatory Data

Factors that help explain the performance of programs, beyond the data collected for SEA monitoring, should be used to help interpret program performance. For example, the national rate of growth in the economy or the value of the dollar relative to other currencies may have a significant impact on the ability of a program to perform to expectations. Also, unique events, such as a dramatic change in the stock market, may impact program performance in an unexpected fashion. These typically will be national or international trends that impact the economy generally, and may have consequences for the performance of economic development programs.

We recommend that federal indicators of the economy be used as a starting point for explaining economic change. The gross national product, value of the dollar, prime interest rate, corporate profits, personal income, new housing starts, the consumer price index, the value of exports and export-related employment, and manufacturers' shipment and orders of durable goods are among the national indicators that programs may track to help explain their SEA.

Exhibit 3-3
Recommended SEA Indicators for Economic Development: Export Programs*

Indicator	Rationale for Selecting Indicator
Inputs:	
Dollars spent on the program's activities	Provide information on the resources available to the program
Number of staff-hours expended by the program	
Outputs:	
Number of export workshop/seminars	
Number of trade shows conducted	Activity measures
Number of catalog shows conducted	
Number of counseling sessions conducted	
Number of foreign trips made	Measure of activities in other countries
Number of different firms participating in trade shows	
Number of different firms participating in catalog shows	Counts of clients
Number of different firms participating in counseling sessions	

Outcomes:

Intermediate outcomes:

Number and percentage of firms that increased their interest in exporting as a result of assistance	Measure of increased interest in exporting
Number of trade leads generated from trade shows	
Number of trade leads generated from catalog shows	Provide information on possible future sales
Number of trade leads generated from international trips	

Longer-term outcomes:

Number of client firms that began export trade activities (sales or production)	Measure of new export activity of clients
Number and percentage of clients that increased their export activity (sales, jobs, etc.)	Measure of increased export activities of clients
Dollar value of actual increased export sales from client firms	Major outcome measure for the program

---

*The recommended indicators presented in this exhibit are illustrative. They are intended to serve as a starting point for use in the development of a comprehensive set of SEA indicators for external reporting of an entity's results of operation. This exhibit does not provide illustrations of indicator disaggregation or of comparison data such as trends, targets, or other comparable entities. Both disaggregation and comparison data are important aspects of SEA reporting. They are discussed in the Economic Development Programs chapter and in the Overview.

Exhibit 3-3 (continued)

Indicator	Rationale for Selecting Indicator
Outcomes (continued):	
Number of actual jobs created from increased exports by client firms	Measure of job creation for client firms
Percentage of clients rating the timeliness of assistance as excellent, good, fair, or poor	Service quality indicators
Percentage of clients rating the knowledgeability of program staff as excellent, good, fair, or poor	
Percentage of clients rating the overall helpfulness of assistance as excellent, good, fair, or poor	
Percentage of clients rating the contribution of assistance received to outcomes realized as high, moderate, or low	Provides information on the contribution of services to observed outcomes
Efficiency:	
Program expenditures per actual dollar of increased export sales by client firms	Measure of the cost of program services for each dollar of increased export sales realized by client firms
Program expenditures per actual export-related job created by client firms	Measure of the cost of program services for each export-related job created by client firms

CONCLUSIONS

The SEA indicators currently used to monitor economic development programs in most state and local governments can be vastly improved. By adopting methodologies that provide better information and by selecting indicators that better reflect program accomplishments, state and local governments can use SEA indicators to guide programs, rather than merely using them to justify a program's existence to the governor or legislature. In areas such as business attraction, financial assistance, and export development, SEA indicators can also provide program managers with the information necessary to improve program performance.

4. Elementary and Secondary Education

Harry P. Hatry and Marita Alexander, The Urban Institute

James R. Fountain, Jr., Governmental Accounting Standards Board

	Page
Introduction	98
Scope	99
Elementary and Secondary Education Goals and Objectives	100
Methodology	101
Current Practices in SEA Reporting	102
Discussion of SEA Indicators	104
Disaggregation	112
Comparison Information to Be Reported	113
Explanatory Data	115
Costs of Obtaining and Reporting SEA Information	117
Conclusions	117

INTRODUCTION

This chapter reviews current practices in assessing and reporting service efforts and accomplishments (SEA) for public elementary and secondary school systems and makes recommendations for external reporting of SEA indicators. We identify both commonly used SEA indicators and selected potential SEA indicators not being widely used, and recommend possible SEA indicators for use as a basis for future external reporting.

This chapter is addressed primarily to administrative and elected officials—at both the school system and the local and state levels—concerned with external reporting practices. However, we hope that the findings and recommendations also will encourage school officials to improve internal SEA indicator reporting practices.

Accountability in public elementary and secondary education is of major national importance. It is the public service with the largest annual state and local government expenditure. More than $155 billion (approximately 20 percent of all state and local expenditure) is spent annually on public elementary and secondary education in the United States.[1] States collect and dispense to local school systems about 50 percent of these public-school dollars.[2]

Education has widespread effects on the American population. The U.S. Department of Education reports that there were approximately 83,500 public schools in the United States during school year 1986–1987. These elementary and secondary schools are now actively serving approximately 40 million students, or almost 17 percent of the U.S. population.[3]

The elementary and secondary education systems in the United States are the major public institutions devoting efforts to prepare our youth to become fully participating members of our society. The

---

[1] U.S. Department of Commerce, Bureau of the Census, "Governmental Finances in 1985–86," Series GF-86, No. 5 (Washington, DC, 1987), Table 29.

[2] U.S. Department of Commerce, Bureau of the Census, "State Government Finances in 1986," Series GF-86, No. 3 (Washington, DC, 1987), Table 12.

[3] U.S. Department of Education, Office of Educational Research and Improvement, Center for Education Statistics, "Characteristics of Elementary and Secondary Schools in the United States, 1986–87," CS88-045 (Washington, DC, 1988).

schools seek to teach their students to read, write, speak, listen, think, and compute clearly and effectively, and to instill in them knowledge of the importance of responsible citizenship and other forms of human behavior.[4]

With responsibility for making a major contribution to achieving results so critical to the future of our country, accountability for the effective and efficient performance of school systems is clearly of major importance for our nation. SEA indicators are an important part of accountability efforts because they help elected officials and citizens see what results they are getting for their money. The information also can be used by school personnel to keep track of their own progress, identify problem areas, and guide efforts to improve performance.

SCOPE

Elementary and secondary educational institutions commonly provide a number of services. These include:

- Regular instruction
- Special education
- Vocational education
- Adult education
- Library
- Extracurricular activities
- Health services
- Transportation
- Food
- Day care
- Support services, such as counseling, building maintenance, and curriculum development.

The focus of this chapter is on regular instruction. We do not include preschool, adult, or vocational education services, nor do we explicitly cover school services such as libraries, extracurricular activities, health, transportation, or support services. However, many (probably most) of the educational SEA indicators we discuss are at least indirectly affected by these other school services.

---

[4]See, for example, Salt Lake City (Utah) School District, "Salt Lake City School District Educational Philosophy Statement" (Salt Lake City: Board of Education, 1985).

ELEMENTARY AND SECONDARY EDUCATION GOALS AND OBJECTIVES

Exhibit 4-1 presents the goals and objectives that often are explicitly stated or implicitly assumed for elementary and secondary education. In general, there is considerable agreement among educators and legislators as to the cognitive objectives (those concerned with providing factual information, basic skills, and skills for future life activities).

Educators and legislators have mixed feelings about noncognitive elements. For example, whether schools should attempt to provide "education" relating to values and ethics is particularly controversial. Other noncognitive objectives, such as helping students achieve sound self-esteem, are less often explicitly articulated but seem to be generally accepted by educators and legislators.

The Commission on Reorganization of Secondary Education (1918) made a historic statement of the goals of public education. These have been labeled the "Seven Cardinal Principles of Education." They are (1) health, (2) command of fundamental processes, (3) worthy home membership, (4) vocation, (5) citizenship, (6) worthy use of leisure time, and (7) ethical character. In 1985, the Educational Research Service polled teachers to see whether they believed these were still appropriate for schools almost seventy years later. Of the responding teachers, 82 percent agreed that the list was still a satisfactory statement of goals for schools. Some teachers wanted to add objectives such as encouraging creativity, developing responsibility and good work habits, and refining critical-thinking skills.[5] Note that of the original seven goals, only the command of fundamental processes and possibly some aspects of health, vocation, and citizenship are explicitly examined and tracked by most school systems.

SEA indicators are closely related to goals and objectives because they are the mechanisms through which progress on achieving the goals and objectives of our elementary and secondary education system can be assessed and the results used to direct efforts to improve the effectiveness of our schools.

---

[5]Glen E. Robinson and Nancy J. Protheroe, *Cost of Education: An Investment in America's Future* (Arlington, VA: Educational Research Service, Inc., 1987), p. 62.

**Exhibit 4-1
Commonly Found Goals and Objectives of
Elementary and Secondary Education**

Cognitive

- To provide basic and higher-order skills (including problem solving)
- To provide "factual" information
- To provide skills for future life activity (including further education and employment)

Noncognitive

- To develop self-esteem and self-concept
- To develop interpersonal skills
- To develop good work habits
- To develop self-discipline
- To develop responsible citizenship
- To maintain mental and physical health
- To encourage students to develop ethical values

Efficiency

- To achieve the above outcomes at minimal cost

Equity

- To enable students of all races, ethnicities, income levels, and genders to be brought to their maximum potential

METHODOLOGY

In performing this research, a selection of the extensive published and unpublished literature on elementary and secondary education pertaining to this topic was reviewed. We also examined materials from ongoing SEA indicator measurement-related projects, particularly those of the U.S. Department of Education and the Council of Chief State School Officers. Specific SEA indicator materials from fourteen states and a number of school systems across the country were then reviewed. The indicators identified during the research were analyzed and considered as to their validity, ability to communicate results (especially for accomplishment of goals and objectives), and contribution to a comprehensive picture of educational performance.

CURRENT PRACTICES IN SEA REPORTING

In June 1989, when the *New York Times* reported that 51 percent of the pupils in the New York City public schools were "unable to read at the level expected of their grade,"[6] the newspaper was reflecting the recent trend of monitoring and reporting on the results of elementary and secondary education. The article explained that reading scores had improved from the previous year, when 54 percent of the pupils were reading below grade level. The information for the story did not have to be researched or dug out by the reporter; it was provided by the New York City Board of Education as part of its annual report on school performance.

In the 1980s, many, if not most, states made major legislative- and executive-branch efforts to improve education, particularly in response to the 1983 report of the National Commission on Excellence in Education.[7] One major element of this trend has been an increase in concern about the accountability of school systems. Legislatures have been calling for increased oversight by the state government. Generally, this oversight requires the use of standardized test scores. More recently, some legislatures have required a wider variety of SEA indicators.

School districts in New York State are required to report the results of certain tests annually at a public meeting of the Board of Education. Illinois school systems are required to make available to the public a "School Report Card" for each school, which includes test results in mathematics, science, social studies, and language, together with selected student characteristics, instructional resources, and financial information.[8] The California State Department of Education prepares a

---

[6]Neil A. Lewis, "51 Percent of Pupils Score Poorly in Reading," *New York Times* (June 30, 1989), p. B1.

[7]National Commission on Excellence in Education, *A Nation at Risk: The Imperative for Educational Reform* (Washington, DC: U.S. Government Printing Office, 1983).

[8]A. T. Woodberry School, "School Report Card. Facts and Figures about Your School: The Better Schools Accountability Report for the 1985–86 School Year" (Centroid, IL, 1986).

"Performance Report for California Schools" for each school.[9] The report includes a detailed explanation of how to read the performance information on six cognitive learning areas, with comparisons of the school's performance to that of a selected comparison group. Information is also provided on statewide averages and targets for California schools for the six areas, and certain explanatory factors are included.

These examples highlight the fact that many states and local school systems are active in measuring and reporting the results of their elementary and secondary education programs. Among those with comprehensive performance monitoring programs that have been reviewed as part of this research are the states of California, Colorado, Connecticut, Florida, Illinois, New York, Pennsylvania, Rhode Island, South Carolina, and Texas. Considerable work is also being performed at the national level by the National Governors' Association (NGA), the U.S. Department of Education, and the Council of Chief State School Officers (CCSSO).

However, in the NGA's second annual report for restructuring American education, the NGA education subcommittee said:

> ... State accountability systems continue to be heavily weighted toward regulating the level and use of educational resources rather than monitoring the outcomes of educational practices. Yet, if new local practice is to be stimulated and supported, state accountability systems must be changed to assess the overall performance of the school and to reward educators at the school level.[10]

In spite of the tremendous effort already being expended on the measurement of elementary and secondary education SEA, serious problems still exist. Usually absent are indicators that compare service outputs and outcomes to inputs, and indicators of noncognitive aspects of learning, such as self-esteem, work habits, self-discipline, physical fitness, and citizenship. Further, reported dropout rates are

---

[9] California State Department of Education, "Performance Report for California Schools, 1987: Epic Senior High" (1987).

[10] NGA, *The Governors' 1991 Report on Education, Results in Education: 1988* (Washington, DC, 1988), p. 5.

plagued by differences in definitions. Standardized tests used across states, such as college aptitude tests, are being questioned as to their value in evaluating high school achievement, and state-level measures of student outcomes are often not comparable between states.

Overall, a variety of school districts appear to be reporting SEA indicators for elementary and secondary education. But these indicators appear to lack consistency in what is measured and how results are measured; there is also a lack of indicators designed to measure efficiency (including cost-effectiveness).

DISCUSSION OF SEA INDICATORS

Based on our research, which drew heavily on the work being done by many organizations and individuals, we believe SEA reporting for elementary and secondary education, and especially the regular instruction component of education, has developed to the level at which broad experimentation with a comprehensive set of SEA indicators is not only warranted but badly needed.

Exhibit 4-2 presents our recommendations for a comprehensive set of SEA indicators—with the rationale for their selection—for use as a beginning point in developing an SEA report that would meet the specific needs of a school, school system, or state.

It is important when experimenting with SEA indicator reporting that the reporting entity use the recommended indicators only as a beginning point and expand or modify those indicators to reflect the school system's goals and objectives and specific areas of performance it considers significant.

School systems should consider reporting on these indicators annually. These reports would include input, output, outcome, and efficiency indicators presented together, as well as key explanatory factors. The data should be backed up by explanations as to the source of the data and definitions (such as in a footnote or an appendix to the report). Narrative explanations of performance for certain indicators should also be included when it is believed they are needed for complete understanding.

Following are our major recommendations regarding these SEA indicators.

1. Continued reporting of standardized tests of student achievement (other than SAT and ACT results) by major subject area is desirable as a principal indicator of schools' service accomplishments. In the future, however, more emphasis should be placed on the results of proficiency tests (e.g., criterion-referenced tests). We believe standardized test score results should be expressed *both* as an overall average (e.g., the average percentile for a school on a particular test) *and* as the percentage of students who are above or below their grade level or specified quartiles. This will provide more information on how test scores are distributed. Results of proficiency tests should also be presented. School systems should, preferably, report the percentage of students achieving each of two or three proficiency levels rather than only one, "minimum" level. Reports should, in the accompanying explanations, clearly describe what the students who reach the reported levels can do. If school systems wish to report college entrance tests, such as the SAT and ACT, these should be clearly labeled as representing aptitude for college.

2. Cognitive testing should be expanded to cover more of the curriculum that school systems actually teach. Existing tests provide coverage of achievement and ability in certain basic and highly important skills, but usually only a small portion of the subject matter and "skills" that schools teach is presently tested for, and that only at certain grade levels. Thus, expansion, especially of the use of annual criterion-referenced (objective-referenced) tests, is needed to permit schools to assess levels of proficiency in a broader range of subjects.

3. School systems should obtain feedback annually from students, including dropouts, and possibly parents to obtain their ratings of the quality and effectiveness of the schooling students have received. (Exhibit 4-3 illustrates the coverage of such a survey.) Such surveys should be administered at, or near, the end of the school year, perhaps as part of the cognitive testing process. We believe it would be appropriate for these feedback surveys to be administered to students ten years of age and older.

4. School systems need to place more attention on attrition and dropout rates, with greater focus on identifying and tabulating the data by reason. Reporting of annual dropout rates, as well as the more-traditional rates of attrition between the ninth grade and graduation, would provide more guidance to officials as to when and where improvements were needed.

Exhibit 4-2
Recommended SEA Indicators for Elementary and Secondary Education*

	Indicator	Rationale for Selecting Indicator

Inputs:	Expenditures[a] (in millions) (may be also broken out by type of activity such as instructional and administrative)
	  Current dollars
	  Constant dollars
		To provide a measure of resources used to provide services

	Total number of personnel	To provide a measure of the size of the organization
Outputs:	Number of student-days (thousands)	To provide a general measure of workload
	Number of students promoted/graduated	To provide a measure of students satisfactorily completing educational requirements
	Carnegie units as percentage of required[b] (with number of required units shown parenthetically—can be reported by major subject area)	To provide an indication of courses taken by students in certain critical subject areas
	Absenteeism rate	To provide a measure of student participation in classes and an indication of their interest in learning
	Dropout rate	To indicate the school's success in keeping students actively involved in the learning process

Outcomes:	Test score results—*for each major subject area*	
	Average percentile on standardized tests	
	Percentage of students above the tests' 50th percentile[c]	To provide measures of student achievement in academic subjects and a comparison with expected achievement and established norms
	Percentage of students reaching their grade level of proficiency or higher	
	Percentage of students achieving grade-level gain on achievement test[d] (may be presented for major subject areas as well as overall)	To provide a measure of student annual progress—the indicator is also used to develop a measure of cost-effectiveness
	Percentage of students scoring higher than prespecified level of self-esteem	To provide an indication of the development of noncognitive skills and abilities generally considered as objectives of formal education
	Percentage of students achieving specified physical fitness test standards	
	Percentage of graduates gainfully employed or continuing education two years after graduation	To provide an indication of the school system's results in preparing graduates for further education or to become members of the workforce

*The recommended indicators presented in this exhibit are illustrative. They are intended to serve as a starting point for use in the development of a comprehensive set of SEA indicators for external reporting of an entity's results of operation.

This exhibit does not provide illustrations of indicator disaggregation or of comparison data such as trends, targets, or other comparable entities. Both disaggregation and comparison data are important aspects of SEA reporting. They are discussed in the chapter and in the overview.

[a] A clear description of which expenditures are included or excluded should be provided.

[b] One Carnegie unit equals five hours per week of instructional class time on a subject for an entire school year.

[c] The 50th percentile is the point that one-half of the students who were used to develop the test norm scored at or above and one-half scored below.

[d] A grade-level gain is the measure of a student's progress by school year, as assessed by a test score, for example, from the 6.1 grade level to the 7.1 grade level.

Exhibit 4-2 (continued)

Indicator	Rationale for Selecting Indicator
Outcomes (continued):	

Percentage of students rating as good, excellent, or improved—their own:
   Work and study skills
   Self-discipline
   Interpersonal skills
   Knowledge gained
	To provide measures of students' perceptions of their acquisition of knowledge and selected noncognitive skills and behavior

Percentage of parents rating their children good, excellent, or improved in:
   Work and study skills
   Self-discipline
   Interpersonal skills
   Knowledge gained
	To provide measures of parents' perceptions of their child's acquisition of knowledge and selected noncognitive skills and behavior; to allow comparison with student perceptions; to indicate the school system's contribution to the acquisition of these skills and behavior

Efficiency (input/output and input/outcome measures):	

Cost per unit of output
   Per student-day
   Per student promoted/graduated
	To provide an indication of the school system's "technical" efficiency of operation

Cost per unit of outcome Per student achieving grade-level score gain or target level for an outcome	To provide an indication of the school system's "true" efficiency in achieving student outcomes

Explanatory Data:

Controllable
    Average number of hours per student in oversized classes (per day)

Not controllable
    Average daily attendance
    Percentage of minority students
    Percentage of students participating in subsidized lunch or other public welfare program
    Percentage of students needing special remedial programs
    Student mobility rate[e]
    Percentage of students with English as a second language
    Student enrollments

} To provide information on factors that are likely to have some effect on student achievement and that can be important in understanding performance indicated by SEA indicators

---

[e] One definition for this is: Percentage of school's beginning enrollment entering, or departing, after the start of the school year.

Exhibit 4-3
Illustration of the Coverage of a Survey Requesting Students, or Ex-Students, to Rate Various Aspects of Their School's Contribution to Noncognitive Outcomes

How much did your education (this past school year) at this school contribute to your personal growth in each of the following areas? Would you say it contributed: Very Much, Somewhat, or Very Little?

1. Working independently
2. Learning on your own
3. Following directions
4. Working cooperatively in a group
5. Organizing your time effectively
6. Recognizing your rights, responsibilities, and privileges as a citizen
7. Planning and carrying out projects
8. Understanding different philosophies and cultures
9. Persisting at difficult tasks
10. Getting projects done on time
11. Caring for your own physical and mental health

Source: Adapted from Northeast Missouri State University, "Alumni Survey 1986." Printed with permission.

---

5. School systems need to undertake measurement and reporting of noncognitive elements more regularly—especially of such elements as self-esteem, work habits, interpersonal relationships, physical fitness, and in-school disruptive incidents. Though these are by no means solely the responsibility of school systems, schools play a major role in student development on these elements.

Self-esteem can be assessed by adding an existing self-esteem scale to year-end cognitive testing or by separate assessments as part of obtaining the student feedback suggested in item 3 (p. 105). Student and parent feedback on the student's progress toward developing *good work habits, self-discipline,* and *interpersonal relationships* can be obtained along with their ratings of the quality of schooling suggested in item 3.

Physical fitness can be assessed using the tests recommended by the President's Council on Physical Fitness and Sports. Physical fitness testing is already done by most schools, so testing in a more systematic manner, with tabulation of information on scores and comparisons with norms, is not likely to present a major problem for most school systems.

Incidents of *in-school disturbances,* such as delinquency, drug use, and violent behavior, have been of increasing concern to many school systems. Though caused in part by many factors outside the direct influence of the schools, these incidents represent safety problems and also indicate a lack of school control and discipline. Key needs here are to adequately define what constitutes such incidents and to tally them accordingly.

6. School systems should continue to expand the development and reporting of efficiency (including cost-effectiveness) indicators. These would include traditional efficiency indicators such as cost per student-day and new indicators that would relate cost to measures of outcome. We recommend experimentation with indicators relating costs to students promoted or graduated and to measures of learning and noncognitive progress, such as the number of students achieving annual target gains on test scores and self-esteem levels.

Because of cost accounting problems, the expenditure figures need to be clearly defined and, if disaggregated (for example, by administrative and instruction costs), carefully calculated and described. To further help users obtain a better understanding of efficiency, school systems can break out costs by major activities such as institution administration, transportation, and support activities.

Because of lack of experience with "cost per unit of outcome" indicators, school systems will need to consider these indicators as very experimental. State departments of education may need to provide technical assistance to school systems to help them introduce such measurements.

7. It is important to report input indicators along with information on outputs, outcomes, and efficiency. This will enable users to examine trends in expenditures and school personnel and to compare these trends with trends in output and outcome indicators. Expenditures should be pre-

sented in constant, as well as current, dollars to give users of the reports a better perspective on how the amount of resources available to school systems is changing after removing the effects of inflation.

8. Student–teacher ratios, if presented, should focus on counting the number of classes that are overcrowded or, better, the number of students in overcrowded classes. Student–teacher ratios are often reported, but past research has raised questions about the relationships between these ratios and learning, at least within the range of ratios that have been examined. Reporting the number of students in overcrowded classes will focus user attention on the main issue and not the *average* student–teacher ratio, which may hide the real problem.

9. Finally, measures of student progress and the effect of education on students are essential. We recommend reporting two indicators that provide information about student progress and its effect on them after graduation. First, schools should report on student grade-level gain in achievement tests. This will provide a measurement of the school's effect on student performance that is tied to the student's beginning level. "Gain" (improvement) may be a more valid indicator than absolute levels of test performance, especially when considering the performance of school systems with high percentages of disadvantaged students. Second, we recommend reporting the percentage of graduates gainfully employed or continuing their education two years after graduation as a partial measure of the effect schooling has had, in the short run, on their ability to function in society.

DISAGGREGATION

The logical starting point for disaggregation of SEA measures is to provide data for individual school systems and schools. In addition, SEA indicators that are broken out by key characteristics of students are likely to be considerably more informative to school officials and the public than merely presenting aggregate figures for each indicator for the school system, or even for individual schools. We urge school systems to break out individual SEA indicators for each *individual school* and by such additional characteristics as:

1. *Race/ethnicity/minority group*—This breakout has attracted public attention and encouraged a number of school systems to focus more on improving the performance of lower-performing groups.
2. *Students receiving subsidized lunches.*

3. *Students with English as a second language.*
4. *Age and grade.*
5. *Gender.*
6. *Subject area.*
7. *Initial levels of the indicator*—So that the extent of improvement for groups of students starting at various levels can be discerned.

For some indicators, other disaggregations may also be desirable. For example, disaggregations of dropout rates by reason for dropping out (as well as by grade, gender, and ethnicity) can be used by the school system and elected officials to help determine where and when actions to correct problems should be directed, as well as to detect trends in such indicators. Disaggregating SEA measures enables schools and school systems to see where specific problem areas exist and make more-detailed policy and program responses to these problems.

COMPARISON INFORMATION TO BE REPORTED

Reporting comparisons of current performance to benchmarks allows users of the information to obtain a better perspective on performance. We believe each of the following types of comparisons should be carefully developed and reported.

First, where nationally developed (or state-developed) norms or other data are available—such as with standardized cognitive tests, self-esteem scales, and physical fitness tests—comparisons with these norms should be used.

Second, states should make comparisons among their individual school systems, and school systems should make comparisons among their individual schools. Comparable schools and school systems need to be selected explicitly by considering factors such as those used by the State of California in developing comparison groups for its performance report. (See Exhibit 4-4.) These factors include parent education level, student mobility, English-language fluency, and family receipt of Aid to Families with Dependent Children benefits.[11] Among other states using criteria to select comparison groups are

---

[11] California State Department of Education, "Performance Report for California Schools, 1987: Epic Senior High," p. 3.

Exhibit 4-4
An Example of a Comparison Display

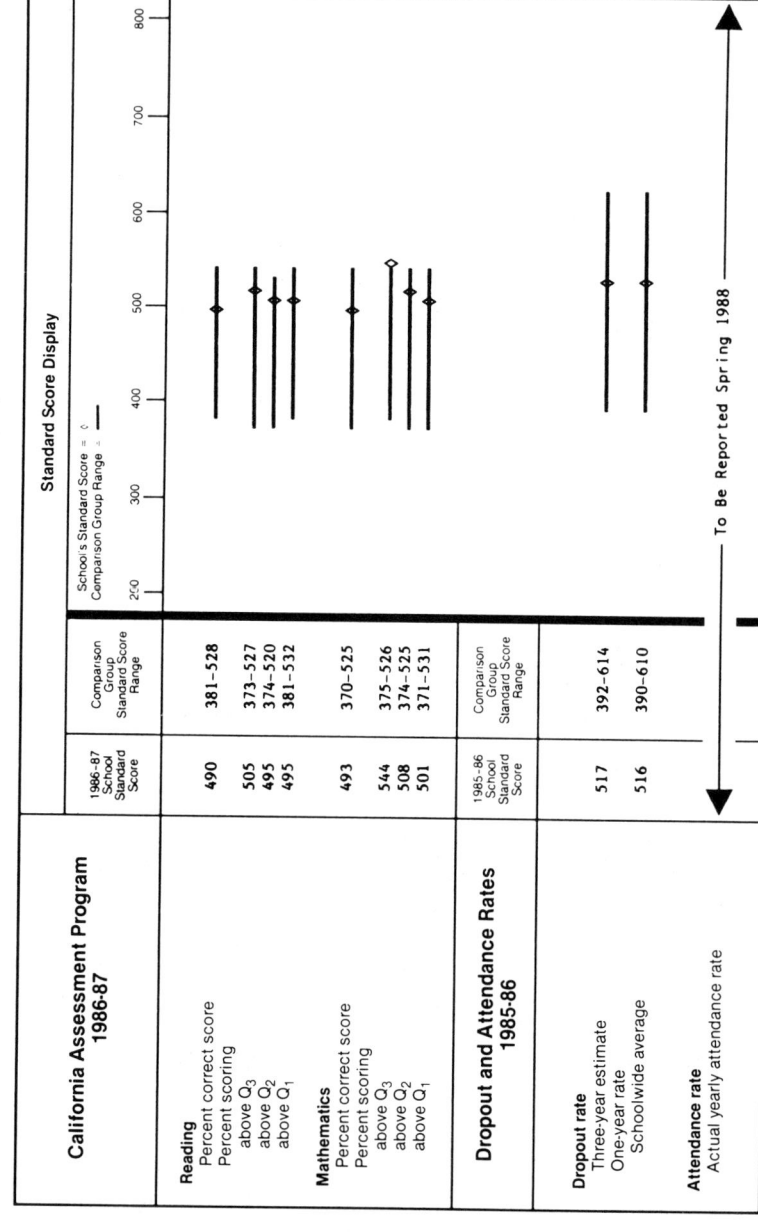

Source: California State Department of Education, "Performance Report," p. 7. Reprinted with permission.

South Carolina[12] and Texas.[13] Of special importance is the percentage of students who are "at risk" (based on such information as percentage participating in school-lunch programs, percentage in special education classes, and student test score levels early in the school year).

Third, school systems should make and report comparisons of results over time. Indicator data should be reported for recent years so that improvements or declines in performance can be identified. This is the most common form of comparison currently used by school systems.

Fourth, school system administrators and other policy officials should annually set goals (targets) for the school system and for individual schools on the specific indicators. Actual performance should subsequently be compared with the targets to determine to what extent the goals were achieved. This can become a very important comparison for individual schools and school systems. Meaningful goal setting, however, is not easily done. Targets should be linked to specific school action plans and should be consistent with school budget and resource levels in order to represent practical, achievable goals.

EXPLANATORY DATA

Exhibit 4-5 lists the candidate explanatory factors that we found in use or that appeared to be potentially useful. A school system might choose to include any or all such factors in its performance reports to elected officials and the public. Each explanatory factor, however, has a unique quality and usefulness and may not be applicable to all school systems.

Most school systems and individual schools will likely prefer to include at least some explanatory information in reports presenting data on various performance indicators. Such information can help readers understand why particular schools (or school systems in the case of statewide reports) are scoring at higher or lower levels on indicators than in previous years or than other schools or school systems.

The small set of recommended explanatory factors in Exhibit 4-5 are likely to be widely applicable and of interest to elected officials and the

---

[12]Michael M. Turner, "Performance Reporting in South Carolina: 1973–1987" (South Carolina Department of Education, Quality Assessment Section, 1987), p. 10.

[13]Irving (Texas) Independent School District, Department of Planning, Evaluation, and Research, "Annual Performance Report for 1986–1987: Achieving Academic Excellence," p. 24.

Exhibit 4-5
Candidate Explanatory Factors

Noncontrollable Factors (e.g., demographic)

1. Student enrollment figures
2. Percentage of students of minority racial/ethnic groups
3. Percentage of students on subsidized lunch program
4. Percentage of pupils in the school whose families receive welfare benefits
5. The total number and percentage of students in families below the poverty level
6. Percentage and number of students in compensatory education programs
7. Percentage of students with "limited English proficiency" and percentage enrolled in "English as a Second Language" classes
8. Percentage of students enrolled in special education classes
9. Distribution of *entering* test scores (such as from the end of previous school year)
10. Mobility rate (e.g., percentage of school's enrollment entering, or departing, after the start of the school year)
11. Per capita income
12. Property value per pupil
13. Percentage of students in gifted or talented programs

Controllable Factors

14. Student–teacher ratios
15. Percentage of student-hours spent in "overcrowded" classes
16. Percentage of teachers with Master's degree
17. Percentage of teachers who passed teacher competency tests
18. Teachers' entry salary (for entrants with a BA or for entrants with a Master's degree) and average teacher's salary after 10 years
19. Average teacher tenure
20. Number and percentage of teachers teaching out of their primary subject area
21. Teacher turnover rate

Note: Factors 1–13 are community demographic characteristics, generally outside the control of the school system. The school system has a significant degree of control over the other factors.

public. In this summary set, we have emphasized explanatory factors that indicate the proportion of the student body that is likely to be "at risk" and that identify schools with greater levels of difficulty in achieving learning and noncognitive development. Narrative explanations, such as unusual circumstances affecting the data, should supplement the table.

COSTS OF OBTAINING AND REPORTING SEA INFORMATION

We recommend that school systems and others experimenting with SEA indicators monitor the costs of gathering, analyzing, preparing, and reporting this information. These costs should then be carefully compared to the benefits derived from use of the information. The added costs of reporting the set of SEA indicators recommended here should be moderate for school systems that already have a basic testing and data-gathering capability. The *start-up* costs for such items as a self-esteem index, more careful follow-up of dropouts (including reasons for dropping out), standardized physical fitness test data collection, annual surveys of parents and students, and even annual surveys of graduates after they have left school (including development of procedures for reporting the information) can be significant (such as for developing and testing the needed procedures), but *annual* efforts and costs thereafter should be reasonable.

Considerably more costly will be efforts to develop tests that cover more of the curriculum being taught, and to test more grades annually. Some states, as noted earlier, are already making important strides in this direction.

CONCLUSIONS

Education has become a primary concern in the United States and receives a major share of public funds. Yet serious questions are still being raised about the quality of the education received by our youth and whether the recent increase in resources has resulted in a comparable increase in results. SEA indicators that are regularly reported to the public and elected officials are necessary for addressing these questions because they present information that provides users with the ability to assess performance over time, against other school systems, and against the major goals and objectives of the school system.

Many experiments are currently being performed by states and school systems in the reporting of SEA data, but there has been no coordinated effort directed at testing a comprehensive set (or sets) of SEA indicators. We believe the public-education community is in a position to make a major stride in the development of effective external reporting of results. We recommend that a program be established to coordinate and monitor a comprehensive experiment in SEA reporting for elementary and secondary education.

We believe the indicators in Exhibit 4-2 provide an excellent point to begin the development of a comprehensive set of SEA indicators and that, if used for expanded experimentation and further research, they can help focus efforts aimed at improving the means of monitoring the performance of our elementary and secondary educational system, without adding unduly to its costs.

5. Fire Department Programs

Robert W. Parry, Jr., Indiana University

Florence C. Sharp, Ohio University

Jannet Vreeland and Wanda A. Wallace, Texas A&M University

	Page
Introduction and Scope	120
Methodology	120
Reporting Service Efforts and Accomplishments	121
Input Measures	121
Overall Fire Protection	121
Fire Suppression	128
Fire Prevention	128
Output Measures	129
Overall Fire Protection	129
Fire Suppression	129
Fire Prevention	130
Outcome Measures	130
Overall Fire Protection	130
Fire Suppression	132
Fire Prevention	133
Efficiency Measures	135
Disaggregation	135
Recommendations	136
Comparison Information and SEA Norms	136
Intercity Comparisons	137
Intertemporal Comparisons	137
SEA Targets	138
Recommendations	138

INTRODUCTION AND SCOPE

The need for fire-prevention and fire-fighting services in this country is extensive. In 1986, 2.3 million fires were reported in the United States, and these resulted in 5,850 civilian deaths, 26,825 serious injuries, and direct property damage of approximately $6.7 billion.[1] In the same year, city governments spent a total of $7.3 billion on fire protection.[2] In addition, hundreds of millions of dollars are spent for temporary shelter, medical care, missed work, and other social costs associated with fires. Given these statistics, fire department operations are of obvious interest to the citizenry. The primary goal of this research project is to identify means of communicating the service efforts and accomplishments (SEA) of fire departments that will assist users in evaluation of fire-prevention and fire-suppression efforts.

Fire departments may provide a broad range of services: emergency ambulance service, nonfire emergency rescue, natural disaster assistance, disposal of hazardous material and toxic substances, nonfire-related water pumping and smoke clearance, building inspections, various social services, and other miscellaneous functions. The two services, however, that appear to be common to all fire departments are fire suppression and fire prevention. This study focuses on reporting the SEA of fire departments in these two areas. The overall goal of fire-suppression activities is presumed to be the extinguishment of fires with the minimum loss of life and property, and the overall goal of fire-prevention activities is presumed to be the reduction of the incidence of fires and the restriction of loss of property and life in the fires that do occur.

Methodology

Extensive literature on fire services was reviewed. This review identified fire department SEA measures that have been considered, the relationship of those measures to characteristics of municipalities, the context in which different measures might be disclosed, and the possible implications of these factors for reporting. A literature review and practice review serve as a basis for suggestions on feasible approaches to reporting on the SEA of municipal fire departments.

---

[1] M. J. Karter, "A Look at Fire Loss in the United States during 1986," *Fire Journal* (September/October 1987), p. 38.

[2] U.S. Department of Commerce, Bureau of the Census, *Statistical Abstract of the United States: 1989* (Washington, DC, 1989), p. 286.

Current disclosure practices were evaluated by examining a sample of municipal financial and budgetary reports. A total of 573 municipalities were asked to provide annual reports, budget information, and other demographic data. The findings are summarized in the full-length research report, and implications drawn are one basis for SEA measures recommended herein.

REPORTING SERVICE EFFORTS AND ACCOMPLISHMENTS

The following discussion focuses on identifying appropriate measures of input, output, outcome, efficiency, and overall SEA measures for fire-suppression and fire-prevention activities. Exhibits 5-1 through 5-3 list the SEA measures considered, classified by category.

Input Measures

Inputs include financial and nonfinancial measures of the resources consumed in the process of providing fire services. Typically, they are expressed in terms of wages paid or man-hours spent on fire fighting or prevention, and these would appear to represent the minimum level of information desirable. Inputs could also include capital expenditures, information on the water supply, the number of fire vehicles or stations per square mile, the type of alarm and dispatch system, and other types of equipment. Used in conjunction with output and outcome data, these input measures may be useful in determining how efficiently outputs are obtained and whether inputs are used effectively.

Overall Fire Protection

The input measures that users would be likely to relate to overall fire protection are number of personnel, total man-hours, and total cost. The cost is often already available in the comprehensive annual financial report (CAFR); however, since total cost may be artificially inflated in any given year due to the timing of capital expenditures, it is recommended that operating expenditures be reported separately from capital expenditures. We recommend the following input disclosures: (1) total operating and capital expenditures for fire services; (2) numbers of full-time, part-time, and volunteer personnel; and (3) total man-hours worked in the period.

Exhibit 5-1
Recommended SEA Indicators for Fire Departments: Overall Performance*

Indicator	Rationale for Selecting Indicator
Inputs:	
Total Operating Expenditures } Total Capital Expenditures }	Provide information on funds used to provide services
Personnel Full-Time Personnel Part-Time and Volunteer Personnel Total Man-Hours Worked	Provide information on labor resources used; available
Outputs:	
Population Served Residential Workforce Tourist, Average Daily Property Value Protected Residential Commercial Public Property	Provide a measure of workload; readily available
Outcomes:	
Percentage of Citizens Rating Performance Satisfactory	Assesses citizen satisfaction and concern
ISO Fire Insurance Rating	An outside measure of overall fire risk

Total Dollars in Fire Losses — Attempts to quantify success (or failure) of all fire department efforts in minimizing property losses due to fire; readily available

Total Fire-Related Deaths — Attempts to quantify success (or failure) of all fire department efforts in minimizing deaths due to fire; readily available

Total Fire-Related Injuries — Attempts to quantify success (or failure) of all fire department efforts in minimizing injuries due to fire; readily available

Explanatory Data:

Area of Responsibility

Area served in square miles for municipality and peer-group cities.
Population density (population per square mile) for municipality and peer-group cities.

Fire Code Compliance

Percentage of buildings in compliance with fire code regulations for municipality and average for peer-group cities.

Other Data

This data should highlight any factors pertinent to fire-prevention or fire-suppression efforts of this fire department. It could include, for example, information regarding climate, rainfall, social disturbances, road conditions, structural conditions, or average age of buildings.

---

*The recommended indicators presented in this exhibit are illustrative. They are intended to serve as a starting point for use in the development of a comprehensive set of SEA indicators for external reporting of an entity's results of operation.

This exhibit does not provide illustrations of indicator disaggregation or of comparison data such as trends, targets, or other comparable entities. Both disaggregation and comparison data are important aspects of SEA reporting. They are discussed in the chapter and in the Overview.

Exhibit 5-2
Recommended SEA Indicators for Fire Departments: Fire Suppression*

Indicator	Rationale for Selecting Indicator
Inputs:	
Personnel	
Full-Time Personnel	Provide information on labor resources used
Part-Time and Volunteer Personnel	
Total Man-Hours Worked	
Total Operating Expenditures	Provide information on resources committed to suppression activity
Total Capital Expenditures	
Man-Hours in Training Programs	Provide information on preparedness
Percentage of Fire Fighters Reaching an NFPA-Recommended Certification Level	
Outputs:	
Number of Fire Calls Answered	A measure of suppression workload; readily available
Outcomes:	
Water Supply	Measure availability of water needed to suppress fires—a measure of fire fighting readiness
Minimum Water Volume Available	
Minimum Water Flow Available	
Population with Access to Adequate Water Supply	

Response Time
  Average Response Time — ⎫
  Percentage of Responses in under 5 Minutes ⎬ Measure success in delivering timely service; currently measured by fire departments

Average Time to Control Fires
  Single-Alarm, Residential
  Single-Alarm, Industry
  Two-Alarm, Industry
Percentage of Fires Spread Limited to X% Square Feet on Arrival
  Single-Alarm, Residential
  Single-Alarm, Industry
  Two-Alarm, Industry

⎬ Measures success in minimizing fire damage

Efficiency:

Operating Expenditures per Capita — Provides per capita cost of service information for operations

Capital Expenditures per Capita — Provides per capita cost of capital investment

Operating Expenditures per $100,000 of Property Protected — Relates operating cost information to value of property protected

Capital Expenditures per $100,000 of Property Protected — Relates capital investment to value of property protected

---

*The recommended indicators presented in this exhibit are illustrative. They are intended to serve as a starting point for use in the development of a comprehensive set of SEA indicators for external reporting of an entity's results of operation.

This exhibit does not provide illustrations of indicator disaggregation or of comparison data such as trends, targets, or other comparable entities. Both disaggregation and comparison data are important aspects of SEA reporting. They are discussed in the chapter and in the Overview.

Exhibit 5-3
Recommended SEA Indicators for Fire Departments: Fire Prevention*

Indicator	Rationale for Selecting Indicator
Inputs:	
Personnel	
Full-Time Personnel }	Provide information on labor resources used
Part-Time and Volunteer Personnel }	
Total Man-Hours Worked	Provides information on labor resources used and workload
Total Operating Expenditures	Provides information on resources committed to prevention activity
Total Capital Expenditures	Provides information on allocation of resources between operations and capital
Outputs:	
Number of Inspections }	
Number of Education Programs Offered }	Measure activity level; readily available
Number of Fire Investigations Performed }	
Outcomes:	
Number of Fires (Reported and Unreported)	Attempts to quantify success (or failure) of efforts to prevent fires

Percentage of Fires Preventable by Inspection or Education	Attempts to quantify need for additional efforts in fire prevention; measures effectiveness of inspection program
Number of Fires of Suspicious Origin	Aids in interpreting fire rates by identifying fires not preventable by education and inspection

Fires in Inspected/Uninspected Buildings
  Industrial
  Other
	Measure effectiveness of inspection program

Citizens Participating in or Aware of Education Programs	Attempts to measure effectiveness of education programs
Efficiency:	
Expenditures per Capita	A measure of per capita cost of service information
Expenditures per $100,000 of Property Protected	Relates operating cost information to value of property protected

---

*The recommended indicators presented in this exhibit are illustrative. They are intended to serve as a starting point for use in the development of a comprehensive set of SEA indicators for external reporting of an entity's results of operation.

This exhibit does not provide illustrations of indicator disaggregation or of comparison data such as trends, targets, or other comparable entities. Both disaggregation and comparison data are important aspects of SEA reporting. They are discussed in the chapter and in the Overview.

Fire Suppression

A number of inputs related to fire suppression have been reported: for example hours or dollars spent in total and for each type of suppression activity, including training, drill, actual fire fighting, administration and planning, and maintenance of equipment. The most frequently reported suppression measure relates to efforts spent on fire fighter training, with the next most frequent being time spent on maintenance and repairs. The popularity of these input measures may be related to the outcome expected to be gained. Schaenman and Swartz recommend that a distinction be made among full-time, part-time, and volunteer personnel.[3] Other inputs reported include miles traveled, hydrants installed, water used, and the number of stations.

The largest number of inputs reported in practice related to fire suppression, disclosing time and dollar inputs for each type of suppression activity. However, our recommended measures would not include such detail. While the large investment required for suppression equipment with a long service life justifies reporting capital and operating expenditures separately, only the following measures are recommended: (1) numbers of full-time, part-time, and volunteer personnel working in fire suppression; (2) total man-hours worked in the period on fire suppression; and (3) total operating and capital expenditures for fire-suppression activities.

Because of the emphasis that fire fighters and their organizations put on training as a means to improve suppression efforts, we believe that some disclosure of the amount or level of training is important. We recommend two measures: (1) number of man-hours spent in formal training programs; and (2) percentage of fire fighters holding/maintaining an NFPA (National Fire Protection Association) recommended certification level.

Fire Prevention

As in the case of overall protection, information on costs and personnel inputs are needed to evaluate efficiency. The cost of fire-prevention activities may not be broken out in the CAFR, so our recommendations

---

[3]P. S. Schaenman and J. Swartz, *Measuring Fire Protection Productivity in Local Government: Some Initial Thoughts* (National Fire Protection Association, 1974).

include: (1) numbers of full-time, part-time, and volunteer personnel working in fire prevention; (2) total man-hours worked in the period on fire prevention; and (3) total operating and capital expenditures for fire-prevention activities.

Output Measures

Examination of municipal reports yielded a total of 66 output measures currently reported. Output measures by themselves are of limited help in evaluating the services provided by a fire department. However, when used in conjunction with input measures, they could be helpful in determining the efficiency with which the resources were used. In addition, if services performed can be related to outcome measures, the information may provide guidance on potential reallocation of services.

Overall Fire Protection

Two basic measures have been suggested for reporting overall fire protection output: population served and property protected. Population can be subdivided into residential population, population in the workforce, and visitors. These provide only rough approximations of fire department activity, perhaps focusing more on community need than on actual service provided. They also facilitate interpretation of other performance measures by allowing computation of losses per population (e.g., deaths per 100,000 population) or per dollar-value property protected (e.g., dollar losses per $100,000 of property protected). Some of this information may be routinely provided in the statistical section of municipal annual financial reports. We recommend the following output measures: (1) population served in three categories (if applicable): residential, workforce, and visitor; and (2) value of residential, commercial, and public property protected.

Fire Suppression

By far, the most frequently reported fire-suppression measure is the number of fire call responses. Although this measure is discussed as a potential outcome measure related to fire prevention, cities are also using it to report on the overall workload of fire fighters in suppressing fires, and it would appear to be useful for both purposes. Classification of responses by type of call, separating out false alarms, could also be useful as a measure of activity level, as could averages by individual fire company. We recommend reporting the number of fire calls answered.

Output measures can be reported for all activities in which fire-suppression personnel are engaged. Municipal reports included numbers of fire hydrants serviced, false alarms answered, fire lanes inspected, cases of arson investigated, and violations corrected, suggesting the feasibility of tracking such measures.

Fire Prevention

Two primary prevention activities conducted by the fire department are inspections and educational programs. Fire investigations also fall into the area of preventive activity to the degree that they discourage arson or identify potential problems. Output measures of these activities are popular in actual reports, and we recommend all three: (1) number of inspections made, (2) number of education programs offered, and (3) number of fire investigations performed.

Outcome Measures

Overall Fire Protection

Schaenman and Swartz suggest two ideal financial measures for the service accomplishments of fire departments: fire losses that did not occur because of effective fire-prevention activities, and fire losses not incurred due to efficient and effective fire-suppression efforts.[4]

Although desirable measures in theory, these outcomes are not measurable in practice. Since losses not incurred cannot be measured, some of the suggested SEA indicators provide information on losses that *were* incurred. The dollar value of property lost, the number of fires, and the number of fire-related deaths and injuries have been suggested as useful measures of performance.[5]

Ramanathan suggests that the reduction in fire insurance premiums due to the existence of a fire department would provide a financial

---

[4]Schaenman and Swartz, *Measuring Fire Protection Productivity,* p. 3.

[5]See M. Getz, *The Economics of the Urban Fire Department* (Baltimore: The Johns Hopkins University Press, 1979); P. S. Schaenman et al., *Procedures for Improving the Measurement of Local Fire Protection Effectiveness* (The Urban Institute and National Fire Protection Association, 1977); Schaenman and Swartz, *Measuring Fire Protection Productivity;* and K. L. Rider, "The Economics of the Distribution of Municipal Fire Protection Services," *The Review of Economics and Statistics* (vol. 61, no. 2, May 1979), pp. 249–258.

measure of the social benefits provided by the fire department.[6] Although an interesting concept, the lack of verifiability of such estimates suggests that other measures would be preferable.

The Insurance Service Office (ISO) rating of the fire department has received a great deal of attention in the literature. Historically, the insurance grading system has stimulated improvements in fire protection, but it has also been criticized for discouraging new and innovative practices.[7] Further, the fact that the final judgment on rate changes reflects the ISO executives' "sense of market conditions"[8] can affect the usefulness of ratings in evaluating fire department activities. Commercial fire insurance rates can be set or adjusted at various organizational levels, which introduces possible measurement error and bias into the resulting insurance premiums. Locale, urban setting, and crime rates with respect to arson activities are among the factors likely to influence such figures. Nonetheless, figures are available on property insurance rates across the country, and perhaps an opportunity exists to report comparative statistics for both ISO grades and insurance premiums as an "outcome" measure of fire department activities. We did not observe any cases of this type of disclosure, but budget objectives of some fire departments included the stated goal of achieving a higher ISO rating.

A final overall measure identified in the literature is the percentage of the population that rates the fire protection service as satisfactory. This type of information can be obtained from surveys. The reports examined included an example of attitude surveys on fire-prevention activity, but this information could easily be obtained on an overall basis. John Hall, director of fire analysis at the National Fire Protection Association, has noted, however, that citizen opinions on fire services obtained from surveys are usually formed in the absence of any direct experience or knowledge because fires are relatively rare events, reducing the number of people directly involved.

---

[6] K. V. Ramanathan, draft working paper: "Social Value Added: A Common Yardstick for Evaluating Diverse Government Services" (March 1988).

[7] See B. B. Gordon, W. Drozda, and G. S. Stacey, "Condensed Report on Cost-Effectiveness in Fire Protection," Project No. 355-8030, 355-8031" (Urban Studies Center, Battelle Memorial Institute, 1969).

[8] G. Stevenson, "Rate Making and Fire Insurance," in C. Rapkin (ed.), *The Social and Economic Consequences of Residential Fires* (Lexington, MA: Lexington Books, D. C. Heath and Co., 1983), p. 390.

Although they may represent the major objectives of a fire department, fires that were prevented, losses that did not occur, or lives that were not lost due to the activities of the fire department cannot be measured. In an attempt to approach those concerns, however, we recommend that four related disclosures be made: (1) level of citizen satisfaction with fire protection services obtained through surveys; (2) ISO fire insurance rating; (3) dollar value of fire losses for the year; and (4) number of fire-related deaths and injuries for the year.

Fire Suppression

Time required to respond to a fire is a popular measure of fire-suppression performance. This performance measure depends on the fire department's communication system, the physical layout and location of fire stations, the ability of fire fighters to get to their apparatus quickly, and the ability of drivers to determine the fastest route and drive to the site of the fire. It should be noted that response time is also affected by road, weather, and traffic conditions, as well as other factors beyond the fire department's control.

Gordon, Drozda, and Stacey,[9] and MacGillivray[10] conducted research indicating that reduced response time is likely to reduce losses or, conversely, that longer average response times are associated with greater fire loss. Rider reported that response time was the most crucial variable in explaining loss of life due to fire in New York City.[11] Specific response measures recommended in the literature are average response time and percentage of responses taking less than a target number of minutes, by neighborhood and type of occupancy.

The availability of water plays an important role in a department's ability to fight fires. Water is usually delivered through a fire hydrant system or from nearby bodies of water, though it is sometimes transported to the scene. The important question seems to be whether adequate water volume and flow can be delivered when necessary, rather than the method of delivery. Important measures of SEA should focus on the minimum volume and flow of water available and the proportion of the population with access to the water supply.

---

[9]Gordon et al., "Condensed Report."

[10]L. A. MacGillivray et al., *Municipal Fire Service Workbook* (Research Triangle Institute, International City Management Association, and National Fire Protection Association) (Washington, DC: U.S. Government Printing Office, 1977).

[11]Rider, "The Economics of the Distribution of Municipal Fire Protection Services."

Because the availability of water is so important in determining a department's ability to fight fires, we recommend two disclosures dealing with water supply: (1) minimum water volume and flow available and (2) percentage of the population with access to an adequate water supply.

The time required to respond to a fire call has been documented as a factor in minimizing loss of life and property, and is frequently reported. We recommend two disclosures on response time: (1) average response time and (2) percentage of responses taking less than *x* minutes.

Other measures of fire-suppression effectiveness include time to control the fire[12] and measures of fire spread after the arrival of the first unit.[13] One city reported the percent of fires confined to the area of origin or less, but none reported measures of spread beyond that. Since the size of the fire upon arrival plays a major role in fire control, stratification by size seems a logical extension for each of these measures.

Much of the literature is devoted to the development of measures of a fire department's ability to control and extinguish fires once fire fighters arrive on the scene. Although there may be some problems associated with developing measures of this type, we recommend that municipalities experiment with various measurement techniques in an attempt to report: (1) average time to control (or extinguish) fires, by size on arrival and type of occupancy; and (2) percentage of fires in which spread after arrival is limited to a target number of square feet, by size on arrival and type of occupancy.

Fire Prevention

Three major areas of fire-prevention activity are building inspection, fire cause investigations, and education. The NFPA has reported a causal effect between building inspections and fire prevention. Education is also viewed as a method of fire prevention. Fire cause investigations will facilitate reporting the percentage of fires that are considered preventable by inspection or education.[14]

The major objective of fire-prevention efforts is to reduce the incidence of fires, but prevented fires are not observable. Therefore, it seems natural that one measure of effectiveness will focus on the oc-

---

[12] Schaenman et al., *Procedures for Improving.*

[13] Schaenman and Swartz, *Measuring Fire Protection Productivity.*

[14] J. R. Hall, Jr., et al., *Fire Code Inspections and Fire Prevention: What Methods Lead to Success?* (Boston: National Fire Protection Association, 1979); and Schaenman et al., *Procedures for Improving.*

currence of fires, which is observable and which the department hopes to minimize. Reported fires has been suggested as an indicator of occurrences.[15] Thus, attempts to report on prevention accomplishments must focus on the department's ability to minimize the number of fires. It should be noted that some fires are not reported. This could cause comparisons across cities to be misleading. Including fires discovered after the fact in the number of occurrences would provide a more accurate count.[16] As one measure we recommend disclosing the number of fires reported and unreported.

The NFPA reported that fire rates are 50 percent lower on average when all or nearly all public buildings are subject to annual inspections.[17] Several of the reports we examined included the number of inspections performed, but none disclosed the number or percentage of uninspected buildings. This made a meaningful assessment of the effectiveness of the inspection program in reducing the incidence of fire, on a proportional basis, nearly impossible.

An outcome measure of fires in inspected buildings would provide information on the effectiveness of the department's inspection program, or on the municipality's building and fire codes.[18] We recommend reporting the rate of fires in both inspected and uninspected (or frequently versus infrequently inspected) occupancies, by type of occupancy and risk class.

The effectiveness of fire-prevention efforts is affected by the prevalence of arson, incendiarism, false alarms, and building code violations. Thus, clearance and conviction rates for these factors may be beneficial to understanding the SEA of fire departments. The percentage of arson and false-alarm cases closed each appeared once in the reports examined. A problem with reporting this type of information, however, is that the legal system plays a very important role in such measures. We recommend that fire departments disclose the frequency of fires of suspicious origin, which is a more subjective measure, but potentially more useful for interpreting prevention efforts.

Surveys can provide measures of citizen awareness and perceived performance. With regard to fire prevention, one city reported on surveys of residents, business owners, and school staff that indicated that

---

[15] Getz, *The Economics of the Urban Fire Department.*

[16] Schaenman and Swartz, *Measuring Fire Protection Productivity.*

[17] Hall et al., *Fire Code Inspections and Fire Prevention.*

[18] Ibid.

50 percent were aware of the fire-prevention program and 80 percent were satisfied with fire-prevention services. While surveys may not establish that citizens follow all fire-prevention precautions taught in education programs, they do indicate the number of people who have read or heard messages on the topic.

We recommend disclosure of citizen satisfaction obtained through survey in the overall fire department activities section. If fire departments use this approach, we recommend that they also obtain data for another disclosure: percentage of citizen respondents who are familiar with or who have participated in fire-prevention education programs.

Efficiency Measures

By combining some of the input measures with output and outcome measures, some efficiency measures can be developed. Because many of the recommended outcome measures are directed toward negative results, such as lost property values, we do not recommend using them to illustrate efficiency. Instead, we suggest that the following measures be reported: (1) fire-suppression expenditures (total and operating) per capita; (2) fire-suppression expenditures (total and operating) per $100,000 of property protected; (3) fire-prevention expenditures per capita; and (4) fire-prevention expenditures per $100,000 of property protected.

Disaggregation

Most of the literature seems to assume that fire department performance will be compared across communities, suggesting aggregation of performance information at that level. Most of the data in reports examined was presented for the city as a whole. In addition, some of the literature on performance suggests that intercity comparisons be made, requiring the use of performance measures by fire station. Hartford, Connecticut reports total responses (fires, false alarms, and smoke scares) by neighborhood.

Users might prefer disaggregation, depending on the issue at hand. For example, if citizens were interested in the relative quality of fire service delivered to their neighborhoods, they would prefer data by fire station. The City of Akron, Ohio Fire Department reports responses to alarms, and incendiary fires, property loss and involved property valuation from incendiary fires by census tract. It would appear reasonable to begin with city data as a desirable level of disclosure with more disaggregation by locale within a city being particularly relevant for large metropolitan areas. Other circumstances may likewise warrant additional detail.

As noted earlier, a number of suggested fire department SEA measures involve disaggregating fire incidence data by type of fire, age or type of building, and population density or type. The City of Akron discloses building fires by both cause and type of building.

Recommendations

Both literature and actual reports suggest that aggregating performance by community provides useful information for intercity comparisons. Currently, much information is already compiled at that level. For external reporting purposes, we recommend that fire department SEA measures should be aggregated by city and disaggregated for major communities.

Particular cities are encouraged to disaggregate data by station or by fire company when the circumstances seem to warrant such disclosure. The preceding section also suggested that a number of SEA measures on fire incidence be disaggregated by type of fire, building, or population.

Comparison Information and SEA Norms

Most of the literature on fire performance measures seems to assume that comparisons will be used to interpret the reported information. The fire chiefs and finance directors surveyed both favored reporting comparative data.[19] The International City Management Association publication *Managing Fire Services* suggests three ways to evaluate productivity of fire departments: (1) Compare productivity measures among communities; (2) compare these measures within a single community over time; and (3) develop optimal performance specifications and then measure current performance against these optimal measures.[20]

---

[19]R. W. Parry et al., "Reporting Performance Measures for Municipal Fire Departments: Theory and Practice" (Indiana University Working Paper, 1990).

[20]J. L. Bryan and R. C. Picard (eds.), *Managing Fire Services* (Washington, DC: International City Management Association, 1979), p. 366.

Intercity Comparisons

It would seem that recommended disclosures should focus on some intercity performance norms. A tie-in to average response time and average fire loss per capita experienced by peer cities, certification programs, and insurance grading systems provides benchmarks that place performance in context. The use of state or national performance norms is unusual in actual practice, but some examples were observed. Tallahassee, Florida reports its Insurance Service Office's (ISO) fire service rating as class 2 and Downers Grove, Illinois cites an objective of progressing toward a class 3 ISO rating. Norfolk, Virginia, using a national training performance measure, states, "250 fire fighters have been trained to certification at NFPA Fire Fighter III level."

Underlying differences in communities that are beyond the control of the fire department, such as population density and age of construction, may affect the quality of intercity comparisons. For this reason, fire chiefs and finance directors surveyed found national averages less desirable than other performance norms.[21] Rather than using performance statistics for all communities in the state or nation, classes of communities that share certain characteristics should be identified for reporting more useful performance norms.

Intertemporal Comparisons

Intertemporal comparisons avoid the problems of lack of comparability across communities, highlighting performance trends that indicate improvement or deterioration. For example, Wethersfield, Connecticut reported that fire losses were reduced 6 percent to $245,205, or $24,000 below the prior four years' average.

Intertemporal comparisons still have some potential comparability problems. Changes in the community over time in such things as traffic patterns, residential patterns, and new construction can make long-term comparisons difficult. In year-to-year comparisons, one bad fire can overwhelm many of the reported measures—especially in smaller communities.

---

[21] Parry et al., "Reporting Performance Measures."

SEA Targets

The use of optimal performance targets means that considerable effort must be devoted to developing a model of performance. Obtaining agreement on optimal specifications can be difficult, and users may be concerned with the objectivity of such standards. Program budgets sometimes include performance targets for the following year, developed by city officials. These could be useful in evaluating actual performance.

A common flaw in presentations regarding objectives and performance measures is that comparisons reported one year's actual, the following year's estimated, and the next year's budgeted or planned amounts. Actual performance was never reconciled to previous estimates in the reports examined. Yet, when two years' consecutive budget reports for a municipality were reviewed, substantial discrepancies were noted between earlier projections and actual achieved performance, with no mention of this in the report. For example, Farmers Branch, Texas reported in its 1984–85 budget report that 2,200 emergency alarms were estimated to have occurred in 1983–84 and 2,200 were projected for 1984–85. Yet, in the 1985–86 budget report, actual alarms handled in 1983–84 were reported at 2,339 and 3,442 were estimated for 1984–85.

Recommendations

Users need a context in which to evaluate SEA. Fire department SEA reports can facilitate evaluation of SEA by providing comparisons over time. We recommend the disclosure of fire department SEA measures for a three-to-five-year period in order to facilitate intertemporal comparisons.

Fire department SEA reports can also facilitate evaluation by providing comparisons with other communities. National fire service organizations gather data to provide national statistics on many SEA indicators, but communities exhibit different characteristics related to demands and constraints on fire service. We recommend that national fire service organizations that gather fire performance data should develop meaningful subgroups of fire service communities for which they compile performance statistics for comparative purposes. The common characteristics of those subgroups should be made available with the performance measures.

Then, assuming that appropriate data is made available, we propose that the disclosure of fire department SEA measures should compare those measures to SEA by peer departments.

Finally, actual performance has more meaning if one knows what planned performance was. We recommend a third standard of comparison: The performance targets established internally for fire departments, if any, should be disclosed for the future period and for past periods. Direct planned-to-achieved comparisons should be made for the periods presented.

6. Hospitals

Richard E. Brown, Kent State University

	Page
Introduction	142
Scope	143
Methodology	143
Current Hospital Reporting Practices	144
Hospital Association and State Activity	144
Accreditation Process	145
Federal Government Role	146
Recommendations	148
Indicators	148
Rationale	149
Disaggregation	152
Comparison Information	153
Explanatory Data	154
Summary of Recommendations	154

INTRODUCTION

This chapter focuses on SEA measurement in hospitals. Health care and hospitals touch the lives of all, which accounts for the great general interest in the topic. This interest often takes the form of performance measurement reporting, although it is not always recognized as such. For example, *USA Today* carried a brief graphic and commentary on the national decline in the average length of a hospital stay, broken down by male and female. Hospitals themselves have used performance measures to make their case to the public. The *Wall Street Journal* carried a story about hospitals using mortality statistics in their ads to attract heart patients. Photographs of the ads were included in the story. General interest has been raised to a new level by the federal government's public release of mortality data for all hospitals with Medicare patients, which includes most hospitals.[1]

The hospital industry in America is an extraordinarily large and complex network. In general, the objective of hospitals is to provide high-quality patient care in a cost-effective manner that allows them to remain financially viable in an increasingly competitive industry. There are approximately 5,700 short-stay or community hospitals in the United States, a decrease of 2.4 percent over the past decade. During that same decade, however, the number of certified beds increased by over 6 percent, to just over 1 million. Of the 5,700 hospitals, 32 percent are controlled by governmental entities, 55 percent are nonprofit hospitals, and 13 percent are proprietary. In the mid-1980s hospitals employed about 3 million individuals and spent over $130 billion.[2] During the past decade hospital admissions remained constant at approximately 33.5 million, but outpatient visits increased by nearly 15 percent

---

[1]"USA Snapshots: A Look at Statistics That Shape the Nation," *USA Today,* October 14, 1987, p. 1; "Hospitals Cite Mortality Statistics in Ads to Attract Heart Patients," *Wall Street Journal* (July 28, 1987), Sec. 2, p. 1; Frank E. James, "Controversy Mounts over Efforts to Measure Quality of Health Care," *Wall Street Journal* (December 17, 1987), p. 29; Michael Waldholz, "Report on Medicare-Patient Death Rates Draws Fire of Hospital Representatives," *Wall Street Journal* (December 18, 1987), p. 44.

[2]American Hospital Association, *Hospital Statistics: 1986 Edition* (Chicago: AHA, 1986), pp. xvii–xxiii.

to approximately 219 million. There were substantial drops in both the average length of stay for patients and the occupancy rate of beds during this ten-year period.[3]

In addition, the proportion of hospital costs associated with patients who are not financially able to pay for the cost of services provided has increased and is straining the capability of some governmental hospitals to provide quality care. There is an increasing awareness that changes must be made in the operation of hospitals if they are to continue to provide quality services at a reasonable cost. Industry organizations have recognized the need for change as stated in *Critical Minutes:* "A key to improving critical care services would be the linkage of reimbursement policy to outcome evaluation and the utilization of resources. A national data base which evaluates patient experience in terms of illness, diagnosis, length of stay, and subsequent quality of life must be developed."[4]

SCOPE

Hospitals, for purposes of this review, means governmental community or short-term hospitals—the kind used by most patients—in contrast to federal, long-term, and psychiatric hospitals, institutions for the mentally handicapped, and clinics for drug and alcohol treatment. Further, the focus is on the measurement of treatment categories associated with hospital inpatient and outpatient care, excluding emergency and auxiliary services (ambulance service, cafeteria, etc.).

METHODOLOGY

To assess the amount and kind of SEA measurement reporting that exists in this complex and large industry, efforts were concentrated on the national organizations in the industry, such as the American Hospital Association (AHA), the Joint Commission on Accreditation of

---

[3]For example, the occupancy rate for government-run hospitals decreased from 40.6 percent in 1985 to 29.6 percent in 1989 (Karen Torrey, "Privatization: An Antidote for Ailing Facilities," *City & State,* March 26, 1990, p. 15).

[4]Foundation for Critical Care, "Critical Care in the United States: An Agenda for the 1990s," *Critical Minutes* (vol. 1, no. 2, Winter 1990), p. 1.

Healthcare Organizations, and the Health Care Financing Administration (HCFA). Contact was then made with state and regional organizations and, last, with several hospitals. Personal interviews were conducted to gather information, and to collect reports and other data. About two dozen officials in the hospital industry were contacted. State and local budget documents were also reviewed for examples of the reporting of SEA measures.

The focus of the research is on existing reporting systems, the data actually being reported, and the SEA indicators being tested in various regional and even national pilot projects.

CURRENT HOSPITAL REPORTING PRACTICES

Hospital Association and State Activity

An enormous amount of performance-based reporting already exists within the hospital industry. Since the mid-1940s the AHA has annually surveyed all hospitals in the United States to collect data on hospital utilization, revenues, expenses, and a variety of other aspects of health care. The volume resulting from this survey, *Hospital Statistics,* is available to all members, as well as other interested parties. Also, since 1957 the AHA has offered a data subscription service to individual hospitals called "Monitrend," which disaggregates this same data by hospital and department and provides comparisons to peer groups of hospitals.

Some state hospital associations provide a similar service, as do some urban and regional hospital associations. The Maryland Hospital Association (MHA) is among the leaders at the state level. Maryland is in the unique position of being the only state with a full waiver from Medicare's Prospective Payment System (PPS), the system under which the federal government normally pays hospitals for services to Medicare patients. Maryland has its own state regulatory commission which sets a uniform rate for all hospitals and payers and which requires quarterly reports from each of the state's 65 hospitals. The state form, *discharge abstract information,* contains 75 to 80 data elements for each discharged patient. Both the state commission and the MHA analyze this data and report back to the state's hospitals on their performance.

The Hospital Council of Western Pennsylvania (Pittsburgh area) is an example of a regional hospital association that is active in SEA reporting. The Council serves 84 hospitals and uses a quarterly "flash survey" to collect performance data. It then reports this data periodically, comparing each hospital member to its peer group.

The Pennsylvania Health Care Cost Containment Act of 1986 establishes a 21-member council and requires all hospitals to report to the council on prices, utilization, and quality. Among the first tasks of the Health Care Cost Containment Council was the creation of a uniform claim and billing form for the collection of patient data. Hospitals are required to submit patient data on gender, date of birth, address, admission date, discharge date, diagnoses, procedures, physicians involved in the case, total charges and actual payments, physician charges and payments to physicians, and primary payer. In addition, hospitals must submit audited financial statements, Medicare and Medicaid cost reports, and status of licensure and accreditation.

Accreditation Process

Still another level of hospital reporting relates to the responsibilities of the Joint Commission on Accreditation of Healthcare Organizations. The Commission requires that, as a part of the accreditation process, all hospitals establish a quality assurance committee and process. Hospitals had been given a great deal of discretion in the identification of performance measures that would be used for internal reporting purposes. Recently the Commission announced a new program called "Agenda for Change," which is testing hospitalwide, cross-departmental, and specialty-specific clinical indicators at pilot site hospitals nationwide. The pilot sites were chosen from more than 100 volunteers and vary in size, ownership, location, teaching status, and system affiliation. In announcing the program, the Commission stated:

> ... Quality of care has become a major public policy issue. When resources were abundant and quality was assumed to be inherent in the system, quality care was an issue left to health care professionals. Today, however, the general public, government, business, insurers, and consumer groups are expressing increased concern.... These

groups have thus been prompted to seek more information about clinical performance and other dimensions of quality care.[5]

The Commission has completed testing of clinical indicators for maternal, newborn, and anesthesia care. They have also completed development of clinical indicators for heart, trauma, and oncology (cancer) care and have selected hospitals to test the proposed indicators. The development of two sets of cross-department indicators—the appropriate and effective use of medications, and the prevention, detection, and control of infections—is in progress.

This broad-scope well-coordinated project to develop, test, and implement a comprehensive set of SEA indicators for the hospital industry is unique and provides an excellent source of SEA indicators for hospitals.

Federal Government Role

The hospital associations and the Commission are, in the final analysis, part of the hospital industry, and thus their efforts at performance measurement and improvement, however well intentioned, are viewed with skepticism by many. This in part accounts for Pennsylvania's Health Care Cost Containment statute which was discussed earlier. Similarly, during the 1980s enormous changes occurred in the federal government's financial involvement in health care, which brought about stronger efforts to monitor hospital performance. The federal government's involvement in hospital affairs is principally through the Medicare and Medicaid programs, programs for the elderly and the needy, respectively. Medicare enrollees totaled over 30 million people in the mid-1980s, or 12.6 percent of the U.S. population. Another 21 million people (about 8.6 percent) received Medicaid services. Of the nearly $400 billion in U.S. health care expenditures at that time, over a quarter of the total was for Medicare and Medicaid patients. While Medicare enrollees constituted only 12.6 percent of the population in 1985, they made up about 40 percent of all hospital admissions.[6]

In 1983 Medicare's PPS began and revolutionized U.S. hospital financial management. In place of what was essentially a cost-reimburse-

---

[5]Joint Commission on Accreditation, "Update: Agenda for Change" (vol. 1, no. 1, September 1987), pp. 1–2.

[6]HCFA, Bureau of Data Management and Strategy, *HCFA Statistics* (September 1985).

ment system in the early years of Medicare, a payment system was created with three key features:

1. The unit of payment is the discharge, which is classified into one of 468 diagnostic-related groups (DRGs). Illustrative DRGs include categories such as birth delivery, appendectomy, heart failure and shock, diabetes age 36 or over, and major joint procedures.
2. The basis of payment is a historical national average standardized cost per case, calculated from Medicare cost report data updated for inflation.
3. The Medicare payment equals the standardized cost per case in the rate year, multiplied by a DRG-specific cost weight.[7]

This major change in the payment concept was accompanied by a tougher performance review system. The key to performance reporting under the PPS is the 1982 Uniform Bill ("UB82"), through which information decreed by HCFA is recorded upon the discharge of each patient. This information is sent to a fiscal intermediary such as Blue Cross, which edits the data, pays the bill, compiles a hospital tape, and passes it on to HCFA. In addition to performing its own analyses, HCFA provides the data to its Peer Review Organizations (PROs). These organizations are private firms under contract with HCFA, and there is roughly one per state. The PROs have the task of reviewing claims for Medicare services provided by hospitals (under stringent HCFA criteria) to determine their reasonableness, medical necessity, and quality of care. In performing their work, the PROs begin by using computer and statistical analyses and also perform on-site hospital visits to review patient files. Nurses and, if necessary, physicians form the nucleus of on-site review teams. The PROs also have considerable authority in recommending that HCFA sanction activities against hospitals and physicians.

The measures HCFA is assessing include length of stay, number of discharges, mortality rates, admission denial rates, and readmission rates. HCFA is currently publishing mortality data by DRG and by hospital, a development that is causing considerable controversy.[8]

---

[7]Ernst & Whinney, *The Medicare Prospective Payment System,* No. J58475, 1987, p. 2.

[8]Ernst & Whinney, *The Impact of PROs on Hospitals,* No. J58693, 1987; also HCFA, *Medicare Hospital Mortality Information* (Washington, DC: U.S. Government Printing Office, 1987), 7 vols.

The controversy has resulted in two U.S. General Accounting Office (GAO) reviews of HCFA's mortality analyses. The second review found significant improvements in the analyses since the first review but still noted a number of shortcomings.[9] The review identified possible problems due to lack of sufficient adjustment for the mortality rates of individual principal diagnoses, the need for validation studies to provide a basis for evaluating whether observed mortality exceeding the projected range can be associated with quality-of-care problems, and the need for improved measures of severity of illness, especially within high-risk diagnostic categories.

HCFA also began an Effectiveness Initiative with the assistance of the Institute of Medicine of the National Academy of Sciences to address the question of "what works in the practice of medicine." The first report of that initiative sets forth the purposes and elements of the Effectiveness Initiative, identifies critical factors to consider in the discussion of clinical conditions, and recommends clinical conditions for initial investigations. It also recognizes as a matter of special concern "the generation and use of reliable and valid outcome measures that relate to functional status and quality of life."[10]

RECOMMENDATIONS

Indicators

The recommended set of SEA indicators includes indicators of input, output, efficiency, and outcomes, as well as accompanying explanatory information. The recommendations draw on existing reporting systems and those still in various stages of experimentation within the hospital industry. The recommendations recognize that many users of the data will probably wish to review information on inputs and outputs (including workload or activity levels), even though scholars may strongly argue the merits of the more-sophisticated measures of efficiency and results. The proposed system also tries to walk the line between reporting so much data that reports are overly complex and reporting data so selectively that it does not portray a comprehensive

---

[9]U.S. GAO, "Medicare: An Assessment of HCFA's 1988 Hospital Mortality Analyses" (Washington, DC, December 1988).

[10]Institute of Medicine, "Effectiveness Initiative: Setting Priorities for Clinical Conditions" (Washington, DC, 1989), p. 11.

picture of the hospital's SEA. The measures, listed in Exhibit 6-1, should be disaggregated, when possible, by major diagnostic-related group when a significant number of patients are being treated in that group.

Rationale

External users will want to have some basic cost or input data in order to be informed about the magnitude of resources being used by a hospital and the trend in their use. The availability of cost information is also important to provide a basis for relating these costs to outputs and outcomes in order to approximate hospital efficiency.

Output indicators have received widespread use for many years and provide users with information about the utilization of the hospital, the mix of the methods of treatment (inpatient versus outpatient), and the hospital's practice concerning duration of stay. Output measures also become the denominator for important efficiency indicators.

The "bottom line" of hospital performance is the quality of care—does the patient receive quality treatment, does he or she get well, and is care provided on a timely basis? Although average length of stay per treatment mode may be viewed as a very simplistic aspect of quality of care, and indeed is usually included (as recommended in this report) as an output indicator, it does address one important dimension of care—as an indicator of the length of time patients spend in the hospital.

If an unusual number of patients were to contract infections while in the hospital, one would certainly have cause to question the quality of care. Surgeries in relation to total admissions attempts to address the issue of unnecessary surgery, while mortality rates is self-explanatory. Patient surveys, while impressionistic in nature, provide important feedback on "consumer satisfaction." Readmission within 31 days offers a check on the danger that hospitals, in an effort to contain costs, will release patients without carefully assessing their condition. An indicator that reports denials of admissions would help control attempts by hospitals to improve SEA by turning away more difficult cases.

Efficiency measures, such as cost per inpatient day or per discharge, when available by DRG or treatment mode, begin to provide a sense of the costs at which a given hospital provides services. This, of course, is important to many users of reports—investors, taxpayers, the county commission, the board of trustees, and so forth. Unfortunately, in the health care field, efficiency and results (quality of care) often seem to be at odds. The cost focus of the federal government's prospective pay-

Exhibit 6-1
Recommended SEA Indicators for Hospitals*

Indicator	Rationale for Selecting Indicator
Inputs: Total cost; Support cost; Medical care costs (nursing, etc.); Physical plant; Full-time equivalent (medical staff, personnel, all staff, etc.)	To provide a measure of resources used to provide services, to permit efficiency calculations, and to encourage resource comparisons
Outputs: Admissions (by payer class); Patient days; Average length of stay; Occupancy rate; Outpatient visits; Discharges	To continue the long tradition of reporting such data, which industry and experienced managers find useful, and to encourage output and efficiency comparisons
Outcomes: Mortality rates; Surgeries per 100 admissions; Infection rates (hospital-acquired); Results of random patient surveys (to collect patient views of care, food, cleanliness); Preadmission or admission denials; Readmission rates (within 31 days); Admission rates (within 31 days for outpatient surgery)	To temper hospitals' quest for efficiency by focusing on a number of indicators of quality of care; "mortality rates" are self-explanatory; "surgeries related to admissions" attempts to identify an unusually high rate of surgeries; "infection rates" addresses care while in the hospital; "patient surveys" provide important clientele feedback on a wide array of issues; "admission denials" focuses on a hospital's possible tendency to admit only healthier patients to maximize Medicare payments, while attention to "readmission rates" reduces the chance that a hospital will release patients prematurely due to cost considerations

Efficiency:
   Total cost per inpatient day
   Labor cost per inpatient day } To provide a variety of measures of efficiency of operations
   Cost per outpatient day
   Cost per discharge
   Nursing hours per inpatient day
   FTEs per occupied bed

   Cost per patient discharged who did not have a hospital-acquired illness during his or her stay } To provide an efficiency measure that relates inputs to service outcomes

Explanatory:
   Severity of illness
   Source of admission (elective, required, emergency)
   Comorbidity or complicating factors (disease factors, not intrinsic to the primary disease, that may have an impact on the patient outcome)
   Age
   Gender
   Staffing level (doctors, nurses)
   Percentage of admitted patients with income below poverty level
} Any explanatory material needed to present clarification of specific measures and to discuss variations in the indicators from peer group and/or historical performance

---

*The recommended indicators presented in this exhibit are illustrative. They are intended to serve as a starting point for use in the development of a comprehensive set of SEA indicators for external reporting of an entity's results of operation.

This exhibit does not provide illustrations of indicator disaggregation or of comparison data such as trends, targets, or other comparable entities. Both disaggregation and comparison data are important aspects of SEA reporting. They are discussed in the chapter and in the Overview.

Note: The SEA report ideally should break out many of these indicators by diagnostic-related group. However, considerations of space, simplicity, and value to the user may require that this level of detail should instead be available on request and as supporting documentation.

The report should contain comparisons over time with relevant peer groups and, as such information becomes public, with individual, competing hospitals.

ment plan has led to the cliche that "patients are being released from hospitals quicker but sicker." The implication is that to remain within HCFA's mandates on patient-cost reimbursement, hospitals are releasing patients before they are well, thereby remaining within HCFA's cost guidelines so that they can make money and survive in an increasingly competitive environment. This paradox, in turn, leads to the need for attention to effectiveness and quality of care, or result indicators.

One experimental efficiency indicator is included in Exhibit 6-1: cost per patient discharged who did not have a hospital-acquired illness during his or her stay. This is not an indicator currently in use. It is included to encourage the public hospital community to identify and report indicators that relate cost to measures of outcome. This will produce a truer measure of real efficiency than the usual cost per patient-day measure.

Explanatory factors are needed to provide a basis for understanding the possible reason for a hospital's performance. Recognizing that certain patient factors often exert as much or more influence on the outcome of care as the quality of care received suggests the necessity of reporting explanatory factors and analyzing the linkage between these factors and patient outcomes. Thus, the proposed blend of indicators reports on different aspects of SEA, but also uses a mix of indicators to reinforce each other in very important ways.[11]

Disaggregation

The principal unit for disaggregation should be by individual hospital, data that is not readily available in current external reporting. Hospitals, the Joint Commission, and the regional and national associations work very hard to protect the confidentiality of individual hospital data. The federal and state governments, however, are beginning to release such data. Beyond the level of reporting by hospital, information currently collected on hospital admission and discharge forms permits a great deal of additional detailed reporting. As requested or required, a hospital should provide a breakdown of SEA indicators by diagnostic-

---

[11] For an alternative but similar view of a performance reporting system, see the study by John R. Griffith, *Measuring Hospital Performance,* An INQUIRY Book (Chicago: Blue Cross Association, 1978), especially pp. 8–9.

related group for DRGs that make up a significant portion of their treatments, for inpatients and outpatients, by source of admission (elective, required, emergency), and by a variety of demographic factors such as age and gender.

Comparison Information

Once the SEA data is available by individual hospital, many combinations of comparative analyses are possible. As previously mentioned, the various hospital associations have long provided such information, and hospitals are quite accustomed to using this data. In many of its reports, the Hospital Council of Western Pennsylvania, discussed previously, uses a series of peer groupings—a regional breakdown (southwest, northwest, east, and western Pennsylvania) and classification by type of hospital (metro teaching, metro nonteaching, urban teaching, etc.). Hospital officials seem less interested in comparisons with hospitals based on economic sector—public, nonprofit, and proprietary. Government funding and regulation seem to have blurred these distinctions. Today many former public hospitals have become nonprofit hospitals, although they may still receive taxpayer support. A part of this movement is due to marketing considerations; another is an effort to avoid government control.

In some ways the most meaningful comparison for a hospital may be its ability to compare its SEA directly with those hospitals it views as its competitors. In time, such direct comparisons could have considerable positive impact on the cost and quality of care.

Reporting systems should also encourage hospitals to compare current SEA performance to that of prior years, and thus a report should present SEA indicators for several years.

Several efforts currently are under way to develop and implement SEA indicators for various clinical and cross-departmental factors of hospitals. The Effectiveness Initiative of HCFA and the Joint Commission's Agenda for Change both hold promise in providing reliable, relevant SEA indicators. But as pointed out by the GAO, much work still remains to be done in validating the indicators and ensuring that explanatory factors such as severity of illness at admission, comorbidity (complicating factors), and patient attitude are considered before meaningful comparisons can be made between hospitals or with norms or standards. Still, comparisons over time and with performance targets established by the hospital can provide indications of variances from expected results.

Explanatory Data

Input, output, and, to a lesser extent, outcome and efficiency indicators have been used for many years in the hospital industry and are fairly well understood. However, the implications of some seemingly negative efficiency indicators may require explanation. For example, a hospital that is "marketing" service (more nursing attention) will want to explain the effect of such a policy on cost per patient day, as well as the effect on quality of care (perhaps a shorter average length of stay). Similarly, a hospital may wish to include explanatory comments relating to quality of care or outcomes. For example, admitting lower-income patients, who may not have had the advantage of satisfactory diet and preventative health care, may negatively impact outcome measures. A willingness to admit patients who are more seriously ill could have a similar impact. A minimum set of explanatory factors has been included in Exhibit 6-1 with the recommended SEA indicators. Care should be taken to present these and other possible explanatory factors in a manner that will assist users in understanding the hospital's performance on the SEA indicators presented, especially where it varies from the comparative information being reported.

SUMMARY OF RECOMMENDATIONS

The general outline and format for a proposed SEA report are shown in Exhibit 6-1. The recommended list of SEA indicators focuses primarily on hospitalwide indicators and includes input, output, outcome, and efficiency indicators. This is not meant to discourage disaggregation of indicators where they can be useful, such as for selected DRGs or by source of admission. In addition, these data should be accompanied by graphics, textual analyses discussing trends, explanatory commentary, and relevant peer group and historical comparisons. Such a report could include as many as 40 or 50 pages. A brief executive summary and series of graphics would make such a lengthy and technical document more useful to trustees and nonhealth professionals. Simplicity should be a key goal of any reporting effort.

This study's conclusion is that an SEA report should be prepared for hospital trustees, oversight governmental units, and public disclosure. Ultimately, a year-end report would be verified by some objective outside party, with the results of such a review also being made public. While the SEA report is seen as a separate document, a summation of it should be included with the hospital's comprehensive annual financial report.

Because of the progress already being made by HCFA and the Joint Commission in developing, testing, and reporting SEA indicators for hospitals, it is appropriate that hospitals wanting to report SEA indicators direct their attention to the work being done by those organizations. The recommended set of SEA indicators included in this report will provide a starting point for choosing a comprehensive set of hospitalwide indicators. But because the ongoing projects of HCFA and the Joint Commission are comprehensive, have developed indicators that are tested and reviewed, and will continue to address other important areas of hospital service, they should be carefully considered before a determination is made as to the SEA indicators to be reported on.

In the case of the hospital industry, it is safe to conclude that experimentation with SEA indicators has begun in earnest and with the backing of several key organizations that have the capability of providing leadership in expanding the use of SEA indicators. The role of interested organizations in this case is to participate in and encourage this already existing process.

7. Mass Transit

Wanda A. Wallace, The Deborah D. Shelton Systems Professor of Accounting, Texas A&M University

	Page
Introduction	158
Scope	160
Goals and Objectives of Services	161
Methodology	161
Summary of Findings and Recommendations	162
Recommended Measures	162
Section 15	163
Measurability, Validity, Comprehensiveness, and Accuracy of Indicators	177
Disaggregation	179
Communication and Display of Information	179
Relevancy and Intended Audience	184
Recommendations	185

The author thanks Jannet Vreeland and Sandra Welch, Ph.D. students at Texas A&M University, and Sindy Rabold, administrative assistant, for their support in the execution of the research to which this chapter relates. The author similarly wishes to express her appreciation of the numerous experts in the area of mass transit who have given so freely of their time, making this chapter possible. This chapter has benefited from the comments of Ronell B. Raaum of the U.S. General Accounting Office and Wendell Cox, transportation consultant, both of whose assistance is particularly appreciated.

> ... [T]he kind of city we live in today is largely a product of the transportation system.[1]

INTRODUCTION

In 1984, state and local governments subsidized transit systems for about 48 percent of their $9.4 billion operating costs, with the federal government contributing 10 percent.[2] These statistics bear out the considerable economic investment in mass transit by the public sector. The decline in federal subsidies from the 1980 level of 18 percent to the 1984 level of 10 percent demonstrates the increasing burden of mass transit operating costs being assumed by state and local governments.

The consequences of this increased burden for state and local governments become even clearer when the trend in transit unit costs from 1965 to 1983 is considered. Such costs have increased by more than double the inflation rate. Moreover, a trend has been observed of declining coverage of such operating costs by operating revenues: In 1967, a 96 percent coverage of operating and capital costs was reported, and by 1977, it had fallen to 53 percent of operating costs, exclusive of capital costs,[3] with another decline by 1984 to 42 percent.[4] In fact, in 1979, Massachusetts Bay Transportation Authority, as one example, was recovering only 27 percent of its operating costs from fares and other operating revenues.[5]

---

[1] Naomi Bailin Wish, "Improving Policy Making in Public Transportation," *Public Administration Review* (November–December 1982), p. 530.

[2] U.S. Department of Transportation, *The Status of the Nation's Local Mass Transportation: Performance and Conditions—Report to Congress* (Washington, DC: U.S. Government Printing Office, UMTA, June 1987).

[3] American Public Transit Association, *1985 Transit Fact Book* (Washington, DC, 1985), plus earlier editions, including 1976, 1978, and 1987, cited by U.S. Department of Transportation, *The Status of the Nation's Local Mass Transportation: Performance and Conditions—Report to Congress* (Washington, DC: U.S. Government Printing Office, UMTA, June 1987).

[4] U.S. Department of Transportation, *The Status of the Nation's Local Mass Transportation*, p. 55.

[5] James Ortner and Martin Wachs, "The Cost–Revenue Squeeze in American Public Transit," *Journal of the American Planning Association* (January 1979), pp. 10–21.

Beyond difficulties in recovery of costs, problems have arisen tied to massive capital investments by mass rail transit systems. For example, delays and cost overruns have caused such investments to mushroom, as exemplified by a subway project in New York City which was reported to have a cost overrun of $650 million (with the original bid of the biggest share of the construction project being $395 million) and a ten-year delay.[6] Beyond such construction problems, acquisition practices have had overcapitalization effects, as indicated by an increase to 49 percent in 1984 in the number of excess vehicles owned over the number needed to provide peak-hour service.[7]

Increasing attention has been directed toward enhancing operating efficiency and effectiveness of public-sector transit operations. The Urban Mass Transportation Administration (UMTA) has adjusted grant formulas (e.g., via the Surface Transportation Assistance Act of 1982) to increase state and local responsibility for mass transportation.[8] Formula grant restrictions of federal funds required that not more than 80 percent of capital expenses or more than 50 percent of operating deficits (with matching funds from state and local governments) be covered; these restrictions were intended to penalize mismanagement. However, some evaluators of UMTA programs have concluded that the actual result of UMTA policies has been to encourage mismanagement, due to past encouragement of practices such as overcapitalization.[9]

Within this context of substantial debate over the resources directed toward mass transit and their use, the time is ripe to evaluate the availability of service efforts and accomplishments (SEA) measures. One purpose of this chapter is to assess SEA measures currently being

---

[6] Stanley Penn, "Tunnel Vision: How a Subway Project in New York Has Led to Doubt and Dismay," *The Wall Street Journal* (October 25, 1985), pp. 1, 15.

[7] U.S. Department of Transportation, *The Status of the Nation's Local Mass Transportation*, p. 81.

[8] U.S. General Accounting Office, "UMTA's New Formula Grant Program: Operating Flexibility and Process Simplification," *Monthly List of GAO Reports* (August 1, 1985), p. 10.

[9] See Richard M. Soberman, "Urban Transportation in the U.S. and Canada: A Canadian Perspective," *Logistics & Transportation Review* (Canada, June 1983), pp. 99–109; Robert Cervero, "Effects of Operating Subsidies and Dedicated Funding on Transit Costs and Performance," *Urban America* (vol. 8, 1984); and Paul N. Tramontozzi and Kenneth W. Chilton, *The Federal Free Ride: The Economics and Politics of U.S. Transit Policy* (St. Louis: Center for the Study of American Business, Washington University, 1987).

used. Another is to evaluate, via interviews with producers and users of performance information, the sufficiency of the various SEA measures in current use, and the merits of possible measures not currently in use. This chapter aims to provide both a set of recommended SEA measures for use in monitoring mass transit system performance and the rationale for each measure, while acknowledging each measure's limitations. Attention will be directed to how such measures might be communicated.

SCOPE

Diverse types of services are provided in the transportation area of municipalities, including:

1. Airports
2. Bus systems
3. Subway systems
4. Train systems
5. Streets and highways
6. Parking and traffic
7. Taxicab regulation
8. Oversight of ambulance services and sightseeing vehicles
9. Transportation service for the elderly
10. Transportation service for the handicapped
11. Parks and recreation transportation systems
12. School transportation
13. Negotiation of contracts with private-sector providers of transportation
14. Equipment maintenance
15. Garage service for city vehicles
16. Promotion of carpooling and similar programs to encourage energy conservation and avoid single-occupant automobiles
17. Support of local land use systems.

This chapter focuses on public bus, subway, and train systems, as well as special related services for the elderly and the handicapped.

GOALS AND OBJECTIVES OF SERVICES

A research review of the stated objectives of a number of mass transit systems is the basis for offering the following common objective of public transportation services:

> The basic purpose is to provide safe, dependable, convenient, and comfortable transportation services at minimum cost to the citizens, including special client groups such as the handicapped and elderly.

Many systems stress their goals of high customer satisfaction, target load factors, and specified costs per passenger. While some systems strive to be self-sufficient in financing, others look toward subsidies, contending that the underwriting of public transportation is consistent with the public good, reducing pollution and traffic, and adding to the economic well-being of the populace. About 30 percent of the objectives reviewed give explicit attention to cost-effectiveness and efficiency as key concerns. However, standards for assessing these cost-effectiveness goals are rarely stated in tandem with such objectives. Recognition of the need to comply with regulations and the importance of marketing transit services to potential riders are suggested in some budget reports. Similarly, a role for environmental concern and the importance of capital improvement and maintenance of vehicles is acknowledged.

METHODOLOGY

The methodology for this chapter encompasses an extensive review of literature concerning SEA measurement, transit operations, and regulatory requirements.[10] It also includes a mailing to 573 municipalities, resulting in 215 responses (a 38 percent response rate), of which 126 provided full annual reports and budgets for assessment of current reporting practices, and formation of a data base of survey responses, Section 15 filings with UMTA, and information in *The UITP Handbook of Public Transport* (Belgium). This chapter also draws on extensive interviews with approximately 80 preparers, auditors, users, regulators, politicians, and other interested parties. Details of each phase of the methodology will be

---

[10]U.S. Department of Transportation, *Urban Mass Transportation Act of 1964, as Amended through May 1983 and Related Laws* (Washington, DC: U.S. Government Printing Office, 1983).

provided in an unabridged report available from the GASB, along with elaboration on the findings and recommendations. The next section of this abridged chapter focuses on the overall recommendations that emerged from the study.

SUMMARY OF FINDINGS AND RECOMMENDATIONS

Based on the evidence detailed in the unabridged report, the following recommendations are offered.

Recommended Measures

For customers (as well as other user groups such as decision makers who operate, finance, and regulate mass transit), a report should be prepared that directs attention to timeliness, economics, safety, and environmental quality. Exhibit 7-1 presents recommended measures by type of indicator (focusing on the purpose the indicator would serve), rationale for inclusion, desired disaggregation level, and limitations noted. Key terms are defined at the end of Exhibit 7-1. Examples of these measures are provided in the unabridged report.

Customers are interested in the following key characteristics of SEA:

1. *Proximity:* How far do I have to go to gain access to the system (a general-purpose dial-a-ride system may pick me up at the house, or I might have to go x distance to reach a bus station) and how far must I walk after it drops me off?
2. *Frequency:* How often does the service run (and during what hours)—on demand, every 15 minutes, every hour, etc.?
3. *Travel time:* How long does it take to make a journey? This is difficult to measure, but could be defined as: Once having accessed the system, a trip of x distance should take no more than y minutes.
4. *Dependability:* Can I depend on a vehicle being there when it is scheduled?
5. *Trip quality:* What is the physical condition of travel and surroundings at stations and stops, and how courteous and helpful are staff?[11]
6. *Information by route:* Can I expect the same performance for this particular route?

---

[11]Wendell Cox, transportation consultant, correspondence, August 2, 1988.

Exhibit 7-1 reflects a variety of measures to address these and related concerns. They could be augmented by cost-effectiveness measures such as cost per satisfied passenger. Variations of outcome measures, including the net cost to the government per passenger or travel time per mile, might be added. The particular selections in Exhibit 7-1 reflect (1) an emphasis on users' needs rather than managers' needs, (2) a preference for the form of measurement already in use, if virtual substitutes exist for some indicators, and (3) a primary focus on nonfinancial measures.

The plausibility of tracking such measures, including those tied to the passengers' environment, is demonstrated in reports already made available by transit systems (e.g., see New York City Transit Authority's quarterly report on the results of a "Passenger Environment Survey"). An example of a "report card" issued by the Straphangers Campaign (a citizens' group in New York City that addresses the needs of subway riders), based on this information, is presented in Exhibit 7-2.

Section 15

Transit systems receiving grants under Section 9 of the Urban Mass Transportation Act of 1964 are required to report certain information to the UMTA. This information is commonly referred to as "Section 15 filings." Despite some unpopularity with transit managers,[12] the Section 15 system has been useful in making information available on a national basis, permitting public-policy makers, researchers, and managers to assess agencies' relative performance. A substantial portion, if not all, of the information required by the UMTA would seemingly be required in order to manage a transit system effectively. Problems identified in Section 15 filings are detailed in the unabridged report; they relate to the timeliness and accuracy of data, the treatment of reconciling items, the determination of the value of contracts and retained earnings when subcontracting, confusion as to the meaning of certain terms, the consistency of enforcement of sampling prescriptions, and the propriety of the prescribed sampling approach to passenger miles. Expectations are that the reliability of this data base will steadily improve and it can be a focal point for developing internal managers' indicators for public reporting.

---

[12] Reflected in Joel Markowitz, "Final Recommendations of the APTA Section 15 Committee." Document prepared for APTA Western and Eastern Education & Training Conferences (April–May 1988).

Exhibit 7-1
Recommended SEA Indicators for Mass Transit*

Indicator	Rationale	Disaggregation Level	Limitations and Suggestions for Explanatory Variables
Inputs:			
Dollar Cost of Service in Constant Dollars and Cash Expenditures	To monitor resources expended and their growth, aside from inflation	Overall system and by type of system	A price index for transit services will suffer from typical shortcomings of any general price-level adjustment.
Unfunded Costs	To evaluate accruals for infrastructure replacement and deferred maintenance and repair	By system	Detection of inadequate rates or other revenue shortfalls by tracking accumulated needs for future replacement funding depends on the ability to assess such needs; explanatory data on the conditions of tracks, bridges, roads, or similar infrastructure dimensions could be useful.
Staff Quantity, Utilization (e.g., labor hours per productive service hour), and Average Compensation (including retirement or fringe benefits)	To evaluate the most significant operating expense and whether transit staff is being used productively	By system and by type of staff (e.g., drivers, mechanics, administrators, and others)	Difficulties can arise in matching staff, particularly drivers, to peak and off-peak workload and some problems could stem from use of part-time drivers.

164

Outputs:

Number of Vehicle Miles	This provides an indicator of extensiveness of service and related demand, providing an indication of length of routes and degree of stress on vehicles, as well as the likelihood of either a cutback of service or a crowded environment; it measures the amount of space or seat capacity delivered	By type of system; by line or route; and by peak a.m. (7–7:59 and 8–8:59), peak p.m. (4:45–5:44 and 5:45–6:44), and off-peak, and reports by weekday, Saturday, Sunday, and holiday
Number of Passengers		
Passengers per Vehicle Mile (a productivity measure)		
Revenue Capacity Miles Delivered		Vehicle miles include deadhead and service miles (but have the advantage of objectivity of measurement from an odometer). Passengers will include fare and transfer passengers. Some averaging is inherent in determining the sum of seated capacity of all active vehicles.
Number of Transit Units Available Divided by Number of Transit Units Required at Peak Hour	Should a breakdown occur, this will provide an idea of the likelihood of replacement of the unit on a timely basis	By type of system, by line or route
		Users must appreciate that too high a ratio may indicate overcapitalization and that some allocations among lines or routes could be arbitrary since sharing across lines occurs.

---

*The recommended indicators presented in this exhibit are illustrative. They are intended to serve as a starting point for use in the development of a comprehensive set of SEA indicators for external reporting of an entity's results of operation. (See definitions of key terms at end of exhibit.)

This exhibit does not provide illustrations of indicator comparison data such as trends, targets, or other comparable entities. Comparison data are an important aspect of SEA reporting. They are discussed in the chapter and in the Overview.

Exhibit 7-1 (continued)

Indicator	Rationale	Disaggregation Level	Limitations and Suggestions for Explanatory Variables
Outcomes:			
Percentage of Population Served by Public Transportation	Assesses the extent to which public transportation facilitates commuting and is used	By system	Socioeconomic conditions, population density, fare and parking rates, and traffic are all likely to influence the propensity of the citizenry to use mass transit.
Geographical Coverage, Route Spacing, Number of Transfers Required by the System Design, and Span of Service (Access) (e.g., area with transit service available within one-half mile of residence—both urbanized area and suburbs)	Convenience is affected by accessibility and operating hours	By service area and type of system; some detail by route and day of week	Population density, employment density, and auto ownership (at household level) affect demand and must be considered in assessing the propriety of the typical required walk to the bus stop; terrain and demand influence transfers.

Measure	Description	Disaggregation	Comments
Percentage of Late Trips (e.g., difference between actual and scheduled times is more than 3 minutes)	This reliability measure addresses the concerns of transit riders that they can arrive at their destination on time and it monitors the reported practice of transit systems as being indifferent to how late service is, once the "on-time" threshold fails to be met	By type of system; by line or route; by peak a.m., peak p.m., and off-peak; and by categories of off-schedule (e.g., 0–3 minutes, 4–5 minutes, 6–10 minutes, 11–15 minutes, 16–30 minutes, over 30 minutes)	To provide maximum service to the most heavily traveled routes, it may make sense to slow up more trips as a means of servicing more passengers: users should consider this trade-off.
Frequency of Service (average headway): Scheduled Time between Bus Arrivals at a Bus Stop (or train arrivals at a station)	This measures planned service to riders	By type of system; by terminal, station, or stop; and by peak a.m., peak p.m., and off-peak	Since scheduled times may not be met, the next metric on actual waiting time must go hand in hand with scheduled headway.
Average Time Past Scheduled Time That a Passenger Waits for a Bus or Train (The presumption is that the amount of time allowed, on average, reflects expectations as to service.)	Measures service to riders and reflects passengers' adaptation to unreliable service	By type of system; by terminal, station, or stop; by route; and by peak a.m., peak p.m., and off-peak	Sampling of bus stops should be statistically based to permit useful disaggregations, and some consideration must be given to geographical terrain and traffic conditions by the evaluator—this can be a very costly measure.

Exhibit 7-1 (continued)

Indicator	Rationale	Disaggregation Level	Limitations and Suggestions for Explanatory Variables
Outcomes (continued):			
Train or Bus Cancellations Including en Route Cancellations and Runs Canceled or Missed (also report as a percentage of scheduled trips)	Such cancellations represent service reductions	By type of system, by route, by peak/off-peak, and by type of cancellation: • car shortage • equipment malfunction • train crew • incoming train is late, delaying start, or creating "bunching" • accident • lack of service due to an event, such as a parade	Controllability should be assessed, as should ripple effects across routes when evaluated using disaggregated information; these figures should be reviewed in tandem with passenger loads, since the cancellation could lead to fewer passengers being delayed for shorter periods.
Mean Distance between Failures (MDBF): Average Number of Miles Subway Cars (or Buses) Travel in Revenue Service during the Month before a Mechanical Failure Occurs Which Is Serious Enough to Cause a Train to Arrive Late at Its Destination	Measures service reliability; the lower the MDBF, the more irregular the service; this metric is most relevant to management	By type of system and by route	Problems arise in defining "late" arrival and in classifying defects found during inspections and preventive maintenance programs; moreover, if failure is a secondary reason for delay (e.g., construction is cited as primary failure), some systems do not track such breakdowns.

Number of Minutes Passed without Seeing a Policeman or Security Officer	Affects the safety of travelers; while both verifiability and reliability can be questioned, visual presence is expected to have a deterrent effect	By platform, bus stop, route, terminal, and station; by time period—peak a.m., peak p.m., off-peak, weekday and weekend, morning, afternoon, evening	Mere visual presence of a policeman does not necessarily deter crime, nor is it the most efficient approach to safety (e.g., audiovisual observation, like banks' security systems might be more effective); perceptions would be measurable through interviews or surveys but may not reflect reality.
Perception of Safety			
Crime Statistics—Violent and Nonviolent (per 1,000 passengers)	Reflects the safety of travelers	By system; by platform, bus stop, route, terminal, and station; by type of crime	Reporting of crime statistics has limitations, particularly due to unreported crimes.
Accidents per 100,000 Miles	Safety indicator	By system and by line or route	Unreported accidents and nonrevenue miles may cause inaccuracies; for comparison, the district traffic accident ratio per 100,000 miles could be reported.
Accidents and Injuries/Fatalities (per 1,000 passengers or 100,000 passenger miles)	Affects the safety of travelers	By system, disaggregated by type: accident at station, collision, or noncollision accident enroute; also, disaggregated by severity of consequences (no injuries or fatalities; injuries; fatalities)	Unreported accidents could distort numbers; controls are required to ensure against omissions.

Exhibit 7-1 (continued)

Indicator	Rationale	Disaggregation Level	Limitations and Suggestions for Explanatory Variables
Outcomes (continued): Passenger Environment Indicators—Percentage of Cars or Buses with • no broken door panels • operative doors • adequate lights • adequate climate control • proper equipment (handrails, straps, seats, mirrors, floor mats, etc.) • no interior graffiti • peeling paint • no excessive litter • no broken or graffitied glass (clear and operative windows) • no heavy dirt on floors • no excessive noise • operative lift features for buses • elderly and handicapped stickers	Affects the comfort of passengers and ease of travel	By type of system and by line or route	Age of units and nature of neighborhood serviced, as well as passenger loads, are likely to affect these metrics; in addition, some measures are fairly subjective in assessment and will require trained observers (except for climate control which can be recorded by measurement devices).

Measure	Detail	Comment
Load Factors (also, percentage of passengers standing; percentage of riders unable to board bus)	By type of system; by line or route; and by peak a.m., peak p.m., and off-peak	Overloading affects the comfort of passengers; underloading affects fare box recovery
Accuracy of Information Provided to Passengers: Response Rate at Telephone Information Center	Overall system information phone lines, printed schedules, and announcements; by station or terminal announcement completeness, audibility, and accuracy; by type of system and by line and route detail for signs and maps	This is difficult to measure in trains, though fare boxes facilitate tracking in buses.
Signs and Map Availability—Percentage of Cars or Buses with • announcements • legible system maps • correctly labeled trains and buses • correct signs		Ease of travel, particularly by new passengers
Customer Satisfaction with Service (e.g., as indicated by number of complaints per 100,000 passengers or surveys of perceptions)	Overall system, by system, by line or route, and by nature of service attribute: • schedule reliability • service reliability • passenger environment • load factors • courtesy of drivers • courtesy of other employees • information services • perceived safety • perceived efficiency • pricing	Feedback provided to address quality dimensions that are otherwise difficult to assess and to monitor overall measurableness of other measures, from a passenger's vantage point. Some subjectivity in tracking exists; this assessment ought to be made by individuals unfamiliar with the system through direct experience and may require surveys of tourists. The inherent limitations of surveys would likely apply, as would problems of perceptions and experiences versus actual performance.

Exhibit 7-1 (continued)

Indicator	Rationale	Disaggregation Level	Limitations and Suggestions for Explanatory Variables
Outcomes (continued):			
Nonriders' Perceptions regarding Public Transportation (e.g., its reliability, safety, etc.)	Provides a means of addressing nonriders' concerns in order to attract them as riders	Overall system	Perceptions (often measured through market research) may have little to do with reality, as by definition nonriders are relatively uninformed.
Efficiency:			
Cost per Passenger	Efficiency measurement	By type of system basis and by line or route	Some adjustment for inflation should be noted across time (e.g., through the use of constant dollars).
Operating Cost per Mile	Efficiency measurement	By type of system basis and by line or route	Same as cost per passenger.
Fare Box Recovery of Operating Costs	Reflects whether services are self-sustaining and reveals cross-subsidization	By type of system and by line or route	System may not have a goal to be self-sustaining.
Required Subsidy per Passenger and per Mile	Reflects sources of financing and the extent of subsidization, other than charges to users	By type of system and by type of subsidy: • UMTA • state • local	Political environments can influence types of financing used; UMTA revenue may be largely uncontrollable.

Explanatory Variables:		
Nature of Services Provided, Particularly Scope of Demand Response Systems for the Handicapped and Elderly	A goal of mass transit frequently includes ensuring mobility to both the elderly and handicapped	By type of system and by service area	The special-interest-group focus of these services likely justifies separate analysis of demand response systems, yet the scope of services provided may affect performance measures for some aspects of operation.
Average Vehicle Age and Remaining Life (quartile information also desirable); Replacement Cost of Fleet	Performance indicators should be viewed in the context of age of system and equipment and its replacement cost	By type of system	The average value can be distorted by having a substantial number of purchases with virtually zero age; the quartile presentation is important in avoiding such a distortion.

Note: Additional relevant demographic information is cited throughout this table in the far right column.

To facilitate longitudinal comparisons, details should be provided for current fiscal year-end, prior fiscal year, and two years ago. To facilitate comparisons to expectations, a budget to actual reconciliation should be reported for each of the three years. In addition, a peer group norm should be reported.

Exhibit 7-1 (continued)

Definitions of Key Terms

"Revenue Vehicle Miles: Total miles traveled by revenue vehicles while in revenue service. Excludes miles traveled to and from storage facilities and other deadhead travel.

Revenue Vehicle Hours: Total number of scheduled hours that a vehicle is in revenue service. Excludes hours consumed while traveling to and from storage facilities and during other deadhead travel.

Revenue Capacity-Miles (Computed): Revenue vehicle miles times the average passenger capacity of the active vehicles in the fleet. Average passenger capacity is determined by averaging the sum of the seated capacity and standing capacity of all active vehicles in the fleet.

Vehicle Miles: The total distance traveled by revenue vehicles, including both revenue miles and deadhead miles.

Vehicle Hours: The total hours of travel by revenue vehicles including scheduled hours consumed in passenger service and deadhead travel.

Fatality and Personal Injury: Accidents in which one or more persons are fatally injured and one or more persons receive personal injury, but no property damage results.

Fatality Only: Accidents in which one or more persons are fatally injured, but no property damage or other personal injury is involved.

Personal Injury Only: Accidents in which one or more persons receive personal injury, but no fatalities or property damage results.

Roadcalls for Mechanical Failure: A count of the revenue service interruptions during the reporting period caused by failure of some mechanical element of the revenue vehicle. (Mechanical failures are to include breakdowns of air equipment, brakes, body parts, doors, cooling system, heating system, electrical units, fuel system, engine, steering and front axle, rear axle and suspension and torque converters. Tire failures and fare box failures are not included.) These revenue service interruptions require assistance from someone other than the revenue vehicle operator (or crew) in order to restore the vehicle to an operating condition. Further, they usually require the transfer of the passengers to another revenue vehicle for the completion of their trip.

Roadcalls for Other Reasons: A count of the revenue service interruptions during the reporting period caused by tire failure, farebox failure, air conditioning system, out of fuel-coolant-lubricant and other causes *not* included as mechanical failures.

Labor Hours for Inspection and Maintenance of Revenue Vehicles: The labor hours of transit system maintenance personnel working on revenue vehicles for the period."

Source: U.S. Department of Transportation, Urban Mass Transportation Administration, *Urban Mass Transportation Industry Uniform System of Accounts and Records and Reporting System*, Vol. 20 (Report No. UMTA-IT-06-0094-77-1) (Washington, DC, January 10, 1977), pp. 8.5-1, 8.6-1, 8.7-1.

Exhibit 7-2
Communication of Information by the Straphangers
TRANSIT REPORT CARD

	DOORS	LIGHTING	MAPS	SIGNS	GRAFFITI	ANNOUNCE-MENTS	AIR CONDITIONING
WEST SIDE IRT (1, 2, 3)	3rd	BEST	2nd	2nd	3rd	4th	BEST
EAST SIDE IRT (4, 5, 6)	2nd	3rd	3rd	3rd	7th	4th	3rd
FLUSHING LINE (7)	BEST	2nd	BEST	BEST	BEST	BEST	2nd
8TH AVENUE LINE (A, C, K, E)	4th	5th	5th	5th	4th	3rd	5th
6TH AVENUE LINE (B, D, F)	5th	4th	7th	4th	5th	2nd	4th
BROOKLYN/QUEENS CROSSTOWN (G)	7th	8th	6th	tied for 6th	2nd	6th	WORST
CANARSIE LINE (L)	WORST	6th	WORST	tied for 6th	6th	WORST	7th
NASSAU STREET LINE (J, M)	6th	7th	4th	WORST	WORST	8th	8th
BROADWAY LINE (N, Q, R)	8th	WORST	8th	7th	8th	7th	6th

	BREAKDOWN RATE	LATE TRAINS	MORNING RUSH HOUR DELAYS	
			UPTOWN	DOWNTOWN
BEST	#4	#7	#1	L
WORST	G	N	A	F

Source: Joseph Rappaport and Gene Russianoff, "The Good, the Bad, and the Ugly" (New York Public Interest Research Center, Inc., 1987), p. 6. Reprinted by permission.

The Section 15 data base will provide the input, output, efficiency, and some explanatory information recommended in Exhibit 7-1, not only for a given entity but also for a defined peer group. Far more detailed efficiency-related information is available through Section 15 for managers' use.

Measurability, Validity, Comprehensiveness, and Accuracy of Indicators

Terminology should be clarified in the areas of reconciling items to Section 15 reporting formats and in measuring purchased transportation retained revenue quantities (e.g., if a city subcontracts for handicapped transportation services with a profit-making entity, how is the quantity of revenue retained by the company or city determined?). Roadcalls should be defined to avoid discretionary alteration of performance indicators.[13] Industry norms with respect to "on-time" definitions and similar attributes should be specified and not subject to redefinition by individual reporters (e.g., British Rail's redefinition of on-time performance to ten minutes from the past benchmark of five minutes, as indicated in its 1986–87 annual report).

Those responsible for data entry should be well trained and monitored to deter possible bias or the creation of adverse incentives and to avoid the potential ill effects of carelessness. Examples of current problems in this regard are detailed in reports by the Office of the Inspector General for the Metropolitan Transportation Authority in New York.[14]

The feasibility of eliciting customer satisfaction measures is exemplified by the "MTA Report Card" pamphlet distributed by the Mass Transit Administration in Baltimore. Exhibit 7-3 presents the form used. This postage-paid feedback mechanism is one approach to gathering information on customer satisfaction. Exhibit 7-4 presents a form for surveying both riders and nonriders—in part, to assess the propensity to use mass transit—that was developed by the Chicago Transit Au-

---

[13] George List, "Recent Developments regarding the Definition of a Roadcall." Prepared for an APTA Bus Equipment and Maintenance Workshop, Working Paper, Rensselaer Polytechnic Institute (March 1987).

[14] Office of the Inspector General, New York Metropolitan Transportation Authority, "An Examination of Selected New York City Transit Authority Performance Indicators for Surface Transportation" (December 30, 1986), and "An Examination of Selected New York City Transit Authority Performance Indicators for the Division of Rapid Transit" (October 17, 1986).

Exhibit 7-3
Eliciting Information on Customer Satisfaction

MTA Report Card

We want to know if we're making the grade. Just take a minute to think about MTA bus and Metro service, and fill out our report card. We promise that when we get our grades in the mail, we will use them to see where we are doing well, and where we need improvement. Then we'll work to do better. Thanks for helping us give you the best service possible.

Please cut along the dotted line, fold so the MTA address shows, staple or tape, and drop into the nearest mailbox.

Thanks for helping us give you the best service possible.

GRADING SCALE
A = Excellent
B = Good
C = Average
D = Unsatisfactory

SUBJECT	GRADE (circle one)
Did the bus or Metro train arrive on time?	A B C D
Did you get to your destination on time?	A B C D
Was the bus or Metro car clean inside and out? Was it free of litter?	A B C D
Was the temperature of the bus or Metro car comfortable—warm in winter, cool in summer?	A B C D
Was the bus or Metro train overcrowded?	A B C D
Was the bus operator or station attendant courteous and helpful?	A B C D
Did the operator drive in a professional manner?	A B C D
If you called 539-5000 and spoke to an MTA information agent, did the agent give you accurate information in a courteous way?	A B C D
OVERALL GRADE Taking each subject into consideration, please give us an overall grade for our service.	A B C D

Please print your answers to the following questions to allow us to know more about your trip. Thank you.

DATE _____ TIME OF DAY _____ AM PM
_____ BUS _____ METRO (check one)
BUS LINE NUMBER _____ VEHICLE NUMBER _____

If you would like a reply, please fill out the following information.
NAME _____
STREET ADDRESS _____ PHONE _____
CITY _____ STATE _____ ZIP _____

What can the MTA do to serve you better? _____
_____
_____
_____

For additional comments, please call the MTA Comment Line at 333-2354 and ask for Information Agent #11.

Note: The third question should separate the assessment of being clean inside the bus or metro car versus outside, with an emphasis placed on the former.

Source: Provided by the Mass Transit Administration, Customer Services Department, 300 West Lexington Street, Baltimore, Maryland 21201-3415. Reprinted by permission.

thority. A mail survey or distribution of surveys on platforms of a mass transit operation may result in nonresponse bias, whereas personal interviews would avoid this problem. Of course, the costs of personal interviews can be substantial.

DISAGGREGATION

The researcher considered disaggregation both by the nature of the measure and by the level of operations, such as per service area, per route, per bus, or per driver. Combinations of stratifications by nature and level are plausible, as well as disaggregation by time or time of day. The disaggregations recommended for each SEA indicator are reported in Exhibit 7-1.

The breakdowns by line/route in Exhibit 7-1, as well as disaggregation by peak time periods, are of major interest to riders. This conclusion is based largely on interviews with users and a careful study of commentaries of the inspector general for New York's Mass Transit Systems.

A distinction between peak and off-peak measures would be particularly useful in maintaining high-quality service,[15] as would breakouts by area of community or by major route. By-route monitoring is imperative for operations and to facilitate the preparation of relevant reports for customers. By-depot details would be useful to passengers, whereas a system-wide level of reporting is too general and would be of limited use to passengers.[16]

COMMUNICATION AND DISPLAY OF INFORMATION

A set of consistent, comparable SEA indicators should be prescribed for inclusion in a transit system's annual report, and that of the city or cities it serves. A separate, easy-to-read pamphlet should be distributed to customers and its contents released to local newspapers regularly, detailing by-route information on performance. Specifically, depend-

---

[15] Eckhard Bennewitz, "Mass Transit," *Productivity Improvement Handbook for State & Local Government,* George J. Washnis, ed. (New York: John Wiley & Sons, Inc., 1980).

[16] Office of the Inspector General, New York Metropolitan Transportation Authority, "Indicators for Surface Transportation" (December 30, 1986), and "Indicators for the Division of Rapid Transit" (October 17, 1986).

Exhibit 7-4
Collecting Information on Both Riders and Nonriders

Nº 7092

YOUR FUTURE CTA SERVICE

We are carrying out a survey of your choice of transportation for your journey to work. We would be grateful if you would help us help you by completing the following questionnaire.

If you wish to take part in a FREE PASS DRAWING, please write your name and address here. *The prizes will be ten monthly passes providing unlimited travel on CTA services.*

Name _____
Address _____
City _____ State _____ Zip _____

1. How do you usually travel to work from home?
   ☐ Drive a car
   ☐ Travel as a passenger in a car
   ☐ Travel by CTA, i.e. bus, rail or both
   ☐ Travel by METRA and/or PACE
   ☐ Walk all the way
   ☐ Other, please explain

2. If you share-a-ride, how many people including yourself travel in the car? _____

3. If you share-a-ride, do you share the travel costs? ☐ Yes ☐ No

4. If you drive your car to work, how much do you have to pay to park the car? $ _____ per week/month

5. About how long does it take you to travel to work? _____ MINS.

6. What time do you arrive at work? _____

7. About how much do you spend per month on your transportation to work? _____ Dollars per month.

8. Do you have any alternative way of travelling to work? ☐ Yes ☐ No
   If yes, please explain _____

9. Why do you not travel by this alternative?
   ☐ Costs more
   ☐ Takes longer
   ☐ Less comfortable
   ☐ Less convenient
   ☐ Other, please explain

10. How many vehicles (car, van, or other) are available to you and members of your household? _____

11. You have a choice: You can either travel to work by car and pay $1.80 per gallon for gas and $200 per month for parking, OR you can spend 10 mins. walking and waiting for public transit (i.e. bus, rail or both) costing $40 per month and taking 10 mins. longer riding time. How would you choose to travel? For the situations given below, please indicate, by checking the appropriate box, your strength of preference for car or transit based on your daily journey to work.

TRANSIT FACTORS		CAR FACTORS		Preference
WALK/WAIT TIME	FARE PER MONTH	TRAVEL TIME DIFFERENCE	GAS PRICE PER GALLON	PARKING COST PER MONTH
10 Mins.	$40	10 Mins. Longer By Transit	$1.80	$200	Strongly Prefer Transit / Weekly Prefer Transit / Indifferent / Weekly Prefer Car / Strongly Prefer Car
5 Mins.	$70	10 Mins. Longer By Transit	$1.80	$100	Strongly Prefer Transit / Weekly Prefer Transit / Indifferent / Weekly Prefer Car / Strongly Prefer Car
5 Mins.	$55	5 Mins. Quicker By Transit	$1.80	$200	Strongly Prefer Transit / Weekly Prefer Transit / Indifferent / Weekly Prefer Car / Strongly Prefer Car
5 Mins.	$60	10 Mins. Longer By Transit	$1.00	$200	Strongly Prefer Transit / Weekly Prefer Transit / Indifferent / Weekly Prefer Car / Strongly Prefer Car

358.07 (rev. 07/87) Strategic Planning

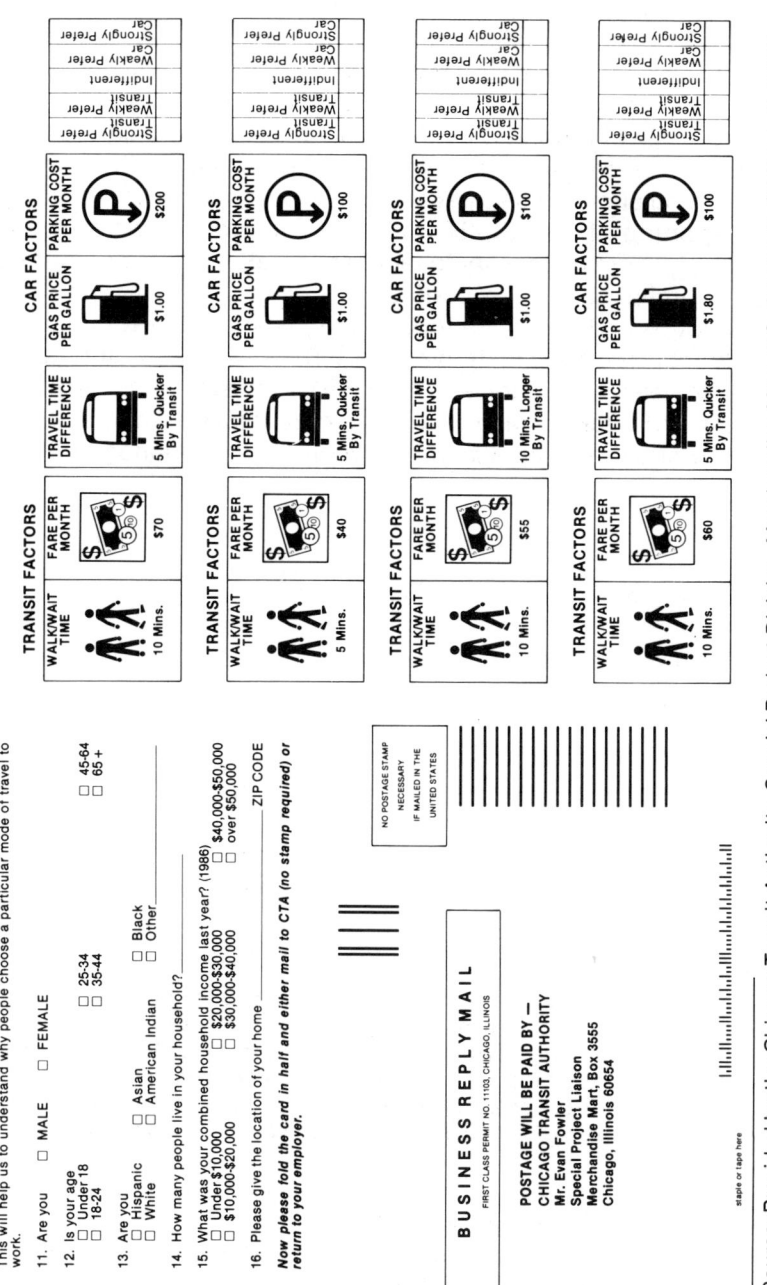

Source: Provided by the Chicago Transit Authority, Special-Project Division, Merchandise Mart, P.O. Box 3555, Chicago, IL 60654. Reprinted by permission.

ability, economics, safety, and environmental measures, as detailed in Exhibit 7-1, should be disclosed. Graphics can be useful in simplifying the messages, in tandem with raw statistics. Jargon, which is prevalent within the industry and in these reports, should be avoided.

The example of reporting by the Straphangers Campaign, presented in Exhibit 7-2, is an effective prototype. As details focus on by-route information and similar disaggregations, caveats can be noted alongside public reporting of quantitative measures, in order to warn users that assumptions were necessary to facilitate breakouts by line, route, time of day, or similar bases of reporting.

Peer groups and overall national averages should be formulated and routinely reported by transit systems.[17] This would entail prescribing what these peer groups are, e.g., through use of size (such as peak vehicle count and peak-to-base ratio),[18] geographical terrain, and type of system criteria including speed and when contract-managed.[19]

---

[17]John M. Greiner et al., *Monitoring the Effectiveness of State Transportation Services* (Washington, DC: U.S. Government Printing Office and The Urban Institute, July 29, 1977); Commonwealth of Pennsylvania Act 76 of 1986; Gordon J. Fielding, Mary E. Brenner, and Katherine Faust, "Typology for Bus Transit," *Transportation Research* (vol. 19A, no. 3, 1985), pp. 269–278; Gordon J. Fielding, Timlynn T. Babitsky, and Mary E. Brenner, "Performance Evaluation for Bus Transit," *Transportation Research* (vol. 19A, no. 1, 1985), pp. 73–82.

[18]Gordon J. Fielding, Marcy Jaffe, and Mark Yamarone, "Using UMTA Section 15 Data for Triennial Reviews," UMTA-CA-06-0213-3 (June 1987).

[19]Gordon J. Fielding and Lee Hanson, "Determinants of Superior Performance in Public Transit," UMTA-CA-11-0029-1 (August 1987).

Section 15 provides a rich resource for reporting benchmarks for comparison. The following items should be reported as peer group and national benchmarks by transit agencies:[20]

- Revenue Generation per Expense: Operating revenue per operating expense

- Operating Safety: 1,000,000 vehicle miles per accident

- Output per $ Cost: Revenue vehicle hours per operating expense
- Utilization of Service: Unlinked passenger trips (i.e., any segment of any trip using a different transit vehicle; unlinked trips may well have a 1.6 ratio to linked trips, on which little uniform data is collected) per revenue vehicle hour
- Labor Efficiency: Vehicle hours per employee
- Vehicle Efficiency: Vehicle miles per peak vehicle required
- Maintenance Efficiency: Vehicle miles per maintenance employee

Such reports should note the public availability of all Section 15 information, so interested users can directly access that data base.

Comparisons among privatized and public lines within a system, as well as competing modes of transportation, are likely to be a motivator to all lines to provide better service more efficiently, and thereby would be of interest to riders.[21]

Time trends should be reported, such as ten-year profiles. Inflation adjustments (e.g., constant-dollar amounts) should be cited as supplementary disclosures for longitudinal comparisons. Explanatory factors of likely relevance, as well as costs associated with the various metrics proposed herein, are detailed in the unabridged report. The use of narratives to explain the nature of operating systems varies substantially.

---

[20]These were developed by Fielding, Brenner, and Faust, "Typology for Bus Transit," with separate analysis of motor buses, demand responses, and rapid rail systems. (U.S. Department of Transportation, *The Status of the Nation's Local Mass Transportation* [1987], discusses the importance of such a distinction.)

[21]Tramontozzi and Chilton, *The Federal Free Ride*.

RELEVANCY AND INTENDED AUDIENCE

Given the realization that about 11 million people ride transit per weekday (an estimate based on the 1980 census reporting a 6.3 percent work trip market share for mass transit), transit systems' capital assets exceed $10 billion, and they consume 412 million gallons of fuel and 2.30 billion kilowatt-hours of electricity,[22] the relevance of SEA information to a broad cross section of individuals concerned with services, financing, conservation, and pollution is apparent. Nonetheless, the recommended focus in developing and reporting on SEA is on internal managers, oversight groups, and customers.

SEA data are being used by states such as Pennsylvania, which currently ties state assistance to transit performance measures (and has since July 1980). Both New York and California similarly base certain types of state assistance on performance systems. Delaware has specified measures for operations assessment, and California mandates performance audits.[23] Since more subsidies are allocated to those with higher performance on selected measures, questions arise as to the sufficiency of the SEA measures in current use. Due, in part, to criticisms of past UMTA policies, in March 1980 the U.S. Senate proposed

---

[22] Adapted from William C. Underwood, "Performance Indicators: A Necessary Management Tool?" *Transit Journal* (vol. 5, no. 1, Winter 1979), pp. 11–16.

[23] See W. G. Allen, Jr. and L. G. Grimm, "Development and Application of Performance Measures for a Medium-Sized Transit System." Presented at the 59th annual meeting of the Transportation Research Board; J. Dockendorf and W. C. Underwood, "Proposed Methodology for Predictable State Mass Transit Funding" (draft) (Harrisburg: Pennsylvania Department of Transportation, 1978), cited in John M. Gleason and Darold T. Barnum "Toward Valid Measures of Public Sector Productivity: Performance Measures in Urban Transit," *Management Science* (vol. 28, no. 4, April 1982); G. J. Fielding, R. E. Glauthier, and C. A. Lave, "Performance Indicators for Transit Management," Institute of Transportation Studies, University of California at Irvine (January 1978), based on *Development of Performance Indicators for Transit* (Irvine: University of California, NTIS #PB278 1977), which is cited in Attanucci et al. (1979); C. A. Keck and N. R. Schneider, "Efficiency, Economy, and Effectiveness: The Development and Application of Multimodal Performance Measures for Transit Systems in New York State," presented at the 59th annual meeting of the Transportation Research Board (Washington, DC, January 1980), cited as a 1980 Working Paper in Gleason and Barnum (1982); T. D. Larson and W. C. Underwood, "Urban Transportation Financing Today." Presented at the Urban Transportation Financing Conference (Bucknell University, 1979), cited in Gleason and Barnum (1982); J. T. Mauro, "Performance Measurement External and Internal," *Transit Journal* (Spring 1980), pp. 57–63, cited in Gleason and Barnum (1982).

that federal subsidies be based on transit performance measures. While not yet adopted, the feasibility of such proposals can be better assessed once a generally accepted set of SEA measures for mass transit is developed, such as the set described herein.

RECOMMENDATIONS

The use of measures outlined in Exhibit 7-1 is encouraged, as is communication of such measures along the lines of Exhibit 7-2. Means of collecting these measures include the tools depicted in Exhibits 7-3 and 7-4. The unabridged report contains details concerning the research that formed the basis for these recommendations.

8. Police Department Programs

Allan Drebin, Northwestern University

Marguerite Brannon, Chicago Tribune Charities

	Page
Introduction and Scope	188
Goals and Objectives of Police Departments	188
Methodology	189
Recommended Indicators	190
Input Measures	190
Output Measures	194
Outcome Measures	196
Explanatory Data	201
Ratios	202
Norms and Comparisons	202
Communication and Display	203
Uses and Users of Data	203
Need for Further Research	204

The authors wish to thank John Jemilo, executive director of the Chicago Crime Commission, and Harold Steinberg, partner of Peat Marwick Main & Co., for their constructive comments on earlier drafts.

INTRODUCTION AND SCOPE

Police departments are an essential operating unit of most local governments. From the standpoint of resources used, both financial and personnel, these units often involve the largest single area of expenditure, approaching half of the general fund budget. In addition to being almost universally provided, police services are an area of great public and news media concern.

Due to the high visibility and importance of police functions, a great deal of data is maintained and disseminated concerning public problems on which police are expected to have an impact. Yet it has not been demonstrated that these data provide potential users with information that is relevant in a decision-making context. The purpose of this chapter is to examine current practices in evaluating the service efforts and accomplishments (SEA) of police departments, particularly in light of their usefulness for decision making; to suggest possible improvements in the measurement process; and to determine whether the available SEA indicators are sufficiently developed to warrant experimentation by governmental units.

Goals and Objectives of Police Departments

Police departments are often called upon to provide a wide range of public services. Their most visible function relates to crime: prevention and suppression of crime and the apprehension of criminal offenders. Traffic control—the regulation of vehicular traffic to promote safety and mobility—is a nearly universal function of police departments. Many hours of police effort are also devoted to providing a multitude of public services that are completely unrelated to crime or traffic. In some jurisdictions the department may be responsible for certain emergency services such as civil defense or emergency medical services.

Previous studies have tried to develop a set of objectives for police departments. Although each jurisdiction must have its own conception of what the police department is responsible for, there seems to be general agreement at the basic level of the essential mission of the department: the protection of persons and property from crime. This leads to a wide array of functions and responsibilities, and many attempts have been made to define these. One definition is found in a study by the National Advisory Commission on Criminal Justice Standards and Goals. The major responsibilities of police noted in the study are:

1. Prevention of criminal activity.
2. Detection of criminal activity.
3. Apprehension of criminal offenders.
4. Participation in court proceedings.
5. Protection of constitutional guarantees.
6. Assistance to those who cannot care for themselves or who are in danger of physical harm.
7. Control of traffic.
8. Resolution of day-to-day conflicts among family, friends, and neighbors.
9. Creation and maintenance of a feeling of security in the community.
10. Promotion and preservation of civil order.[1]

Because of the diversity of police functions, measures of accomplishments in various functional areas are not likely to be comparable. In order to focus on the major issues involving measurement, this study concentrates only on the crime-related functions. It is not intended to suggest that the other areas of police service are any less important, only that this preliminary study must be limited in scope. It must also be recognized that many police services use common resources; patrol, for example, which is the largest single function for most police departments, is directed toward traffic as well as crime. Thus, any conclusions must be viewed in light of these relationships.

Methodology

This study's approach was to obtain information regarding current practices in measurement of police SEA, classify and evaluate these practices relative to their possible uses, and suggest refinements or improvements in the practices to overcome weaknesses identified. The

---

[1] National Advisory Commission on Criminal Justice Standards and Goals, *A National Strategy to Reduce Crime* (Washington, DC: Government Printing Office, 1973), p. 72.

process began with a survey of pertinent literature: Books, articles, and other materials relating to the measurement of police performance were gathered and summarized. Computer searches were used to find additional sources of reference material.

Documents were also gathered from many governmental units to obtain a sampling of current reporting practices. Some were extracted from the comprehensive annual financial reports (CAFR) or special reports of the jurisdictions, and others were found in budget documents. It was rare to find this information in end-of-period reports. When it *was* found, it most often was included in pre-period documents such as budget requests, and based on projections rather than historical results.

Interviews were conducted with knowledgeable individuals involved in using or preparing such information. No attempt was made to identify a representative or statistically valid group of interviewees; they were selected simply because it was believed that their knowledge would be useful in identifying significant issues in the measurement process.

RECOMMENDED INDICATORS

Based on our survey of current reports and the review of pertinent literature, several police SEA indicators appeared to merit consideration. These measures span the full range of measurement categories outlined above and are discussed in greater depth in the following pages.

The usefulness of any indicator is affected by its validity and measurability. Validity implies not only accuracy and verifiability but also that the measure faithfully represents the attribute being evaluated. Measurability is a practical concern; the availability of data needed to produce a measure could constrain its use. These issues are discussed where appropriate for each of the measures considered.

Input Measures

Expenditures: Expenditures are the most valid indication of the efforts expended in police crime-suppression activities. With limited resources, jurisdictions must make difficult allocation choices, and spending money on this objective expresses the preferences of the community. It also provides some perspective on all the other measures. Although expenditures are an input, any outcomes must be viewed in relation to the resource commitment involved. The primary difficulty is in measurement, due to the many common costs associated with police functions. For example, patrol activities relate not only to crime prevention but to traffic and public service. It is believed, however, that accounting and budgeting techniques can be developed to overcome these problems if the information is to be reported.

Equipment, Facilities, and Vehicles: Equipment, facilities, and vehicles are inputs that are frequently reported, particularly in the statistical section of the CAFRs. While this information indicates to the reader the size and scope of the department and the resources devoted to police service, it is not meant to tell how efficiently or effectively these resources are used to achieve departmental objectives. When combined with output or outcome measures, it may be used to develop ratios that can indicate how efficiently or effectively services were provided with resource constraints.

We suggest reporting the dollar cost of equipment used in crime-suppression activities. The validity of such a figure would be affected by such factors as inflation and regional cost differences. These same problems pervade all monetary measures, including financial reports, but this is not a reason to ignore the measure. Cost figures would provide some degree of comparability among jurisdictions and among time periods. Additional information regarding physical units can be made available in notes or supplementary reports.

Number of Personnel; Hours Expended: The most important input to the police function is human resources. Police departments measure and report this input in a variety of ways: as work-days, worker-years, personnel deployment, number of employees or officers, and hours of operation per month. However, simply reporting the number of employees could be misleading, as some employees work less than full-time. For evaluation purposes, the number of personnel hours required to complete a given task is the most relevant measure. In order to make comparisons over time or with similar communities, the measure should be considered over the budgetary time period (i.e., personnel-hours expended per year).

Reporting the number of officers per thousand population might seem to lend itself to comparisons between cities. However, certain caveats should be kept in mind. The number of businesses in and visitors

Exhibit 8-1
Recommended SEA Indicators for Police Departments*

Indicator	Rationale for Selecting Indicator
Inputs:	
Budget expenditures	To provide a measure of financial resources used to provide services
Equipment, facilities, vehicles	To provide a measure of nonpersonnel resources used to provide services
Number of personnel; hours expended	To provide a measure of the size of the organization and the human resources used to provide services
Outputs:	
Hours of patrol	To provide a measure of the quantity of patrol service provided; patrol is generally regarded as a primary product of police efforts
Responses to calls for service	To provide a measure of the quantity of response service provided
Crimes investigated	To provide a measure of the quantity of services provided by investigation units
Number of arrests	To provide a measure of the success of police efforts in apprehending criminal offenders
Persons participating in crime-prevention activities	To provide a measure of the quantity of service provided by crime-prevention units
Outcomes:	
Deaths and bodily injury resulting from crime	To provide a measure of the effectiveness of police efforts in reducing the incidence of personal harm attributed to criminal activity
Value of property lost due to crime	To provide a measure of the effectiveness of police efforts in reducing the incidence of property loss due to criminal activity

Indicator	Purpose
Crimes committed per 100,000 population	To provide a measure of the effectiveness of police efforts in reducing criminal activity
Percentage of crimes cleared	To provide a measure of the effectiveness of police efforts in detection of criminal activity and apprehension of criminal offenders
Response time	To provide a measure of the quality of police response to calls
Citizen satisfaction	To provide a measure of the overall effectiveness of police efforts in meeting citizen needs
Efficiency:	
Cost per case assigned; cost per crime cleared	To provide an indication of the cost efficiency of police efforts
Personnel-hours per crime cleared	To provide an indication of the productivity of personnel in providing police services
Explanatory Variables:	
Population by age group	
Unemployment rate	
Number of households; number of business firms	
Percentage of population below poverty level	To provide information on factors that are likely to affect the incidence and effects of criminal activity so that measures of output, outcome, and efficiency may be viewed in proper context
Land area	
Dollar value of property within jurisdiction	
Demand	
Calls for service	
Cases assigned	

*The recommended indicators presented in this exhibit are illustrative. They are intended to serve as a starting point for use in the development of a comprehensive set of SEA indicators for external reporting of an entity's results of operation.

This exhibit does not provide illustrations of indicator disaggregation or of comparison data such as trends, targets, or other comparable entities. Both disaggregation and comparison data are important aspects of SEA reporting. They are discussed in the chapter and in the Overview.

193

to the community are not taken into account,[2] the makeup of the populations may be quite divergent, and the expanse of area to cover for the same size population may vary greatly.[3]

Personnel-hours provides a basic measure of the human resources used in police crime-suppression activities. The measure is readily comparable among jurisdictions and among years, and is not affected by cost variations.

Output Measures

Output measures reported include hours of patrol, miles patrolled, calls for service responded to, surveillances conducted, warrants served, and arrests made. The data are prevalent in police reports and include a wide range of measures. The indicators have the advantage of being objectively determinable and could be subjected to audit. The problem with them is that they do not directly relate to why the police department is performing these services. Nevertheless, they do represent the direct outputs of police activity and are thus important in evaluating accomplishments.

Hours of Patrol: Typically, police officers allocate a significant percentage of their time to patrol. Hours spent on patrol may be objectively measured. The number of hours of patrol is a measure of the quantity of services delivered in a period of time, but it does not indicate whether department objectives have been met.

Even without strong evidence to support its effectiveness in preventing crime, most citizens feel that police patrol is a worthwhile service. In this sense, hours of patrol may be regarded as an end product, and reporting patrol hours is important for evaluating police SEA. These data should be disaggregated according to communities served to help determine quality and equitable distribution of services.

Responses to Calls for Service: Although officers on patrol may be called upon to respond to specific calls for service, call responses are

---

[2]Harry P. Hatry et al., "Crime Control," in *How Effective Are Your Community Services* (Washington, DC: The Urban Institute and International City Management Association, 1977), pp. 88–89.

[3]Interview with Sheldon Greenberg, associate director of management services, Police Executive Research Forum.

regarded as quite distinct from the patrol function. With patrol, the officers are actively looking for problems that may require police attention. When citizens call, they have a specific problem that they feel requires police intervention.

Counting the number of calls for service provides an indication of the demand for police assistance in the community. However, it does not indicate the degree to which the police were helpful in responding to the citizens' needs. To obtain some basis for evaluating the police crime response, calls for service can be logged by category. Calls involving crime should be separately reported and further broken down by type of crime.

Crimes Investigated: The number of criminal investigations provides an indication of the amount of service provided by investigation units. In many cases, detectives are assigned to pursue a reported crime to determine the cause and gather evidence necessary to prosecute the offenders. Documentation of reported crime can be extended to show the police response. Officers can maintain a log of cases they are working on, so data collection may not be difficult and the numbers reported are likely to be objective. The number can be related to reported crimes to give an indication of the department's response to reported crimes.

One problem with this measure is that some crimes or circumstances call for more hours of investigation or entail a greater level of difficulty than others. Thus, it may be possible to report a large total number of investigations by concentrating efforts on simple or easy cases while ignoring complex or more-difficult cases. This weakness could be overcome by reporting the amount of time involved in the investigation process.

Another problem relates to multiple crimes stemming from a single incident or offender. Is a mass murder one crime or several? In many cases an individual may be charged with several crimes relating to the same event. It has been suggested that crimes be categorized by the relative need for and potential value of investigation.

Number of Arrests: Arrests are a direct product of police activity. This measure includes arrests and warrants served. Although protecting persons and property by suppression of crime is the end objective of police activities, apprehending offenders and bringing them to justice is also an important part of law enforcement. Because arrests are not the final step in the process, this measure is classified as an output, as opposed to "crimes cleared," which is an outcome. The number of arrests can be related to the number of crimes investigated to indicate a level of success in the criminal investigation activity.

Because police departments must maintain records of individuals arrested, data for this measure are readily available. One problem that does occur is the comparability of units used with other proposed measures. For example, the definition of clearance permits only one clearance for each crime, regardless of how many arrests are made. If there are multiple suspects for a single crime, several arrests could result from one investigation. For this reason, potential users of these figures should be aware that the totals are not comparable. Arrest data should be disaggregated by type of crime to provide some sense of the direction in which the department's activities are headed, and to indicate the degree of success in apprehending suspects involved in particular types of crimes. Further breakdowns by geographic area (neighborhood) and demographic character of the suspect and arrestee are also recommended.

Crime-Prevention Activities: Crime prevention is an important element of police service. If crimes can be prevented, the safety of citizens and their property will be enhanced. Although the responsive activities (investigation, apprehension, and so forth) should act in the long run as a deterrent to crime, most police departments have programs that are specifically aimed at crime prevention. These activities include the provision of educational programs to eliminate the opportunity for crime to occur, and home and business security surveys.

The results of successful prevention activities would presumably show up in outcome measures such as crimes committed. Because so many variables are likely to affect that measure, however, it is impossible to ascribe a causal relationship to prevention activities. However, the service efforts can be indicated by the number of presentations made and populations reached.

Due to the diverse nature of crime-prevention programs, it is not likely that counting numbers of presentations would provide objective data that would permit reasonable comparisons among jurisdictions or among years. Therefore, it is recommended that the number of participants be reported, while presentations may be described in narrative fashion in notes or supplementary reports. The number of participants can be measured through direct counts or attendance records.

Outcome Measures

The primary objective of police crime-suppression programs is to protect persons and property within their jurisdiction. In the final analysis, then, the results of police activities must be viewed with reference to their impact on protecting lives and property. Since there is difficulty in isolating the effect of police actions from other factors, measures more directly related to police activities must also be used. If an objective of a department is to reduce the opportunities for the commission of certain crimes, its effectiveness may be evaluated with reference to the actual crimes committed.

Quality Measures: Quality is subjective and thus many people believe that it does not lend itself to measurement. In the police field, however, some attributes of quality can be measured and indeed are widely reported. Perhaps the most prevalent of these is response time for emergency calls. Quality is frequently indicated by minimizing negative results. For example, minimizing undesirable outcomes such as false arrests and charges of excessive force are important factors in evaluating police services. Thus, quality measures include citizen complaints and the length of time citizens must wait for various services.

Deaths and Bodily Injury Resulting from a Crime: The number of persons killed or injured as a result of crime is the most relevant measure of the product of crime prevention and suppression programs. Although homicides are usually reported and can be counted, bodily injury is quite difficult to measure objectively. The severity of the injury is an important dimension, yet it cannot be quantified with any degree of precision. Nevertheless, the importance of this factor suggests that reporting would provide useful information.

To provide an objective basis for discriminating between serious and minor injuries, it is suggested that the measure of the number of injuries be limited to those involving admission to a hospital. This would provide objective measures because hospital admissions are routinely recorded. Despite the difficulty of obtaining an objective measure, the importance of injuries as a final outcome of crime-suppression activities makes it worthwhile to report as an indicator of police department accomplishment.

An alternative would be to estimate the number of days of productive activity[4] lost because of the injury. This would provide some measure of the severity, although it would not indicate the degree of pain and suffering sustained by the victim.

Value of Property Lost: Protecting property is an important element of police crime-suppression activities, so the value of property lost

---

[4]Productive activity is not limited to remunerated employment. It could include attending school or enjoying social events. It is not intended to measure personal loss in monetary terms.

would be a key indicator of the accomplishment of these activities. The difficulty with this measure is obtaining objective data to estimate its magnitude. Losses covered by insurance usually require a police report to document the claim, so there likely will be a certain amount of data available. Automobile thefts, particularly, are usually reported to the police, and registration information should be useful for estimating current values from used-car price books. Unfortunately, many property crimes that do not involve insurance claims go unreported. Victimization surveys might be helpful here, but depending on an individual to place a reasonable value on property that was lost or damaged by criminal acts at some previous time seems unreasonable.

An alternative measure often used in police reporting is the "value of property recovered." Although it is easier to draw conclusions regarding the police department's role in accomplishing the return of stolen property, in the final analysis the police should be concerned with what the citizens lose, rather than how much they recover. Recoveries should be netted against the loss figures to provide an indication of the effect of the crime. Adjusting figures by a price index (such as the Consumer Price Index) would make year-to-year comparisons more meaningful.

Crimes Committed: Virtually all police departments maintain records of reported crimes within their jurisdictions. Since these statistics are compiled and published by the FBI in Uniform Crime Reports, these figures have a great deal of visibility. They are frequently made the subject of news stories, particularly comparing the local jurisdiction with comparable jurisdictions elsewhere.

The use of reported-crime statistics, including the Uniform Crime Reports, has been criticized because of its reliance on reporting, which has been found to severely understate the amount and severity of actual crimes. Several studies of crime reporting have found that actual victimization was substantially higher than the reported rates.[5]

It is recommended that reported crimes be used as a measure of the outcome of police activity. In addition, victimization surveys should be conducted periodically to provide a means of assessing the validity of the reported-crime data. Reported crimes (as compiled in the Uniform Crime Reports) are readily available in nearly all departments, and the FBI guidelines for reporting these figures provide some degree of uniformity among jurisdictions. Victimization surveys are relatively costly

---

[5]For a detailed discussion of victimization surveys citing several of these studies, see Wesley G. Skogan, *Victimization Surveys and Criminal Justice Planning* (Washington, DC: National Institute of Law Enforcement and Criminal Justice, 1978).

to administer, and their continual use probably would not provide much additional information. On a periodic basis, however, they can provide a mechanism for determining the validity of reported data. If estimates of crimes committed from both crime reports and victimization surveys converge, it can be assumed that the crime reports are valid. If victimization surveys repeatedly indicate a substantial degree of underreporting in certain jurisdictions, the reported-crime figures may be increased accordingly to provide reasonable comparative data.

Since the relationship between police activities and outcomes is critical to evaluating police effectiveness, disaggregation of crimes committed to reflect those that are likely to be affected by police intervention would provide important information. Thus, separating categories such as homicides (which police do not affect very much) from those such as auto theft (which police action is likely to reduce) would be useful.

Crime Clearance: Since police departments do not have complete control over the commission of crime (many factors such as economic conditions, employment, street lighting, and even weather conditions have been correlated with crime), many departments have attempted to measure what they regard as the final product of their work. Most prevalent in this area is a so-called clearance rate. This is usually defined as the number (or percentage) of crimes that have been "solved" by arrest or "exceptional" means.

Clearances are reported in the FBI's Uniform Crime Reports. The FBI defines clearance by arrest as follows:

> An offense is "cleared by arrest" or solved for crime-reporting purposes when at least one person is:
>
> 1. arrested;
> 2. charged with the commission of the offense; and
> 3. turned over to the court for prosecution.[6]

A problem with this definition is that a crime is considered to be cleared when only one person is arrested, even though several persons may have participated in the crime. This makes the data not compatible with arrests, and also gives credit for solving a crime even though not all suspects have been apprehended.

---

[6]U.S. Department of Justice, Federal Bureau of Investigation, *Uniform Crime Reporting Handbook* (Washington, DC, 1974), p. 44.

A somewhat controversial and often misunderstood variation of a clearance is an "exceptional clearance." The FBI provides for this possibility in the Uniform Crime Reports, counting cases in which the suspect has not been arrested but the case still is considered closed. Examples given for exceptional clearances include the death of the suspect and denial of extradition. Although there may be a reasonable basis for crediting the police department for clearing crimes under these circumstances, the potential for intentionally puffing this measure of SEA is great. It is recommended that clearance data be limited to those that qualify as clearance by arrest.

Response Time: The time it takes for police to respond to calls for assistance is one of the most widely reported SEA measures. Since response time is only one factor influencing the ultimate impact of crime on citizens and their property, this measure might be categorized as an output measure, as opposed to an outcome. To many observers, however, response time is an indicator of the quality of police service, and thus is an element of the outcome.

As response time is so prevalent in reporting, not only by police but also by other emergency services such as fire and ambulance, it should be included in reports of police accomplishments. Most departments have dispatchers who log calls and record the time at which a car arrives. Sound-recording equipment coupled with time recorders are widely used to document calls for service and personnel arriving at the scene. Thus objective, verifiable data can be obtained without much added cost.

Many departments report an average response time. However, this is not the most-relevant information. Important factors to be considered are whether the reported crime is in progress, whether there are injured people at the scene of the crime, and how soon after the crime was committed the police were called. Assuming there is a critical time beyond which lives may be endangered or the probability of stopping a crime in progress diminishes, faster responses may not add any value. Yet the faster response would bring down the average time. A better measure would be the percentage of responses below a predetermined critical limit. Data should be classified according to relevance to crime or other services, and further broken down by urgency and location.

Citizen Satisfaction: Citizen satisfaction with police service is an indication of the quality of service delivery. Many departments report numbers of citizen complaints. Records are also maintained on disciplinary proceedings and charges of excessive force. Such negative indicators may not be representative of the evaluation of the entire population.

Surveys of citizens to determine their satisfaction with police services would provide more-representative data. Citizen responses are the best indicator of how well the police are meeting local community needs. This is an important factor, because not all communities share the same attitudes toward police services, which makes some of the other measures difficult to evaluate. In some communities, the citizens prefer very strict enforcement of all laws, so a high number of arrests might be a sign of effective police efforts. In other communities, however, the citizens prefer more-relaxed enforcement, permitting petty violations. In this situation, a large number of arrests may be a sign of excessive enforcement, not consistent with community standards.

Although there may be problems with obtaining objective results from citizen surveys, the community's assessment of how well the department is performing its mission is essential to the evaluation of accomplishments. Surveys seem to be the only effective way to determine the degree of satisfaction with police department SEA, so it is recommended that an annual survey of citizens be conducted. Although the survey may logically include many dimensions of service, responses to a key question of "How satisfied are you with the overall performance of the department?" should be reported. These data would not be comparable from one jurisdiction to another, but a trend of results for a single jurisdiction might indicate whether the degree of citizen satisfaction was improving. The survey data should be disaggregated according to the age, sex, and community of respondents, and whether they (or a close relative) have recently been the victim of a crime. This will display differences in levels of satisfaction among different groups of citizens.

Explanatory Data

Explanatory data that can be helpful in evaluating SEA include data regarding the community served: population, number of households, land area, and the dollar value of property within the jurisdiction. Data that have been correlated with crime occurrence—such as educational level, unemployment rate, family income, and age—should be particularly important. These factors can be helpful in developing ratios to place different jurisdictions on a comparable basis. Certain data may be used in compiling ratios to be reported, but providing the raw figures permits the user to prepare other ratios as well. This information tends to be readily available from external sources such as the decennial census.

Demand Measures: Demand measures can be helpful in putting data on service efforts into perspective. If the number of responses to calls is to be measured, the number of calls for service should be reported to make the measure meaningful. Similarly, if the number of investigations is reported, the number of cases assigned should be reported.

Numbers of calls for service and cases assigned generally are available in departmental records. Dispatchers maintain logs of calls, and interviews indicated that these data are regarded as highly reliable.

Ratios

Ratios can be helpful in interpreting data. If the information contained in both the numerator and the denominator appears elsewhere in the document, then reporting the ratio does not provide any additional information. Still, providing the ratio gives the reader a convenient presentation and may assist in understanding. From the standpoint of comparability, ratios are necessary to place different jurisdictions on the same scale. For example, one would expect the number of crimes to be higher in a large city than in a smaller city. Dividing by population to show the number of crimes per thousand population permits the figures to be compared on an equal basis.

Many ratios could be reported using data suggested above. We will suggest two that are widely used and very important: crimes per thousand population (crimes committed divided by population) and clearance rates (crimes cleared divided by number of crimes). These ratios are currently included in the FBI Uniform Crime Reports.

NORMS AND COMPARISONS

The potential uses of SEA data might be enhanced by the availability of benchmarks to permit comparisons with other jurisdictions, with other years for the same jurisdiction, and among organizational units of a single jurisdiction.

Although there may be dangers in making comparisons with noncomparable data, it is clear that such comparisons are made and people are interested in them. The Uniform Crime Reports statistics in particular receive a great deal of visibility, and newspapers regularly compare their own jurisdiction's crime rates with those of other jurisdictions. It is recommended that data aggregated from a small number (about five) of "comparable" jurisdictions be reported for comparison purposes. The comparable jurisdictions should be named in notes to the statements and should not be changed from year to year.

COMMUNICATION AND DISPLAY

Indicators of police department SEA should be distributed widely in the community. Ideally, they would be included in an annual report for all the jurisdiction's departments.

We recommend displaying the measures in a table with comparative data for previous years. Data for a representative group of comparable jurisdictions should be included, so that readers can place the data in proper perspective.

USES AND USERS OF DATA

An important use of the indicators is to demonstrate the department's achievement to those groups to whom it is held accountable. The police are accountable to the public through their elected representatives. These representatives—city councils or similar bodies—must have information on how the police department is performing to fulfill their oversight responsibilities.

A basic function of legislative bodies is to appropriate funds for police as well as other public agencies. In allocating financial resources, it is important to estimate the cost of providing services. Rational decisions should also be based on estimates of results that are expected to be derived from the services. Thus, they need data relating changes in resources, such as personnel, to expected outcomes.

If the public has an interest in evaluating the effectiveness of police departments, the basic question they pose is, "Is the police agency effective in fulfilling its responsibilities to the community?"

Interviews with news reporters indicate that they are very interested in data regarding crime in their communities, feeling this reflects their readers' interest in such statistics. They do not indicate an interest in the effectiveness of the police department as an organizational unit, but rather the characteristics of their community, perhaps in comparison with comparable communities.

NEED FOR FURTHER RESEARCH

While holding public officials accountable for achieving the objectives of their functions, the citizens have delegated the managerial responsibilities to professional managers. Although the managers who are responsible for selecting strategies and assigning personnel must be informed of the impact of their managerial decisions, the citizens do not need to know the details of how a task is performed, only the results.

Many of the measures currently provided by police departments in public documents are not useful to citizens or legislative bodies. Data such as miles patrolled or response time could be quite useful to managers in choosing strategies or assigning personnel, but the public has no way of comprehending their importance to their concerns. (Arguably, response time could be regarded as an indicator of the quality of police services, but the public should be more concerned with the results of the response; e.g., was a life saved, a burglary in progress stopped, an offender apprehended?)

A large amount of data is published on the occurrence of crime, which relates to the end objective of police activity, but this usually is too broad to assign responsibility to the police department. Many variables beyond the control of the police department have been shown to affect the amount of crime.

In addition to preventing crime, we have assumed that an objective of police departments is to identify criminal offenders, apprehend them, and participate in subsequent court proceedings. Although the overall purpose of this objective is consistent with the higher-level objective of reducing crime (bringing offenders to justice is supposed to deter subsequent criminal activity), this objective is more clearly identifiable with police activity. Thus the apprehension and prosecution of criminal offenders becomes an end objective rather than merely a means of accomplishing a higher-level objective.

Here, the so-called clearance rates—crimes resolved through investigation, apprehension, and prosecution—seem relevant. Independent verification is necessary to ensure the integrity of the data. However, this indicator comes very close to measuring results at a level that police departments can reasonably be expected to assume responsibility for.

Statistics such as the Uniform Crime Reports are important for assessing crime in a community. The public clearly is concerned about crime. People want to live in a safe environment. Thus, crime statistics can highlight a need for action, even though the appropriate action might not involve police. Still, police departments are the most-appropriate agencies for gathering and disseminating these data. It would not be economically sound to establish another agency to process this information.

We recommend that police departments continue to provide data on reported crimes in their jurisdictions, classified as is currently done with the Uniform Crime Reports. Starting with these data as a base, however, additional breakdowns should be provided that help explain the relationship of police activity to the reported crimes.

Further research is needed to establish the linkage between intervention and commission of crime. Until such information becomes available, criteria such as location, which might logically be linked to the usefulness of police intervention, should be used to break down crime statistics. Research is needed to develop valid models for classifying such situations objectively.

A major problem with reported-crime statistics is their validity. Experiments have shown significant underreporting of crimes when compared with victimization surveys. Previous studies have recommended that victimization surveys be used as an integral part of the crime-reporting system. However, such surveys are expensive and their results are not of proven validity. We suggest that more effort be expended to improve the reliability of the reported-crime data. Victimization surveys should be used periodically to provide a benchmark and to monitor crime reports.

If victimization surveys showed there was no actual increase in particular crimes, it might be concluded that the increase was due to better reporting (a good sign). Also, if the locations indicated no increase in street crimes, it would help to explain the police role in dealing with the crime, although crimes in other locations should not be treated lightly.

9. Public Assistance Programs

*Sharon Wagner, Richard E. Brown, and James B. Tinnin,
Kent State University*

	Page
Introduction and Scope	208
Description and Objectives of Cash Assistance Programs	208
Methodology	210
Recommended Indicators	210
Input and Output Indicators	210
Outcome Indicators	211
Efficiency Indicators	214
Summary of Indicators	215
Disaggregation	215
Explanatory Data	220
Conclusions	221

INTRODUCTION AND SCOPE

This chapter investigates the use and reporting of service efforts and accomplishments (SEA) indicators in the area of public assistance. The enormous and complex range of public assistance programs could not possibly be covered in a single chapter. Therefore, the scope of this examination has been limited to SEA indicators for cash assistance programs. More specifically, the chapter focuses on SEA indicators for two cash assistance programs: Aid to Families with Dependent Children (AFDC) and General Assistance (GA). It does not include other well-known assistance programs such as Food Stamps, Medicaid, or Supplemental Security Income, nor does it cover the myriad of job-training and workfare programs associated with cash assistance programs.

DESCRIPTION AND OBJECTIVES OF CASH ASSISTANCE PROGRAMS

AFDC was established by Congress in 1935, under the Social Security Act. It is the largest cash assistance program serving needy families with children, having grown enormously since the early 1960s. Between 1965 and 1970, AFDC recipients more than doubled (from 4.3 million to 9.6 million), while costs of payment tripled (from $1.6 to $4.8 billion).[1] By 1986, the number of recipients had leveled off at around 11 million, but costs continued to climb to over $16 billion.[2]

AFDC is funded by federal, state, and sometimes local governments, and is operated by the states or local governments under broad provisions set by the federal government. Within each state, the program may be state-administered or state-supervised. "There may be county offices under both organizational patterns, but in a state-administered program the office is a unit of the state agency, and in a state-supervised program the office is a unit of local government."[3]

---

[1] Evelyn Z. Brodkin, *The False Promise of Administrative Reform: Implementing Quality Control in Welfare* (Philadelphia: Temple University Press, 1986), pp. 3–4.

[2] U.S. Department of Commerce, Bureau of the Census, *Statistical Abstract of the United States: 1989*, 109th ed. (Washington, DC, 1989), p. 366.

[3] U.S. Department of Health and Human Services, *Characteristics of State Plans for Aid to Families with Dependent Children* (Washington, DC: Office of Family Assistance, 1986), p. 9.

The AFDC program provides monthly payments to families that are determined to be eligible by county or local offices. Actual grant amounts vary between states and depend on factors such as family size, income, and state augmentation. The primary objective of the AFDC program is:

> To ensure a basic standard of living for children who lack parental support due to absence, death, disability of one or both parents or the unemployment of the principal wage earner in an intact family.[4]

Secondary administrative goals are:

1. To operate the program as accurately and economically as possible.
2. To operate it in a time-efficient manner.
3. To help parents in these families become self-sufficient.[5]

General Assistance (GA) and General Relief (GR) are cash assistance programs operated by many state or local governments in addition to AFDC. The state programs provide assistance to needy adults who do not meet the eligibility criteria for AFDC or Supplemental Security Income. The programs primarily serve single persons and couples without children. GA programs vary widely between states. Some states mandate a GA program to be state-funded and administered (e.g., Vermont, Massachusetts) or county-funded and administered (e.g., California). Other states have no mandate for the program, but it *may* be funded and administered on a local level (e.g., Florida, Iowa). Absent the state mandate, it is possible that no one is providing GA within a state. This appears to be the case in Oklahoma and Arkansas, where the state governments have recently discontinued the GA program.

---

[4]State of Missouri, "Executive Budget, Fiscal Year 1989," p. 11-16.

[5]Secondary objectives are a composite of several state and county programs. See, for instance, County of San Diego, "Proposed Program Budget, 1987–88," Vol. 1, p. 423; State of Kansas Budget, Fiscal Year 1988, pp. 2–43; State of Georgia, "Budget Report, Fiscal Year 1988," p. 227; and North Carolina State Budget, "Volume 3—Human Resources, 1987–88 Biennium," p. 0(3)–3.

In 1980, almost 800,000 adults received GA assistance, and the cost of payments was over $1 billion.[6] The primary objective of GA is:

> To provide income maintenance for persons who do not have income or resources sufficient to meet their basic subsistence needs....[7]

Secondary objectives of GA are the same as for AFDC.

METHODOLOGY

Several sources were utilized to determine the types of SEA indicators being used in cash assistance programs. State and county budgets were examined. Federal, state, and county officials were interviewed, and publications from agencies such as the U.S. General Accounting Office (GAO) and the U.S. Department of Health and Human Services (DHHS) were reviewed.

RECOMMENDED INDICATORS

The costs of cash assistance programs have risen dramatically since the 1960s. This has caused legislators, administrators, and the general public to question whether the programs are being operated as efficiently and effectively as possible. In order to make this determination, it is critical that SEA measurement of the programs become more sophisticated than simple measurement of inputs and outputs. The following SEA indicators are recommended for both AFDC and GA programs.

Input and Output Indicators

Input and output indicators by themselves are not indicative of a program's efficiency or quality, and effort should be directed toward meaningful rather than voluminous sets of indicators. The following input indicators should be considered for reporting:

---

[6]U.S. Department of Commerce, *Statistical Abstract, 1989*, p. 366.

[7]State of Michigan, "Executive Budget, 1987–88 Fiscal Year," Social Services Section, p. 5.

- Administrative cost of the program (current and constant dollars).
- Total cost of the program including amount of benefits provided (current and constant dollars).
- Total staff-hours used to operate the program.

The following output indicators are recommended:

- Total number of recipients assisted.
- Total amount of assistance provided (current and constant dollars).

Outcome Indicators

Outcome indicators address quality of service and program results. The former indicates how well services are being delivered, and the latter indicates if the right services are being delivered. Effectiveness, when used, refers to the quality of results.

One area of SEA measurement in which progress has been made is the measurement of the quality of services. Quality control indicators include measures of timeliness and accuracy. Specific indicators that should be considered for reporting include:

- Percentage of total applications processed within 45 days.
- Percentage of cases with a redetermination within 6 months.
- Percentage of fair hearing (appeal) decisions made within 90 days.
- Eligibility error rates.
- Agency case accuracy rates.
- Client case accuracy rates.
- Overpayments recovered as a percentage of overpayments identified during the fiscal year.

Eligibility errors include overpayments and payments to ineligibles (positive errors) as well as underpayments and nonpayment to eligibles (negative errors). Agency case accuracy rates indicate how accurate caseworkers have been when making case decisions. Client accuracy rates indicate how accurate clients have been when providing information.

The above measures are recommended for two reasons. Most importantly, they allow the user to gain an idea of how well the program is being administered. Promptness and accuracy (particularly above what is federally required) are excellent indicators of programs that are operated well.

A second reason for reporting these indicators is cost-effectiveness. The indicators are currently required by the federal government for the AFDC program. Thus, the information is already collected and it should be relatively easy and inexpensive to publish it for wider use. States and counties especially need to report these indicators in their areas, since the U.S. DHHS no longer publishes its annual *Profiles of Performance.*

Effectiveness (quality of results) indicators are the most lacking in current reporting. SEA indicators should be tied to program objectives. As defined above, accuracy, promptness, and efficiency are secondary objectives of most cash assistance programs. The primary objective is to ensure a basic standard of living for all those eligible for assistance. Therefore, governments should measure and report their achievement of this objective. This means that governments not only should report the percentage of underpayments (as indicated by negative payment error rates), but should attempt to indicate their efforts to ensure payment to all eligible persons. Thus, governments should also present indicators that report the *number of potential recipients* discouraged from applying or completing the application process due to lines, procedures, waiting periods, and hostile or unhelpful workers.

Attention to effectiveness indicators is especially important if other indicators are receiving increased attention. The current emphasis on preventing overpayments sets workers up to err on the side of stringency. If agencies are evaluated only on the basis of their accuracy and efficiency when processing clients, this may reduce motivation to assist applicants through the process. For this reason, it is recommended that agencies attempt to measure the degree of difficulty of the application process. This could be measured by a survey of applicants or independent evaluation of the application process. Measuring the percentage of initial applicants who complete the process (were denied or given assistance) could serve as another indicator of the difficulty of the application process. Both of these indicators are proposed as experimental indicators and have clear drawbacks; neither of the indicators includes the number of potentially eligible recipients who never apply. However, they could serve as initial indicators of governments' efforts to ensure that all eligible applicants receive assistance. It should be recognized that all SEA indicators are subject to refinement and improvement.

Governments should also try to determine if those receiving assistance actually have enough resources to achieve a basic subsistance level, another primary objective of the program. Factors that indicate a basic standard of living may include health, housing, and existence *not below* the poverty line. Clearly these indicators are subjective, and governments will have to decide where to "draw the line." These indicators are limited by the fact that the provision of resources and assistance at an adequate level does not mean that the recipients will achieve a basic level of subsistance. This is because recipients have discretion in spending resources and may allocate resources to items not contributing to subsistance level. Nevertheless, these types of indicators are essential for assessing whether the primary objective of public assistance is being achieved. Governments should consider a random survey of recipients to get an indication of their standard of living.

A final effectiveness measure would be to indicate whether assistance programs are helping recipients to gain or regain self-sufficiency, a secondary objective of most programs. Self-sufficiency cannot be measured simply by counting the number of cases referred to work programs or the number of cases closed. If recipients gain employment at an inadequate wage, self-sufficiency may be illusory. Thus, in addition to "number of grants reduced due to employment," it is recommended that agencies measure the number of grants increased that had been reduced due to employment, as well as the percentage of cases that are reopened within one to two years.

To summarize, the following effectiveness indicators should be considered for regular reporting:

- Negative case accuracy rate.
- Degree of difficulty of the application process.
- Percentage of initial applicants who complete the application process.
- Percentage of surveyed recipients who meet predetermined physical health levels.
- Percentage of surveyed recipients who live in adequate housing.
- Percentage of surveyed recipients who do not live below the poverty line.
- Percentage of grants reduced due to employment.
- Percentage of grants increased that had been reduced due to employment.
- Recidivism rate, i.e., percentage of cases reopened within one year.
- Percentage of cases not reopened within two years.

Efficiency Indicators

In addition to input, output, and outcome indicators, governments should report on how efficiently cash assistance programs are being operated. There is a distinct difference between quality and efficiency. The former indicates how well activities are performed; the latter indicates at what cost they are performed. The following efficiency indicators should be considered for regular reporting:

- Number of accurate case decisions made per worker.
- Administrative cost per case.
- Staff-hours expended per accurate case action.
- Administrative costs per dollar dispensed.

Both quality and efficiency indicators are important, and a balance must be struck between the two. In other words, if *extreme* care is taken to be 100 percent accurate in case decisions, the timeliness of case activity would suffer, as would efficiency. On the other hand, in order to be as productive as possible, one could give little regard to accuracy, which would surely suffer as a result.

The GAO has recognized the potential trade-off between quality and efficiency: ". . . There may be, and in theory will be, a point at which decreases in payment errors may only be achieved at the expense of productivity. This needs to be watched for and studied."[8] The GAO report goes on to state, however, that "productivity and quality are not incompatible goals. . . . One point should not be emphasized to the detriment of the others, as long has been the case for productivity."[9] The GAO concluded that a "standard, national system for measuring and reporting productivity is needed to emphasize efficiency," just as the nationwide quality control program has encouraged efforts to reduce payment errors.[10] Thus, not only must efficiency be measured and reported, but targets need to be set, and the indicators need to receive national attention equal to that given to quality control.

The efficiency indicators recommended above are an attempt to encourage quantity of output without forsaking quality. Only accurate

---

[8]GAO, *Federal and State Initiatives Needed to Improve Productivity and Reduce Administrative Costs of the Aid to Families with Dependent Children and Food Stamp Programs* (Washington, DC, 1984), p. 16.

[9]Ibid., p. 21.

[10]Ibid., p. 18.

case actions are included in the efficiency ratios of the first and third indicators. This is analogous to removing defective products when counting any organization's output. Furthermore, since accuracy rates are already determined, the indicator would require neither further collection of data nor inordinate amounts of time for computation.

It should be noted that one of the U.S. DHHS efficiency measures—average caseload per worker—is not recommended. This measure is better considered as a workload measure or as explanatory information, since it says nothing about how much output has been produced.

SUMMARY OF INDICATORS

Exhibit 9-1 illustrates the SEA indicators recommended for regular reporting in cash assistance programs. The format should allow for comparison and explanation of SEA data. Of the budget documents reviewed, San Diego County, California, in its 1989–90 Program Budget, came closest to the recommended format. (See Exhibit 9-2.) While not every state and local government is likely to include all of the recommended indicators in a single report, they should be available and accessible to anyone interested, in a variety of reports. If SEA of cash assistance programs is to improve, not only must it be measured, but measurement must be widely reported so that the public can hold government accountable for its performance.

DISAGGREGATION

The principal unit for disaggregation of public assistance SEA data should be geographic. SEA data within states should be disaggregated by county and region to allow for easy and useful comparisons. Since county governments may have more than one public assistance office, the indicators should also be disaggregated by individual office.

A second unit for disaggregation should be differences in caseload. For example, some counties/states have a high percentage of recipients who work part time. Indeed, part-time employment is encouraged to help recipients attain self-sufficiency. However, clients who work require more case activity than nonworking clients; income must be verified continually. Thus, caseworkers with a high number of working clients may

Exhibit 9-1
Recommended SEA Indicators for AFDC and GA Programs*

Indicator	Rationale for Selecting Indicator
Inputs:	
Administrative cost of program (current and constant dollars)	Will provide basic information regarding total resources committed to program; can be used in ratio to determine program efficiency
Total cost—administrative cost plus benefit payments (current and constant dollars)	
Total staff-hours used to operate program	
Outputs:	
Total number of recipients	Can easily be calculated to allow gross comparison over time; can be used in ratio to determine program efficiency
Total amount of assistance provided	
Outcome Indicators:	
Percentage of applications processed within 45 days	Provide information as to how well service is being delivered; give an idea of whether secondary objectives of programs are being achieved; use of indicators is also cost-effective, since they are already required by the federal government for AFDC program
Percentage of cases redetermined within 6 months	
Percentage of fair hearing appeal decisions made within 90 days	
Positive payment error rates (overpayments)	
Negative payment error rates (underpayments)	
Overpayments recovered as a percentage of overpayments identified during the fiscal year	
Negative case accuracy rate	
Degree of difficulty of the application process	Provide information regarding the effectiveness of assistance programs in ensuring assistance for all who are eligible
Percentage of initial applicants completing the application process	

Percentage of surveyed who meet predetermined levels of physical health
Percentage of surveyed who live in adequate housing ⎫
Percentage of surveyed who do not live below poverty line ⎬ Provide information on effectiveness of assistance programs in achieving basic standard of living

Percentage of grants reduced due to employment
Percentage of grants increased that had been reduced due to employment ⎫
Percentage of cases reopened within one year ⎬ Provide information regarding the effectiveness of assistance programs in achieving the secondary objective of self-sufficiency
Percentage of cases not reopened within two years

Efficiency Indicators:

Number of accurate case actions processed per worker
Administrative cost per case ⎬ Provide a meaningful assessment of cost of assistance programs relative to accomplishments; will enable more valid comparisons of program cost over time and between jurisdictions
Staff-hours per accurate case action

Administrative costs per dollar dispensed — Provides an indication of administrative cost-effectiveness

Explanatory Data:
Examples are:
  Unemployment rate
  Number of cases per worker
  Number or percentage of working recipients
  Changes in regulations
  Staffing problems

---

*The recommended indicators presented in this exhibit are illustrative. They are intended to serve as a starting point for use in the development of a comprehensive set of SEA indicators for external reporting of an entity's results of operation.

This exhibit does not provide illustrations of indicator disaggregation or of comparison data such as trends, targets, or other comparable entities. Both disaggregation and comparison data are important aspects of SEA reporting. They are discussed in the chapter and in the Overview.

Exhibit 9-2
County of San Diego, Proposed Budget, 1989–90

Program: Aid to Families with Dependent Children **Department: Social Services**

Performance Indicators	1986–87 Actual	1987–88 Actual	1988–89 Actual	1988–89 Budget	1989–90 Budget
Workload (monthly)					
Preapplication	3,758	3,772	3,824	3,484	4,050
Eligibility determination	2,895	2,856	2,749	2,851	2,947
Cases supervised	36,080	39,275	41,830	40,191	45,648
Efficiency					
Cases per eligibility technician	94.8	99.0	106.6	102.7	107.5
Effectiveness					
Percentage of eligibility determinations made within 20 days of application	68%	72.0%	75.5%	80%	80%
Percentage of immediate need determinations made within 1 day of application	85%	78.8%	67.3%	100%	100%
Percentage of benefits paid with no dollar errors	97%	92.0%	95.63%	97%	97%

Source: County of San Diego, Proposed Budget, 1989–90.

Program: Eligibility Review

Department: Social Services

Performance Indicators	1986–87 Actual	1987–88 Actual	1988–89 Actual	1988–89 Budget	1989–90 Budget
Workload (monthly)					
State/county hearing issues	658	708	765.6	770	770
Field investigations completed	56.25	60	96	90	90
Total prevention investigations completed	658	689	757	808	808
Asset match investigations completed	46	37	22	36	36
Quality control audits completed	160	173.4	173.2	192	190
Efficiency					
Appeal issues per staff-year	650	607	680.4	660	660
Investigations per staff-year	450	301	403.8	357	357
Field investigations per staff-year	93	90	88.6	108	108
Total prevention investigations per staff-year	877	722	825	722	722
Asset match investigations per staff-year	137	112	132	144	144
Quality control audits per staff-year	164.1	174.9	177.7	192	190
Effectiveness					
Percentage of appeal issues resolved without hearing	66.2%	83%	87.3%	75%	75%
Dollars saved due to fraud prevention program (monthly)	$174,395	$155,493	$178,000	$155,000	$178,000
Overpaid dollars identified for collection by overpayment specialist activity (monthly)	$434,864	$489,030	$554,000	$430,000	$600,000
Percentage of state hearing decisions implemented within 30 days of receipt	77.2%	87%	79.6%	90%	90%
Overpayments discovered by asset match (monthly)	$ 73,349	$ 38,732	$ 26,700	$ 35,000	$ 30,000
Dollars saved due to GR fraud prevention (monthly)	N/A	$ 10,696	$ 20,300	$ 21,392	$ 21,392

appear to be less efficient, if staff-hours per accurate case action is used as an indicator. It would therefore be helpful to disaggregate the indicators on the basis of whether or not recipients work.

Another criterion for disaggregation, in the case of AFDC, should be whether programs are state-supervised or state-operated. This type of disaggregation would allow a comparison of whether one type of administration is more efficient/effective than the other. Similarly, in the case of GA, indicators should be disaggregated based on how much authority counties are given in administering their programs.

Other bases for disaggregation should include race/ethnicity of the client, and type of household, such as single-parent or not. This would enable analysis of whether service efforts are related to the type of client being served.

EXPLANATORY DATA

In addition to SEA indicators, governments should report other data that may explain trends in these indicators. Major factors that need to be considered are number and type of incoming cases, the number of cases per caseworker, and key national or local economic influences. For example, the national economic recession of the early 1980s resulted in high unemployment, which in turn increased the number of welfare recipients. Not only did caseworkers have higher caseloads, but they were likely to have more two-parent cases than before. SEA is sometimes affected by external forces beyond the control of the government, and this should be explained.

Another factor that warrants explanation is the percentage of cases in which one of the recipients works. The working recipient requires more of the caseworker's time to verify income and ensure continued eligibility. Likewise, some caseworkers have more responsibility than others to help recipients locate employment. If these factors are not considered, the worker who is actually helping recipients to become more self-sufficient may appear to be less efficient than the worker who is less involved in achieving this important objective.

Governments should also consider explaining federal and state mandates for performance. For example, the federal government has decided that payment error rates for the AFDC program are not to exceed 3 percent. The local government could explain this, and whether it has been achieved.

CONCLUSIONS

A number of SEA indicators have been discussed for public assistance programs. These have all been offered for consideration, refinement, and improvement. Not all need to be reported by any one government in any one report. Governments will need to decide which indicators are appropriate for particular reports.

Governments rightfully may be concerned about the costs of collecting data and reporting SEA indicators. If costs are exorbitant, collection and reporting simply may not be feasible. The majority of the indicators discussed above would appear to require minimal extra costs, especially for AFDC programs. Governments already routinely collect input, output, and quality control information. AFDC administrators are required by the federal government to report many of the suggested indicators, and GA administrators commonly collect similar information for their programs.

Clearly, the most problematic indicators, in terms of cost, are the outcome (effectiveness) indicators (which may be why they are most lacking). It has been suggested that governments consider surveying applicants regarding the difficulty of the application process. A survey of recipients' standard of living has also been recommended. It is recognized that these surveys would be an additional expense to government. Creative administrators may be able to offset this expense. One possibility would be to apply for grants to cover the costs; another, to seek the cooperation of a local university in conducting a survey of recipients. It should also be kept in mind that the surveys would not have to be conducted annually. Once baseline data were collected, they could be updated biennially, or even less frequently. The government would still have an indication of whether the primary objective of its program was being achieved, and whether it improved or deteriorated over time. This knowledge would seem to be worth some extra effort and costs.

10. Public Health

Vivian L. Carpenter and John B. Waller, Jr., Wayne State University
Linda Ruchala, Indiana University

	Page
Introduction	224
Scope	224
Goals and Objectives of Public Health Programs	225
Recommendations	226
Chronic Disease	227
Output (Process) Measures	227
Outcome Measures	227
Efficiency Measures	230
Sexually Transmitted Diseases (STD)	231
Development of AIDS SEA Measures	231
Maternal and Child Health (MCH) Care	234
Output (Process) Measures	234
Outcome Measures	235
Efficiency Measures	235
Control of Stress and Violent Behavior	240
Output (Process) Measures	240
Outcome Measures	240
Other Reporting Issues	241
Disaggregation	241
Explanatory Data	241
Comparison Information	243
Costs and Feasibility	244
Conclusions	244

INTRODUCTION

The primary objective of this chapter is to consider the potential for reporting service efforts and accomplishments (SEA) information by public health agencies in financial reports and other external documents. This chapter includes an overview of the public health service area and provides recommendations on reporting SEA data by public health agencies.

The provision of public health services is a rapidly growing and diverse responsibility of many state and local governments. From 1983 to 1986, state and local government expenditures on public health programs increased 40 percent to more than $9.4 billion.[1] Two national initiatives are currently under way to help public health agencies focus their resources on high-priority health problems and assess their performance. These projects are the Model Standards project and the federally sponsored Objectives for the Nation project.

The Model Standards project was organized in 1977 as a collaborative effort involving public health experts from the American Public Health Association (APHA), the Association of State and Territorial Health Officers (ASTHO), the National Association of County Health Officials (NACHO), the U.S. Conference of City Health Officers (USCCHO), and the U.S. Public Health Service. Reports were issued in 1979 and 1985.

The development of SEA measures for public health agencies is also being influenced by the 1990 *Objectives for the Nation,* which identifies public health programs targeted for special attention by the U.S. Surgeon General.[2] The *Objectives* document is the result of a federal government mandate to promote and evaluate key preventive community public health programs.

Scope

The 1990 *Objectives* report identifies 15 public health program priorities and the Model Standards project has identified more than 40 major public health programs. Because it was not possible for our project to consider all programs in detail, we focused on the following four areas,

---

[1] Public Health Foundation, *Public Health Agencies 1988: An Inventory of Programs and Block Grant Expenditures* (Washington, DC, 1988).

[2] U.S. Department of Health and Human Services, *Promoting Health/Preventing Disease: Objectives for the Nation* (Washington, DC: U.S. Government Printing Office, 1980).

which encompass many of the program priorities established in the *Objectives* report: (1) chronic diseases, (2) sexually transmitted diseases, (3) maternal and child health care, and (4) control of stress and violent behavior.

Goals and Objectives of Public Health Programs

The traditional goals of public health have included pursuing the optimal health status obtainable for the populations served and correcting, to the extent possible, the health problems that impinge upon the physical, social, and mental well-being of the community.

The chronic disease program's goal is to prevent and control the effects of irreversible pathological alterations in the body which often damage increasing amounts of body tissue.[3] Chronic diseases normally require long-term care and often result in costly medical treatments. Most chronic diseases are characterized by periods of recurrence and remission. Because there are no cures for most chronic diseases, the treatment goal is control of the progression of the disease. Examples of chronic diseases are: arthritis, cardiovascular disease, cancer, dementia, diabetes, epilepsy, and hearing impairments. Chronic disease programs include screening, prevention services, and rehabilitative services.

The goal of the sexually transmitted diseases (STD) program is to reduce infectious disease "spread by transfer of infectious organisms from person to person during sexual contact."[4] Acquired immunodeficiency syndrome (AIDS) is generally considered an STD, although transmission can occur through hypodermic needle sharing and blood transfusions. The STD program provides the following services: screening, diagnosis, treatment, patient education, and public information.

The goal of the maternal and child health (MCH) program is to improve the health of mothers and their children. Specific program objectives are to reduce maternal mortality rate, infant mortality rate, and growth retardation due to dietary inadequacies and substance abuse, to reduce the incidence of childhood preventable diseases, and to prevent birth defects. MCH services include prenatal care services, immunization, nutrition education, and routine child health examinations.

---

[3] Toba S. Kerson with Lawrence A. Kerson, *Understanding Chronic Illness: The Medical and Psychosocial Dimensions of Nine Diseases* (New York: The Free Press, 1985).

[4] U.S. Department of Health and Human Services, *Promoting Health,* p. 25.

The final area of focus involves a new public health goal: the control of stress and violent behavior. The U.S. Surgeon General has recognized stress and violence as important factors contributing to premature death and disability in this country. Therefore, there is a need for public health intervention with a focus on reducing mortality and morbidity rates associated with stress, abuse, and violence. The control of stress and violent behavior program seeks to reduce the number of stress-related deaths and disability cases due to homicides, assault, child abuse, spouse abuse, abuse of older persons, and stress-related diseases. The control of stress and violent behavior program services include stress management education, parenting education, crisis intervention, abuse investigation, and emergency placement services.

The four areas of focus represent important community health programs. The areas of focus were selected to represent a broad mixture of public health agency experience with service provision and reporting SEA measures.

RECOMMENDATIONS

This section contains recommendations on SEA indicators for each of the four program areas that we believe are useful in stimulating debate and experimentation with reporting SEA data among interested public health administrators and elected officials. Recommended SEA measures are classified into three groups, corresponding to the program objectives recognized by the Centers for Disease Control (CDC) of the U.S. Department of Health and Human Services. Recommended SEA indicators are classified based on the CDC recommendations, as well as input, output, outcome, and explanatory information. CDC terms are placed in parentheses where applicable.

The CDC makes several recommendations for the development of program objectives. First, outcome objectives are designed to measure changes in health status achieved (e.g., reducing morbidity or mortality) over a specified period of time or for a specific target group. Second, impact objectives outline more immediate and specific program activities that are necessary for achieving outcome improvements. Third, process (output) objectives are designed to measure the amount of services provided.

For all program areas the level of expenditure broken down by program or activity is recommended as an input measure to provide an indication of resources used in service delivery. In addition, some efficiency measures have been recommended for programs where their usefulness in evaluating the financial management of programs is clear. Experts in the field suggested that problems with the validity and reliability of cost per unit of service data limit the usefulness of these measures, so care should be taken in their use.

In recommending SEA measures, we considered several factors. These factors include availability of data, experience in collecting the data and frequency of occurrence in practice, validity of the measure, and usefulness to users of the report.

Chronic Disease

Recommended SEA measures for the chronic disease program are contained in Exhibit 10-1. A wide variety of potential SEA indicators exist for this program because of the large number of diseases that are classified as chronic and the range of services and intervention programs it includes.

Output (Process) Measures

Several activity type measures that can be tied to the accomplishment of program objectives—such as percent of target population screened for a specific chronic disease, percent of target population and health care providers participating in training and education programs, and average worker-hours per client—are recommended as output (process) measures.

Outcome Measures

Two types of data are leading candidates for use as SEA outcome measures: mortality and morbidity data. Mortality data is recommended as an SEA outcome measure because it is readily available, has low cost, has benchmark data, and is widely accepted as an outcome measure. Morbidity data was selected because of its wide acceptance as an outcome measure.

The validity of morbidity comparisons may be compromised because of the lack of uniform reporting methods among state governments: Some conduct statistically valid surveys to gather morbidity data, others do not.

Generally, mortality data has a high degree of validity, is measurable, and is available down to the census tract level. There are, however, limi-

Exhibit 10-1
Recommended SEA Indicators for Chronic Disease*

Indicator	Rationale for Selecting Indicator
Inputs:	
Expenditures (may be broken out by program or activity) in current and constant dollars	Measure of resources used to provide services
Output (Process):	
Number of Patients Treated	Widely accepted measures used by public health professionals to measure program outputs
Number of Persons Screened	
Number Participating in Education Programs	
Number of Clients/Training Sessions	
Average Worker-Hours per Client	
Percentage of Target Population Served	
Outcome:	
Mortality Rates	Measure of death due to chronic diseases
Morbidity Rates	Indication of prevalence of chronic diseases
Target Group with Controlled Conditions	Indication of program effectiveness
Restricted-Activity Days per Person	Indication of quality of life after onset of chronic disease
Bed-Disability Days per Person	
Percentage of Patients (Target Group) with Controlled Conditions	Indication of the accomplishment of short-term program objectives

Efficiency:

Cost of Medical Supplies per Unit — Measure of agency's efficiency in acquisition of supplies

Program Costs/Number of Patients with Controlled Chronic Disease — Indication of agency's costs in achieving each case of controlled chronic disease

Projected Costs Saved/Prevention Program Costs — Indication of agency's efficiency in reducing future public health costs

Program Hours per Controlled Chronic Disease Case — Indication of program hours employed to achieve each case of controlled chronic disease

---

*The recommended indicators presented in this and succeeding exhibits are illustrative. They are intended to serve as a starting point for use in the development of a comprehensive set of SEA indicators for external reporting of an entity's results of operation. This exhibit does not provide illustrations of indicator disaggregation or of comparison data such as trends, targets, or other comparable entities. Both disaggregation and comparison data are important aspects of SEA reporting. They are discussed in the chapter and in the Overview.

tations on its usefulness. First, mortality data may not reflect the impact of current chronic disease prevention programs. Second, many chronic diseases do not reduce life expectancy but do affect the quality of life. Third, care must be used in interpreting long-term trend mortality data since other confounding factors (such as the effects of environmental contaminants and changing lifestyles of the population) may have more influence on the mortality statistics than the chronic disease prevention programs under evaluation.

Since chronic diseases are the leading cause of disability, several outcome measures are recommended to assess the level of disability in the population. Chronic diseases have no cure or have irreversible effects. Therefore, outcome measures that assess the effectiveness of programs in controlling the effects of these diseases are important. For example, hypertension represents a chronic disease that may be controlled through medication, diet, and stress management, but not cured.

Because of confounding factors, we recommend the development of intermediate SEA outcome (impact) measures for chronic disease programs. Intermediate outcome measures should allow assessment of whether or not the program is accomplishing short-term objectives using realistic, measurable, and specific data. Percentage of patients with controlled chronic disease effects after one year in a hypertension program is an example of a very useful chronic disease impact measure.

Efficiency Measures

Two types of efficiency measures are recommended. First, the direct cost of medical supplies is recommended because collection costs are low in relation to the potential benefit of reducing waste and fraud. This measure has a high degree of validity as an efficiency measure for the procurement function of chronic disease programs and benchmark data is available. The cost of medical supplies can be used to assess the allocation of public health monies to medical supplies in relation to other types of expenditures.

If a statistical link can be established between the provision of a particular chronic disease prevention or intervention program and the number of disability days prevented, years of life lost, or number of related chronic disease cases prevented, then a second type of efficiency measure can be developed. This measure requires that the costs of prevention programs be divided by the economic cost savings of projected cases of a specific chronic disease prevented. An example would be the ratio of the projected hospital costs saved due to prevented cases of hypertension-related stroke—based on patients with controlled blood pressure in the program—to the cost of the hypertension control program. For a hypertension program to be efficient in terms of costs, this efficiency ratio would have to be greater than one.

Sexually Transmitted Diseases (STD)

The CDC has been providing leadership in the development of SEA measures for the STD program. The recommended output (process), outcome, and efficiency indicators are presented in Exhibit 10-2.

The incidence of STD cases by type is recommended as an outcome measure because of its frequent use in practice. This measure also provides the best available indicator of the population's health status as far as STD is concerned. The output measures recommended were selected because of their frequency in practice or because they were identified in the *Model Standards Data Benchmark Workbook.*

The STD program has developed SEA measures based on projected economic savings of STD prevention or intervention programs. Projected economic savings can be used as both an output (process) and outcome (impact) SEA measure. The projected economic savings of STD programs, derived from an estimate of the cases prevented divided by the program costs, is recommended as an SEA efficiency measure.

Development of AIDS SEA Measures

AIDS is classified as an STD by most health departments even though it can be transmitted by means other than sexual contact. However, AIDS has several features that distinguish it from other STDs. First, there is no cure for AIDS; it appears to be a fatal disease. Second, sexual contact is only one means through which the disease can be acquired. Third, once an individual is infected with the HIV virus, it takes an average of eight years to develop symptoms significant enough for most doctors to diagnose the case as AIDS.

The collection of incidence data on AIDS is also complicated by different state regulatory environments, difficulties in diagnosis, and the social stigma and fear associated with AIDS.

Presently two statistics are leading candidates for AIDS SEA outcome measures: reported cases of AIDS and reported deaths from AIDS. We must emphasize that both of these SEA measures have serious measurement problems. The CDC argues that reported cases of, and deaths from, AIDS are not appropriate SEA indicators because they

Exhibit 10-2
Recommended SEA Indicators for Sexually Transmitted Diseases*

Indicator	Rationale for Selecting Indicator
Inputs:	
Expenditures (may be broken out by program or activity) in current and constant dollars	Measure of resources used to provide services
Output (Process):	
Number of Persons Screened	Widely reported measures in practice that provide an indication of program outputs
Number of Screened Infected Patients That Were Treated and Time Factors Related to Service Delivery	
Number of Interviewing/Counseling Sessions Assigned per Worker with Time Factors Related to Service Delivery	
Number of Investigations Completed and Time Factors Related to Service Delivery	
Outcome:	
Incidence Data by Type of STD	Widely reported measure, provides an indication of spread of STDs
Projected Number of STD Cases Prevented	Indication of the accomplishment of short-term objectives
Percentage of Positive Gonorrhea Cultures for Females Who Return for Test of Cure	

Efficiency:

Economic Savings from Prevented Cases/Program Costs — Indication of the agency's efficiency in reducing the economic impact of STD cases

Education and Counseling Hours/STD Cases — Commonly reported efficiency measure that provides an indication of efficiency in reported cases due to outreach efforts

Cost per Patient or Visit — Indication of the efficiency of patient treatment operations

---

*The recommended indicators presented in this and succeeding exhibits are illustrative. They are intended to serve as a starting point for use in the development of a comprehensive set of SEA indicators for external reporting of an entity's results of operation. This exhibit does not provide illustrations of indicator disaggregation or of comparison data such as trends, targets, or other comparable entities. Both disaggregation and comparison data are important aspects of SEA reporting. They are discussed in the chapter and in the Overview.

measure success in recognizing the AIDS threat eight years ago and not how well AIDS programs are performing currently. Clearly, reported AIDS cases and deaths cannot be used as outcome (impact) SEA measures. However, we believe that reported AIDS cases and deaths should be used as SEA measures because over time they are indicators of the accomplishment of long-term program objectives and, therefore, do represent valid long-term outcome measures. Since reported AIDS cases and deaths are the best data available and provide important information on the spread of AIDS, we recommend that they be used in a time trend with clear management explanations.

Recommended SEA measures for the AIDS program are contained in Exhibit 10-3. Reported AIDS cases and deaths are recommended as outcome measures because of their frequency in practice and their relation to accomplishment of program objectives. Over time, the number of reported cases and deaths from AIDS should become a valid measure of program accomplishment. The prevalence of the HIV virus in the population based on statistically valid survey methods is also recommended as an outcome measure, although we recognize that this may not be politically feasible in many communities. However, this measure is recommended because it is the only way to accurately monitor the spread of AIDS.

Recommendations for the reporting of outcome and output measures were based on interviews with CDC and a review of CDC documents. Because of the difficulty in developing valid outcome measures for the AIDS program, we recommend that AIDS SEA reports rely primarily on output (process) measures.

Maternal and Child Health (MCH) Care

Maternal and child health (MCH) care may be the most advanced public health program in terms of current reporting of SEA data. Most public health agencies are ready to report MCH program SEA data. Recommended SEA measures are presented in Exhibit 10-4.

Output (Process) Measures

Several process measures that relate to attainment of specific MCH program objectives are recommended. These measures were selected based upon their frequent use in practice and their validity as a measure of service effort. For example, the number of women receiving medical care in the first trimester of pregnancy is an accepted output (process) measure for MCH programs.

Outcome Measures

The infant mortality rate is recommended as an outcome SEA measure for the MCH program because it is widely used in practice, is easy to measure, is readily available down to the census tract level, and is an indicator of the accomplishment of a primary program objective. However, this can be a very unstable statistic when the service population is very small.[5] Therefore, infant mortality rate may only be a useful outcome SEA statistic for agencies that serve large populations.[6] Despite potential validity problems for small service populations, we recommend infant mortality rates, low birth-weight rates, childhood death rates, and maternal death rates as SEA outcome measures for the MCH program.

Although the use of intermediate SEA outcome (impact) measures in the MCH program is not common, we selected several which appear to have a high degree of validity in assessing short-term program accomplishments. Such measures are especially useful when they capture the effectiveness of specific intervention programs. For example, the percentage of teenage pregnancies among those participating in sex education programs compared to baseline teen pregnancy rates provides an indication of whether these programs are effective in reaching their audience.

Efficiency Measures

Three SEA efficiency measures are recommended to help monitor the management of MCH programs: cost per unit of supplement, cost per immunization, and number of premature deaths/number of patients. These efficiency measures are selected because they are not sensitive to the staff patterns used by the agencies or the way service provision is organized (e.g., the use of nurse practitioners versus nurses' aides, emphasis on home visits, etc.).

---

[5]Rita Zemach, "Comments on 'State Trends in Infant Mortality,'" *American Journal of Public Health* (vol. 76, no. 6, June 1986), p. 688.

[6]J. C. Kleinman, "State Trends in Infant Mortality, 1968–83," *American Journal of Public Health* (vol. 76, no. 6, June 1986), pp. 681–687.

Exhibit 10-3
Recommended SEA Indicators for Sexually Transmitted Diseases—AIDS*

Indicator	Rationale for Selecting Indicator
Inputs:	
Expenditures (may be broken out by program or activity) in current and constant dollars	Measure of resources used to provide services
Output (Process):	
Number of AIDS Antibody Tests Given	
Number of AIDS Educational Seminars	
Number of AIDS Cases Treated	Indication of AIDS prevention and treatment program outputs
Number of True/False Positive Results for AIDS	
Community Plan to Control the Spread of AIDS	
Measure of Attitudes of the Target Population Based on Surveys	
Outcome:	
Reported AIDS Cases and Deaths	Widely reported measure that may be legally required in some states
Percentage of Population or Number of Persons with the HIV Virus Based on Statistically Valid Sample Survey Methods	Indication of the prevalence of the HIV virus
Rate of Newborn Babies Testing Positive for HIV Virus	Indication of spreading of the HIV virus

Percentage of Target Population That Has Attended AIDS Workshops That Report a Change in Risky Behavior

Level of AIDS Knowledge in Population Based on Survey Data

Percentage of Population That Has Changed Risky Behavior, Based on Survey Data

} To provide an indication of the accomplishment of short-term objectives

---

*The recommended indicators presented in this and succeeding exhibits are illustrative. They are intended to serve as a starting point for use in the development of a comprehensive set of SEA indicators for external reporting of an entity's results of operation. This exhibit does not provide illustrations of indicator disaggregation or of comparison data such as trends, targets, or other comparable entities. Both disaggregation and comparison data are important aspects of SEA reporting. They are discussed in the chapter and in the Overview.

Exhibit 10-4
Recommended SEA Indicators for Maternal and Child Health (MCH) Care*

Indicator	Rationale for Selecting Indicator
Inputs:	
Expenditures (may be broken out by program or activity) in current and constant dollars	Measure of resources used to provide services
Output (Process):	
Number of Clients Admitted to MCH Program	
Number of Clinic Visits per Month	
Number of Prenatal and Postnatal Mothers Contacted	Widely reported measures that provide an indication of MCH program outputs
Number of Persons Receiving Family Planning Services	
Number of Pregnant Women Receiving Care in First Trimester	
Outcome:	
Infant Mortality Rate	
Low Birth-Weight Rates	
Teenage Pregnancy Rate	
Rate of Lead Poisoning Cases	Widely accepted measures used by public health officials to measure MCH program outcomes
Reported Cases of Preventable Diseases in Children	
Maternal Death Rates	
Death Rates for Children	

Number of Clients Authorized to Be Served and Actually Served by WIC	
Percentage of Low Birth-Weight Babies in Target Population	Widely reported measures by MCH program to provide indicators of the accomplishment of short-term MCH program objectives
Percentage of Teenage Pregnancies among Those Participating in Educational or Training Programs	
Projected Low Birth-Weight Births Prevented	
Projected Infant Deaths Prevented	
Cases of Measles Prevented	

Efficiency:

Cost per Immunization	Indication of the agency's efficiency in providing immunizations
Cost of WIC Supplements per Unit	Indication of the agency's efficiency in purchasing WIC supplements
Number of Premature Births/Number of Patients	Indication of the agency's efficiency in reducing premature births
Projected Health Care Costs Saved through Routine Check-ups/Costs of Routine Check-ups	Indication of agency's efficiency in reducing future health care costs

---

*The recommended indicators presented in this and succeeding exhibits are illustrative. They are intended to serve as a starting point for use in the development of a comprehensive set of SEA indicators for external reporting of an entity's results of operation. This exhibit does not provide illustrations of indicator disaggregation or of comparison data such as trends, targets, or other comparable entities. Both disaggregation and comparison data are important aspects of SEA reporting. They are discussed in the chapter and in the Overview.

Control of Stress and Violent Behavior

The medical literature is starting to document the relationship between stress, diet, health, and death. Public health programs involving control of stress and violent behavior have been given priority status in 1990 *Objectives for the Nation.* Recommended SEA measures for the control of stress and violent behavior program are contained in Exhibit 10-5.

Output (Process) Measures

Very little reporting of SEA data in this area was found in practice, in large part because few programs have been implemented. Until public health agencies establish control of stress and violent behavior as a priority, reporting of SEA measures is unlikely. Given the few agencies concerned with this priority, we conclude that most public health agencies are not ready to begin reporting control of stress and violent behavior SEA data. The recommended output (process) measures were selected because they have been previously reported and provide an indication of program effort.

Outcome Measures

Child abuse and other forms of family violence, which pose difficult measurement problems, continue to threaten the physical and mental health of many Americans. Even though the actual number of children abused or neglected is expected to be greater than the number of cases reported, we recommend the number of reported criminal child-abuse cases as an outcome SEA measure because of its availability and usefulness as an indicator of program effectiveness. While information about child abuse and neglect may not be easily captured through reported incidence figures, violence resulting in death from homicide, suicide, or legal intervention is available and can be disaggregated down to the census tract level.

We further recommend the use of crime and judiciary statistics as outcome SEA measures because they are available and are indicators of the accomplishment of program objectives related to control of violent behavior.

Intermediate SEA outcome (impact) indicators are recommended based on the relevance of the measure in assessing the accomplishment of short-term objectives for the control of stress and violence program. For example, the percentage of patients with controlled blood pressure after participating in stress management training programs is recommended as an impact measure.

OTHER REPORTING ISSUES

Disaggregation

We recommend disaggregating SEA data by various relevant demographic and socioeconomic factors. The disaggregation of SEA measures should be by age, race/ethnicity, income, geographic area, and other program-relevant factors.

There are two major reasons for this recommendation. First, public health agencies often target certain subpopulations for specified programs to increase the efficiency of service provision. Second, certain public health problems disproportionately affect certain age, ethnic, or income groups. Unless measurements are disaggregated to focus on those "high-risk" populations, the real health status of those groups may be obscured by "averaging" those subpopulations in with lower risk groups.

The major inhibiting factor in using SEA data in assessing the performance of health departments is the high cost of developing disaggregated measures at the state and local levels for some types of SEA measures. Much of the national data related to morbidity is based on national surveys that were not designed to provide reliable estimates of the prevalence of disease at the state and local levels of government. Random surveys of the population may be very expensive, especially if they are designed to develop statistically valid estimates for specific geographic regions and subgroups in the population.

Explanatory Data

The explanatory section of SEA reports should clearly indicate that the SEA measurements are in an early stage of development and will be refined as experience dictates. Since the incidence of any disease or condition can be influenced by a variety of factors not directly related to the effectiveness of a particular public health program, we recommend that SEA indicators be plotted over time, with some narrative in-

Exhibit 10-5
Recommended SEA Indicators for Control of Stress and Violent Behavior*

Indicator	Rationale for Selecting Indicator
Inputs:	
Expenditures (may be broken out by program or activity) in current and constant dollars	To provide a measure of resources used to provide services
Output (Process):	
Number of Rape Counseling Hours	To provide an indication of program outputs related to training and counseling sessions that are commonly used interventions in the control of stress and violent behavior
Percentage of Target Population in Stress Management Training and Programs	
Number of Child Abuse Training and Counseling Sessions	
Outcome:	
Suicide Death Rates, 15–24 Years of Age	Readily available statistics that can be used to provide an indication of health and death outcomes related to stress and/or violent behavior
Death Rates from Homicide and Legal Intervention	
Incidence of Hypertension	
Reported Rape Cases	
Violent Crime Rates	
Number or Rate of Permanent Disability Cases Due to Violence	
Reported Child Abuse Cases	
Patients with Controlled Blood Pressures Participating in Stress Management Training Sessions	To provide an indication of the accomplishment of short-term program objectives related to control of stress and violent behavior
Potential Years of Life Saved Due to Intervention Programs	

*The recommended indicators presented in this and succeeding exhibits are illustrative. They are intended to serve as a starting point for use in the development of a comprehensive set of SEA indicators for external reporting of an entity's results of operation.

This exhibit does not provide illustrations of indicator disaggregation or of comparison data such as trends, targets, or other comparable entities. Both disaggregation and comparison data are important aspects of SEA reporting. They are discussed in the chapter and in the Overview.

terpretation provided by program managers. It is unlikely that external readers will be able to understand appropriately the recommended SEA measures without such an interpretation.

To further assist external readers, we recommend that behavioral risk factors be included in SEA reports of state and local public health agencies. Behavioral risk factors associated with the prevention of premature disability and death include: the prevalence and treatment of hypertension, seatbelt use, smoking habits, alcohol and drug use, weight, and physical lifestyle.

Since health departments may not have control over all programs and conditions that affect their community's health, we recommend explaining the organizational and responsibility structures so that external readers can assess the agency's responsibility for specific interventions and programs. For example, few health departments have control over public water systems, yet many diseases, including hepatitis, can be transmitted through these systems.[7] Also, explanations regarding important adverse natural and environmental conditions (e.g., flood plains, water contamination, air pollution, etc.) or special service-delivery problems (e.g., large rural areas or island populations) should be included as explanatory data.

Comparison Information

Comparing SEA measures across jurisdictions may be difficult for several reasons. First, there may be insufficient benchmark data to provide a frame of reference for making comparisons. Second, the organization of state and local health departments differs from state to state and local agency to local agency. In addition, some health departments may have overlapping geographic responsibilities for the delivery of public health services. Third, reporting standards may vary even among related jurisdictions because all departments do not produce the required data in all categories and a lack of uniformity exists in program definitions. Differences in organizational structure, service delivery, and availability of benchmark data may make it difficult to make meaningful comparisons with SEA data across geographic areas.

Although there are several reasons why SEA measures should not be used to make assessments across jurisdictions, there are still valid comparisons that can be made. For example, comparisons can be made to na-

---

[7]G. Berg et al., *Viruses in Water* (Washington, DC: American Public Health Association, Inc., 1976).

tional objectives, state objectives, and/or local objectives. Moreover, comparisons can be made to disaggregated outcome measures and over time. SEA data disaggregated by race and gender can provide useful comparative information. These comparisons are useful in assessing the health status of a community in relation to the nation and may indicate significant health challenges for a particular health agency. In addition, comparisons of outcome measures, such as infant mortality rates by health districts within a state, may be useful in assessing the need for services and hence the targeting of state resources.

Costs and Feasibility

The costs associated with implementation of the recommendations contained in this chapter will be affected by an agency's current level of sophistication in data collection and the quality of reports desired. Large public health agencies, such as state governments, may already have access to up-to-date computer technology which could reduce the costs associated with producing SEA reports.

For local health departments that do not have a high level of computer capability, the relative costs of data collection and report preparation could be high. The current state of an agency's Management Information System is a critical variable in determining the costs of implementing recommendations contained in this chapter. In the near future, state and local health departments may be assisted in their efforts to establish Management Information System capabilities by a project under development at the CDC. The CDC is developing an on-line public health data base that will provide epidemiological data down to the county level of government.

CONCLUSIONS

We believe that public health represents an excellent area for experimentation in SEA measure development and reporting. Several national projects are currently under way to improve the ability of public health agencies to assess their own performance. Public health associations are also committed to improving the ability of their members to produce SEA data. Furthermore, the public health area has programs where careful attention has already been and is being given to the development of SEA measures. Moreover, the computer technology enabling the reporting of data has been greatly improved. All of these conditions have created an environment that should foster the reporting of SEA data for selected public health programs.

With the major challenges facing public health, both public health professionals and the public must be provided with the information necessary to evaluate the allocation of public health monies and the effectiveness of public health programs.

11. Road Maintenance

William A. Hyman and Joan A. Allen, The Urban Institute

Page

Introduction and Scope	248
Maintenance Defined	249
Objectives of Road Maintenance	250
Methodology	250
Recommended Indicators	251
Inputs	252
Outputs	253
Measures of Quality/Outcomes	253
Measures of Efficiency	255
Other Issues	256
Disaggregation	256
Comparison Information	257
Explanatory Data	261
Verifiability of Statistics Produced by Indicators	262

INTRODUCTION AND SCOPE

All levels of government combined spend approximately $65 billion annually on highways, including $17 billion on maintenance and operations.[1] A large but not readily determinable amount of additional funds is spent on local street maintenance. Most transportation agencies' maintenance budgets are stretched thin, and they find it imperative to use their maintenance funds wisely.

It is generally agreed that roads should be maintained to a standard of reasonable quality over their useful lives rather than be allowed to wear out prematurely. A total lack of, or deferral of, maintenance usually results in significant increases in long-run total costs to both agencies and users. Maintenance (including repairs) retards or offsets the deteriorating effects of weather, aging, traffic, wheel loads, and vegetative growth. It also helps overcome damage, vandalism, failure of materials, and shortcomings in pavement design and construction.

Many agencies have implemented maintenance management systems or pavement management systems in order to assist them in allocating maintenance funds more efficiently and effectively. These systems, if well designed, offer significantly improved data on current road conditions and maintenance histories and result in more productive use of scarce funds, labor, material, and equipment. Enhanced financial accounting systems also provide information that can be used to assess the efficacy of road maintenance programs.

Most of the information collected and analyzed by road maintenance agencies is used for internal management and reporting purposes. Relatively little progress has been made in developing road maintenance service efforts and accomplishments (SEA) measures for presentation to the public, elected officials, and others outside road maintenance agencies. Even when suitable SEA measures are available internally, it is only the rare and exemplary organization that has also targeted such information toward external audiences.

The purpose of this chapter is to describe road maintenance SEA indicators that should be considered for communication to citizens and elected officials. Here we examine the ways local and state governments measure and report what they get for the dollars they spend on road maintenance: inputs to maintenance operations, the quantity and

---

[1]*The Status of the Nation's Highways: Conditions and Performance,* report of the Secretary of Transportation to the U.S. Congress (Washington, DC: U.S. Government Printing Office, June 1987).

quality of work accomplished, the productivity of maintenance resources, and the efficiency with which road maintenance is carried out. The recommended SEA measures are illustrative of the type most suitable for external communication.

SEA measures aimed at external audiences can be helpful in obtaining increased funding by more objectively demonstrating the maintenance needs of the roadway system to budget officers and elected officials, such as city council members or legislators. When an agency has surpassed its performance or productivity goals, such information can communicate maintenance successes to the public, including improved quality of roads. SEA measures may also help to determine whether it is more efficient to carry out various types of maintenance using agency personnel or by contracting with private firms. In addition, SEA measures tailored for external use improve the communication and interaction between in-house maintenance managers and appointed or public officials who must respond to the public concerns about road maintenance problems. Another valuable use of SEA measures is to provide information to the financial community to help, for example, bond raters assess the fiscal condition of various government jurisdictions.

Maintenance Defined

This chapter is generally confined to maintenance of the traveled way and the roadside and does not include cleaning, traffic signs, or traffic control. It does include some common maintenance activities in urban areas such as curb, gutter, and drainage repairs.

While definitions of maintenance are not clearly differentiated in practice and vary among jurisdictions, it is common to regard maintenance as actions that enable a road to achieve its intended useful life, rather than extend the road's life. Typical maintenance activities include pothole repair, crack filling, patching, applying seal coats, roadside vegetation control, roadway striping, guardrail maintenance, upkeep of roadside rest stops, blading of gravel roads and shoulders, and clearing drainage ditches and pipes of debris.

Some agencies also regard certain low—capital improvement options, such as bituminous resurfacing, as maintenance. The American Association of State Highway and Transportation Officials (AASHTO) defines physical maintenance of the traveled way as the resurfacing of hard surfaces with bituminous material less than three-quarters of an inch thick or replacement of the traveled way in kind for less than 500 continuous feet.[2]

Another way to characterize road maintenance is to distinguish among actions that are demand-responsive, routine, or periodic. Demand-responsive maintenance arises due to a sudden, urgent, or pressing need for maintenance. When pavements suddenly present hazards such as potholes or blowups, a "demand" is created for maintenance or repairs. In many agencies certain maintenance activities are routine, such as crack sealing. Other maintenance may occur periodically, such as blading gravel shoulders.

Objectives of Road Maintenance

The principal objectives of road maintenance are:

1. To provide a smooth, comfortable, expeditious, and safe ride for the public;
2. To reduce such user costs as fuel, repairs, accidents, and travel time;
3. To utilize labor, equipment, and material efficiently; and
4. To ensure that pavement lasts as long as it should, thereby reducing future costs, such as for rehabilitating or reconstructing it.

The widespread availability of powerful computers has resulted in the practical objective of providing the proper type and level of maintenance at the right time in the right location to bring overall maintenance costs to near the minimum.

Methodology

To determine what SEA indicators are used by local and state governments and how widely they are reported, we reviewed approximately 36 state budgets and 30 city and county budgets or performance documents. We also reviewed the literature pertaining to road maintenance

---

[2]American Association of State Highway and Transportation Officials, *AASHTO Maintenance Manual 1987* (Washington, DC: AASHTO, 1987).

practices, including information on maintenance and pavement management systems. From these materials, we identified jurisdictions that collected and reported service efforts, efficiency, and quality data.[3]

We identified several state and local governments that seemed to have made substantial progress in the identification and use of SEA indicators. We interviewed officials of 11 state and local governments in order to understand more fully the collection, use, and reporting of those indicators.

RECOMMENDED INDICATORS

The vast majority of states and large numbers of counties and cities collect data on the type and amount of work accomplished; funds expended for labor, equipment, and material; labor hours; equipment hours; material used by type and amount; and equipment types or classes used.

Most states have developed production standards (e.g., daily rates of accomplishment for different types of maintenance work) as part of performance standards that are intended to ensure uniform quality of each type of maintenance activity.[4]

---

[3]See, for example:

City of Cincinnati, *The Public Works Story,* 4th ed., January 1987.

City of Winston-Salem, North Carolina, *Annual Budget Program 1984–85.*

City of Alexandria, Virginia, *FY 1987 Budget.*

City of Dallas, "General Description of the Street Inventory," memorandum to Councilman Craig Holcomb, November 5, 1986.

City of Dallas Street and Sanitation Services Department, "Street Maintenance Issue Paper," July 26, 1985.

City of Portland, Oregon, "Report by the Office of the City Auditor," February 1988.

Pennsylvania Department of Transportation, "Districts' Parallel Activities to Those in Bureau of Maintenance," quarter ending December 1987.

New York City Department of Transportation, *Street Smart: A Plan to Improve & Equalize Street Smoothness Conditions in New York City,* March 1988.

Mississippi House of Representatives, Legislative Service Office, "Report to the Fiscal Affairs and Government Operations Committee of the Southern Legislative Conference," October 5, 1987, pp. 1–2.

New York State Department of Transportation, "The Pavement Condition of New York's Highways: 1984," December 1984.

[4]Donald R. Anderson, *Maintenance Management Systems,* National Cooperative Highway Research Program Synthesis of Highway Practice, Report 110 (Washington, DC: Transportation Research Board, National Research Council, October 1984).

In addition, many maintenance organizations have developed "level-of-service goals" against which accomplishments can be compared. Level-of-service goals sometimes serve as thresholds for determining when a certain type of maintenance work needs to be accomplished.[5] A particularly useful level-of-service goal is one that says, for example, that no more than 10 percent of the streets should be in "poor" condition, where *poor* is defined in some reasonably objective manner. As long as funding permits, when a street deteriorates into "poor" condition, this signals a maintenance need. Agencies can track the extent to which they are able to achieve level-of-service goals over time. If agencies are falling short of such goals, the shortfall can be used as a basis for requesting additional funding, or the level-of-service goal can be changed to reflect economic and political realities.

All states and a large number of cities and counties already have some type of pavement management system.[6] By early 1993, all states will be required to have a pavement management system acceptable to the Federal Highway Administration.[7] Therefore, current and historical data on pavement condition and distress should be routinely available at the state level and in many local jurisdictions.

Maintenance SEA has many dimensions, but the bottom line is productivity, efficiency, and cost-effectiveness. SEA measures are constructed from information concerning the inputs, outputs, and outcomes of maintenance programs.

The following paragraphs give examples of the types of information that should be used for regular external reporting of road maintenance SEA.

Inputs

The standard inputs to road maintenance should be reported: overall funding; funding by maintenance activity; person-hours; physical quantities of the most common material used, such as asphalt; and the number of different types of equipment that are representative of or account for the bulk of equipment used. Costs of each of the inputs should be reported in proper units and expressed in both current and inflation-adjusted dollars.

---

[5] R. Kulkarni et al., *Maintenance Levels-of-Service Guidelines,* NCHRP Report 223 (Washington, DC: Transportation Research Board, National Research Council, June 1980).

[6] C. L. Monosmith et al., "Pavement Management at the Local Level," briefing document for meeting at Turner Fairbank Highway Research Center, April 8, 1988.

[7] 23 CFR Part 626, FHWA Docket No. 87-16.

Outputs

A road maintenance agency should convey how much work has been performed. Typical measures of outputs are:

- Miles of roads seal-coated.
- Number of potholes repaired (or tons of premix applied).
- Miles of curb/gutter/sidewalk replaced.
- Number of street utility cuts repaired.
- Miles of roadway striping.

These measures could be strengthened significantly if information on accomplishments were compared to the total need or the goal for the year. Better measures of output would be:

- Percentage of roads seal-coated out of total mileage requiring such work.
- Actual pothole repairs in comparison to planned pothole repairs.

Accomplishment should include preventive maintenance. Although what constitutes preventive maintenance is not generalizable from one agency to another, maintenance managers usually hold strong convictions concerning which type of maintenance can avoid or postpone more costly future actions.

The time period for which output measures apply should be clearly reported. Outputs reported in budget documents, budget requests, or reports aimed at the public are likely to be expressed in annual terms. Daily rates of accomplishment could be reported, but most agencies regard these as productivity figures rather than achievements of the maintenance organization.

Governments should overcome the great temptation to use only measures of output, to the exclusion of quality and efficiency indicators.

Measures of Quality/Outcomes

Road maintenance agencies should provide yearly reports on the condition of their roads to public officials and the public. Among the best indicators are:

- "Rideability" ratings, as determined by machines and/or trained observers.
- Measures of distress that have a direct bearing on maintenance SEA and needs, such as the miles of road that suffer from a specific type of cracking of a given severity and covering a certain percentage of the surface.
- Annual change in sufficiency scales, deficiency scores, or other composite indexes that reflect a variety of factors that contribute to road condition; these include roughness and pavement distress.
- Percentage of roads equaling or exceeding level-of-service goals such as "maintain in satisfactory condition" or "keep the present serviceability rating at 2.5 or above."
- Number of lane miles in poor, satisfactory, good, and excellent condition.

Quality assurance data are becoming more widespread, and more transportation organizations can be expected to administer surveys to assess public perceptions of road conditions and agency performance, although survey data is not without shortcomings. Examples of SEA indicators based on quality control efforts, evaluations of responses to citizen complaints, and well-designed citizen surveys are:

- Average and year-to-year change in response times to maintenance problems reported by the public.
- Miles of short bituminous resurfacing work whose "rideability" rating fell to an unacceptable level within three years compared to the total miles of such work done.
- Ratings from citizen surveys as to the quality of road maintenance practices and results.

Another good measure of outcomes is the average service life of different repairs and types of improvements. Many maintenance activities have service lives that can be well defined, for example, blading of gravel roads or shoulders.[8]

---

[8]K. J. Feighan et al., "Estimation of Service Life and Cost of Routine Maintenance Activities," *Highway Maintenance Planning,* Transportation Research Record 1102 (Washington, DC: Transportation Research Board, National Research Council, 1986), pp. 13–21.

In addition, maintenance will affect the service life of pavement betterment and construction jobs, so that a measure of outcomes is the annual change in service life for such improvements as resurfacing, recycling, and reconstruction.

Another potential measure is the added cost to users of less-than-adequate road conditions. While agencies have attempted to estimate the effect of pavement condition on accidents and vehicle operating costs, this type of analysis is only now becoming widely practical as pavement management systems are being implemented throughout the country.

Measures of Efficiency

Most agencies do not make a distinction between productivity and efficiency indicators, though there is an important difference, and both should be reported. Productivity indicators reflect how well various inputs are used: money, labor, equipment, materials, and time. Unit costs, such as dollars per cubic yard of hand patching, are insufficient productivity measures. They need to be supplemented by separate productivity measures for each nonmonetary input, such as labor, equipment, materials, and time. An example is cubic yards of hand patching per person-hour of labor.

One way some agencies have portrayed productivity is to express the extent to which a certain maintenance activity is performed to production standards (daily production rates). For example, if the production standard is "x miles of chip seal per day," one could report the number of days per year when chip seals were being applied and the number of days the production standard was equaled or exceeded.

Efficiency measures portray the benefits the public receives in terms of better roads given *all* the maintenance resources used. It is recommended that efficiency measures be developed in addition to productivity measures. An example of a practical efficiency measure suitable for public reporting is the number of miles of road in a specific road category maintained in a satisfactory or better condition per dollar of expenditure on the road category. The categories should be defined so that roads are reasonably uniform in important characteristics such as surface type and expected service life.

A refinement of this measure would involve the use of a pavement-condition rating scale: "the number of miles of a category of road maintained with a pavement serviceability index (PSI) of 2.5 or better per dollar of expenditure."

Efficiency and productivity measures should be reported for two or more periods. To reflect accomplishments of the maintenance organization, it is not enough to present a figure that pertains to a single point in time; there must be a way to measure change in SEA.

Measures of productivity and efficiency should be developed not only for the entire maintenance program but also for key components of interest to the public, for example, pothole repairs, surface treatments such as seal coats, and maintenance resurfacing.

These measures are not without their problems. Changes in pavement condition can be attributed to many things besides the productivity of the maintenance organization, and it is important that public officials or others outside the agency understand when unusual weather, rapid increases in truck traffic, or other factors distort measures of efficiency or productivity.

Exhibit 11-1 provides a summary of recommended road maintenance SEA indicators with a rationale for each.

OTHER ISSUES

Disaggregation

SEA indicators should be tailored to the audiences for which they are intended. They should also be sufficiently detailed to be illuminating but not so detailed that the information cannot be quickly absorbed and interpreted. These precepts should affect the level of disaggregation of the data. If the audience consists of public officials, not only is overall information about the maintenance program appropriate, but the data should be broken down according to jurisdictions of concern to public appointees, legislators, and city council and county board members. When addressing the public, maintenance agencies will find that truckers will be most interested in information concerning truck routes while the average motorist is primarily interested in commuter routes and roads and gateways to recreational and vacation areas.

Maintenance accomplishments and efficiency are likely to be related to the type of road and traffic levels (especially truck traffic), and so breakdown by functional class within a jurisdiction is appropriate (e.g., interstate, other freeways and expressways, principal arterials, minor arterials, collectors, and local streets). Disaggregation by type of pavement also conveys useful information, for example, flexible versus rigid pavements. Additional breakdowns by climate and terrain are useful if road maintenance activities are spread over areas with different climate conditions and geography that significantly affect maintenance SEA and road conditions.

In some cases, the most reasonable level of disaggregation may be by maintenance district. This type of breakdown avoids presenting SEA measures subject to misinterpretation because of differences in staffing levels, experience, or time and distance to travel to maintenance sites.

Finding out what legislators and the public most want to know about road maintenance and giving them that type of data or level of disaggregation might produce the best results in terms of interest and support for the government's road maintenance program.

Comparison Information

SEA measures should be compared over time and geographically to national or other sources where appropriate. Comparisons should also be made with regard to level-of-service or other goals, or to standards or objectives set by maintenance managers, other top management, or public officials. In addition, where possible, maintenance performed in-house should be compared to maintenance contracted out.

Year-to-year comparisons are best suited for public presentations. Historical information that spans many years is more useful than short-run changes in road maintenance SEA measures.

Public officials frequently wish to compare the performance of their jurisdiction with others. To make these types of comparisons useful, they need to be performed with care. Comparisons should be made among jurisdictions with similar characteristics, that is, within "peer groups." States frequently compare the condition of their roads with others in the same region. Large cities should look to their populous counterparts in similar climatic regions to make comparisons. Smaller cities in similar circumstances make suitable mates.

Annual accomplishments should be compared against level-of-service goals. For example, if a jurisdiction decides that no more than 10 percent of the street mileage should be in "unsatisfactory condition" at the end of the year, one can compare the number of streets actually in unsatisfactory condition to this goal.

To improve efficiency, an agency's goal might be to achieve a 5 percent reduction in the cost per year to keep the same mileage of roads in "satisfactory condition." At the end of the year, it is possible to com-

Exhibit 11-1
Recommended SEA Indicators for Road Maintenance*

Indicator	Rationale for Selecting Indicator
Inputs:	
Expenditures (current and constant dollars)	
Total	
By activity	Data normally gathered; provides a breakdown by type of resources used
Labor hours	
Quantity of material by type	
Equipment hours by type	
Outputs:	
Pavement miles resurfaced	
Pavement miles seal coated	
Number of potholes repaired (or tons of premix applied)	Measures accomplishments of maintenance program
Miles of curb/gutter/sidewalk replaced	
Number of street utility cuts repaired	
Number of storm inlets repaired/cleaned	
Miles of preventive maintenance	Important measures that require careful definition and typically must be based on engineering judgment
Miles of deferred maintenance (i.e., postponed work)	
Outcomes/Quality:	
Number and percentage of lane miles of road whose condition was either improved or maintained at a satisfactory level (i.e., PSI > 2.5)	Ties maintenance accomplishments to changes in road condition and level-of-service goals
Lane miles in poor, fair, satisfactory, and excellent condition	

Indicator	Description
Road rideability as measured by such devices as Mays Meter	A reliable, repeatable, and commonly used method for measuring roughness
Pavement distress indicators measured by visual condition surveys that relate to maintenance performance (e.g., number of lane miles with severe alligator cracking)	Easy to collect, but considerable engineering knowledge required to correlate with maintenance outcomes, quality, or needs
Percentage of lane miles at acceptable rating level	Relates pavement condition to level-of-service goal
Percentage of roads seal coated out of total requiring such work	Compares accomplishments to needed work
Average quality assurance measures achieved on completion of maintenance resurfacing (e.g., average smoothness)	Measures on-site work quality; quality assurance/control is becoming increasingly important in road work
Year-to-year change in the average service life of different types of maintenance work on different categories of highways	Indicates whether maintenance work is longer lasting
Citizen perceptions of road condition based on public opinion surveys	Measures perceptions of users
Average time to respond to citizen complaints	Measures responsiveness to concerns of road users

*The recommended indicators presented in this exhibit are illustrative. They are intended to serve as a starting point for use in the development of a comprehensive set of SEA indicators for external reporting of an entity's results of operation.

This exhibit does not provide illustrations of indicator disaggregation or of comparison data such as trends, targets, or other comparable entities. Both disaggregation and comparison data are important aspects of SEA reporting. They are discussed in the chapter and in the Overview.

Exhibit 11-1 (continued)

Indicator	Rationale for Selecting Indicator
Efficiency:	
Ratio of inputs to outputs: Average unit dollar cost for labor, equipment, and material for particular types of repair such as average labor-hours per mile of street resurfaced	Measures efficiency in a widely used and easy-to-compute manner
Measures related to outcomes/quality: Number of miles maintained in a "satisfactory" or better condition per dollar of expenditure by road category (i.e., PSI > 2.5)	Relates productivity to changes in road condition and level-of-service goal
Number of miles improved to or maintained at PSI > 2.5 per dollar of expenditure by road category	Relates productivity to quantitative level-of-service goal
Comparison of performance measures for in-house and contract labor by maintenance activity	Helps determine whether different types of maintenance should be contracted out
Explanatory Data:	
Weather (degree days, freeze-thaw cycles)	
Terrain (flat, rolling, mountainous)	
Type of road (flexible, rigid)	Helps explain exceptional or unusual values of performance indicators
Traffic volume and percentage of trucks (or equivalent single-axle loads)	
Average time or distance to work sites	
Lane miles of agency maintenance responsibility by road type	
Pavement age distribution	
Other unusual work circumstances	

pare the change in cost from the previous year to the goal of the 5 percent cost reduction, assuming one is judging cost performance for the same number of miles of road.

It is strongly recommended that maintenance agencies jointly develop level-of-service goals with public officials who have budget responsibility. Other interested members of the public should also participate. In this way, a reasonable consensus can be developed concerning the desirable or acceptable condition in which roads should be maintained. Also, level-of-service goals can serve as a benchmark for the accomplishment of different types of maintenance work.

As the role of the private sector grows in road maintenance, it will be increasingly important to compare the cost of performing maintenance work in-house to contracting with a private firm. Agencies should seek competitive bids to use as a basis for comparison. Where the same type of work is being performed both in-house and by contractors, then inputs, outputs, quality indicators, and measures of productivity and efficiency can potentially be compared.

Explanatory Data

It is important for appropriate explanatory data to be reported along with SEA indicators. Explanatory data are particularly useful in explaining SEA significantly above or below norms a government is using or to account for failure to achieve goals and objectives.

Explanatory data is necessary to make full sense of comparisons. If the "number of lane miles of maintenance resurfacing" declined from one year to the next, what is the reason? Reduced productivity, a drop in funding, inflation in road maintenance costs, an unusually long winter, equipment breakdowns, heavy turnover of personnel, or work on roads with much higher traffic, trucks, and loads? Explanatory data concerning these and other factors, such as terrain and absenteeism, can help explain unusual variations in SEA indicators.

If SEA measures are found to be unreliable year after year because of various extenuating circumstances, then the agency should attempt to devise a new set of measures that will more reliably communicate to external audiences the agency's service efforts and accomplishments.

The governments to which we talked and from which we received budget documents and other literature almost never include explanatory data information when reporting SEA data. This information gap should be filled.

Verifiability of Statistics Produced by Indicators

SEA indicators should be as accurate as possible. Thus, there should be ways to check the data that underlie the SEA measures. Verifiability can be enhanced if:

- Field data is checked for accuracy before entry into the computer.
- The original data concerning inputs—labor, equipment, material, and time—are retrievable for at least three or four years.
- Information for maintenance management systems, pavement management systems, accounting systems, and fiscal reporting use the same data and are fully coordinated. Reporting periods should be identical and, where relevant, accounts should balance to the dollar both within and between systems.
- Ratings of rideability and distress are repeatable. A random sample of road sections should be double-checked periodically to ensure accuracy.
- Road roughness equipment is calibrated to ensure annual and geographical comparisons are meaningful.
- Sample data for SEA measures are statistically sound.

12. Sanitation Collection and Disposal

Marc A. Rubin, Miami University

	Page
Introduction	264
Scope	264
Objectives of Solid-Waste Collection and Disposal Services	265
Current Practice	265
Recommended Indicators	266
Solid-Waste Collection	266
Input Indicators	266
Output Indicators	267
Outcome Indicators	267
Efficiency	270
Explanatory Information	271
Solid-Waste Disposal	271
Input Indicators	271
Output Indicators	271
Outcome Indicators	272
Efficiency	273
Explanatory Information	273
Street Sweeping	281
Input Indicators	281
Output Indicators	281
Outcome Indicators	281
Efficiency	281
Explanatory Information	284
Disaggregation	284
Comparison Information	284
Conclusions	286

INTRODUCTION

Local spending on solid-waste services totaled over $7.3 billion in 1987.[1] The cost trend for these services suggests that per capita costs for sanitation collection and disposal will continue to rise at a relatively rapid rate. Results from a survey conducted by the International City Management Association indicate that recent per capita costs of local government refuse departments are increasing at a higher rate than either police or fire protection.[2] Rising costs, environmental problems, and the considerable amount of media attention given to solid-waste collection and disposal all point to concern over solid-waste issues and the need for SEA indicators relating to these services.

Any discussion of reporting SEA indicators for solid-waste collection and disposal should consider the differences in the services offered by service providers. For example, some governments use a government public works department to collect solid waste, others contract with private companies, others provide a franchise to selected private companies, and some do not provide the service at all, but leave businesses or residents to make arrangements to dispose of the solid waste either by hauling it themselves or contracting with a disposal service. Some localities use a combination of these methods to provide sanitation services. In addition, services may vary in regard to the frequency and location of pickups, types of solid waste collected, and other characteristics affecting the quantity or quality of services.

SCOPE

The most common method of solid-waste disposal in the United States is open dump or landfill. At present, approximately 80 percent[3] of all solid waste is disposed of in landfill. The environmental drawbacks of landfill disposal and the lack of future landfill sights have focused much attention on alternative methods of disposal, such as incineration (waste-to-energy) and recycling. SEA indicators for each of

---

[1] U.S. Department of Commerce, Bureau of the Census, *Government Finances in 1987–1988*, GF-88-5 (Washington, DC, 1990).

[2] Gerald J. Hoetmer, "Police, Fire, and Refuse Collection, 1987," in *The Municipal Year Book, 1988* (Washington, DC: International City Management Association, 1988).

[3] U.S. Congress, Office of Technology Assessment. Cited in *City & State* (November 20/December 3, 1989).

these disposal methods are addressed in this chapter. Indicators for street-sweeping services are also covered. However, this chapter does not address SEA indicators for all functions that may be assigned to sanitation departments. For example, functions not covered by this chapter include illegal dumping, snow removal, weed control and tree trimming, wastewater and sewage, street repair, or sensitive issues surrounding hazardous waste (functions that are sometimes assigned to sanitation departments).

OBJECTIVES OF SOLID-WASTE COLLECTION AND DISPOSAL SERVICES

The general objective of sanitation collection and disposal services is to provide, in the most efficient and effective manner, for the collection and disposal of solid waste, leaving an environment that is aesthetically pleasing and free of the health hazards associated with solid waste. The convenience of the service to recipients should also be considered in the assessment of sanitation collection and disposal services.

CURRENT PRACTICE

The current state of reporting SEA measures related to solid-waste collection and disposal varies widely among governmental units. Although most governments report budget data and actual expenditure data, few other measures are disclosed with significant regularity. The most common measures besides budget and expenditure data relate to either inputs or outputs. Very few outcome and efficiency measures are regularly reported. The most common SEA measure disclosures are discussed below.

With regard to waste collection, the most common information disclosed besides budgeted and actual expenditures includes the number of collection vehicles, the amount of solid waste collected, and the number of customers served.

Although few SEA measures are regularly reported for landfills, some governments provide information on remaining capacity, tons of solid waste processed, and cost per ton of solid waste processed. Waste-to-energy facilities are still not very common and thus little information is known regarding relevant SEA measures. Limited data suggest that the only waste-to-energy SEA measures regularly provided concern operating capacity and amount of waste burned. Recycling—which is another method of solid-waste disposal, and one that is rising in popularity—also has few well-developed SEA measures. Most recycling SEA measures relate to the number of tons of recyclable waste collected or the number of households participating in the recycling programs.

Currently used SEA measures concerning street sweeping include number of vehicles, number of personnel, and miles of streets swept.

RECOMMENDED INDICATORS

The following recommendations concerning solid-waste indicators are based on a review of current literature, a review of governmental financial reports and budgets, and responses to a survey questionnaire sent to government officials. These recommendations are meant to provide a basis for developing a set of SEA indicators that will form a suitable beginning point for broad experimentation with external reporting and should not be perceived as being a complete or final set.

Within each service area, recommendations are organized by input indicators, output indicators, outcome indicators, efficiency (ratio of input to output) and cost-effectiveness (input to outcome) indicators, and explanatory information. Decision makers need to use a combination of indicators along with explanatory information to appropriately assess how well the objectives of the government have been met in providing the service.

Solid-Waste Collection

Exhibit 12-1 contains the recommended SEA indicators for solid-waste collection and the rationale for recommending each indicator.

Input Indicators

Recommended indicators of input for solid-waste collection include actual expenditures (current and constant dollar), the number of vehicles, and the number of personnel (including first-line supervisors) responsible for collection services. These indicators provide users with information regarding total inputs and a breakdown of inputs between capital and labor. If possible, this information would allow more thorough assessment of services if it could be disaggregated by the district and by the type of unit served (single- or multiple-residential, commercial).

Output Indicators

The number of customers served (by type) and the tons of solid waste collected are suggested as workload indicators. They provide a good indication of the volume of work performed. It is likely that they either are already computed and reported or will not require excessive additional costs to collect. Because of the wide variety of environmental conditions and service levels, these output indicators may be difficult to interpret and compare among jurisdictions. They can, however, be useful to discern trends over time within the same jurisdiction and, with other information, as a basis for comparison with similar districts.

Outcome Indicators

Outcome indicators recommended for consideration include percentage of missed collections, percentage of collections not completed on schedule, percentage of streets rated acceptably clean, and customer satisfaction as indicated by either customer survey or number of customer complaints. The first three indicators attempt to quantify the success of reaching service goals; the final indicator attempts to capture customer satisfaction with this effort.

Percentage of missed collections and percentage of collections not completed on schedule are relatively easy to calculate and interpret, and in many cases are already available. The information necessary to compute these indicators should be collected by an individual who is unrelated to the direct provision of the services to ensure greater confidence in the accuracy of the measures.

A weakness of missed collections and the percentage of collections not completed on schedule as indicators is their inability to address the objective of aesthetically pleasing or to measure whether the environment is free of health hazards. In addition, these indicators are not easily compared among jurisdictions having different inputs and factors impacting collection. For example, the percentage of missed or late collections may be affected by such things as the weather conditions, number of vehicles, average age of vehicles, or frequency of collections.

The percentage of streets (or alleys) rated acceptably clean, although not extensively used, is a good overall indicator relating to the general

Exhibit 12-1
Recommended SEA Indicators for Solid-Waste Collection*

	Indicator	Rationale for Selecting Indicator

Inputs:	Expenditures
	  Current dollar[a,b]
	  Constant dollar[a,b]
		Provides information on total resources input

	Number of personnel Number of vehicles[b]	Provides a breakdown of resources by labor and capital
Outputs:	Number of customers served[a,b] Tons of waste collected[a,b]	Provides a measure of workload; enables comparison over time; provides data for unit costs
Outcomes:	Percentage of scheduled collections missed[a,b] Percentage of scheduled collections not completed on schedule[a,b]	Attempts to quantify whether service goals were reached, data are readily available
	Percentage of streets rated acceptably clean[b]	Objective assessment of service goal
	Average customer satisfaction rating[a,b] Number of customer complaints	Assesses customer satisfaction with the service
Efficiency:	Cost per ton of solid waste collected[a,b] Cost per customer served[a,b]	Indicates efficiency; already widely used; will enable comparisons with other jurisdictions
	Tons of solid waste collected per employee[a,b]	Useful in assessing employee efficiency

Explanatory Information:

{ Frequency of collections[a,b]
Location of collections[a,b]
Composition of solid waste
Climatic conditions
Terrain
Average wages of employees
Type of agency(ies) providing the service
Type of contract with service provider (if relevant)
Average number of customers per collection route-mile[a]
Types of vehicle
Crew size on vehicle
Type of containers used by customers
Percentage of recyclable waste recycled
Transfer costs } Indicates level of convenience to customer; usually readily available

*The recommended indicators presented in this exhibit are illustrative. They are intended to serve as a starting point for use in the development of a comprehensive set of SEA indicators for external reporting of an entity's results of operation.

This exhibit does not provide illustrations of indicator disaggregation or of comparison data such as trends, targets, or other comparable entities. Both disaggregation and comparison data are important aspects of SEA reporting. They are discussed in the chapter and in the Overview.

[a]Designates an indicator for which it would be desirable to disaggregate by customer type (commercial, single-residential, multiple-residential).

[b]Designates an indicator that should be disaggregated by district.

objective of providing an aesthetically pleasing environment. An overall indicator such as this can also aid in the allocation of resources among districts; the reliability of this type of indicator appears to be considerable. (See the New York City reports, including "The Mayor's Management Report" and "The State of Municipal Services" by the Citizens' Budget Commission, for discussions of the use of street cleanliness ratings.) One problem, however, with using such ratings is that they appear to be relatively costly to introduce and maintain, and their interpretation may be more difficult than interpreting other indicators.

Indicators of customer satisfaction may be worthwhile measures (and thus may provide feedback to the government agency) of SEA, but they can be expensive. In obtaining an indicator of customer satisfaction via a survey, care is needed to ensure that the sample of customers is representative of the population and the information is elicited in such a way as to be useful and free from bias. Differences among customers' perceptions and expectations of the service may create difficulty with comparisons and interpretations of customer ratings. Using the number of customer complaints is a less expensive measure of satisfaction, but it may be less accurate as well.

Efficiency

Recommended indicators of input to output include cost per ton of solid waste collected and cost per customer served. Both measures are widely used and should be readily available. The cost per customer served should be disaggregated by the type of customer (single- or multiple-residential, commercial) and district. These indicators relate cost to quantity of output and are useful as efficiency indicators; however, they do not address the effectiveness of sanitation collection services. Although comparative data from other jurisdictions are available, the difference in inputs and environmental factors from jurisdiction to jurisdiction needs to be considered in the interpretation of comparative data.

Another potentially useful indicator is the number of tons of solid waste collected per employee. This indicator is useful in assessing employee efficiency and can be compared over time within the same organization. Comparisons between cities reporting this indicator would need to consider explanatory information such as the type of collection vehicle (for example, two-person or three-person vehicles), collection location, and geographical and other environmental characteristics.

Explanatory Information

Disclosing sufficient explanatory information is paramount to properly interpreting SEA information regarding any sanitation-related service, particularly if interjurisdiction comparisons are attempted. As mentioned before, the types of services offered, environmental factors, and departmental constraints will vary considerably among governments and will have a significant impact on SEA indicator results.

Factors such as frequency and location of collection, terrain, climate, customer waste composition, customer density (customers per route-mile), and type of collection containers can have a significant effect on collection services. These factors, therefore, should be disclosed to aid in interpretation of the SEA information. Additional information that should be disclosed includes the average wages and fringe benefits of employees (to aid in cost comparisons), the percentage of recyclable waste recycled, the average distance to disposal or transfer site, the transfer costs associated with collection, and the type of organization and contracting used for solid-waste collection. A useful categorization of the disclosed explanatory information is to divide the information into factors that can be controlled at some point by the government (for example, collection containers, contracts, wages) and factors that cannot be controlled (for example, climate and terrain).

Solid-Waste Disposal

Exhibit 12-2 illustrates the recommended indicators for solid-waste disposal and the rationale for selecting each indicator.

Input Indicators

Actual expenditure data (current and constant dollar), number of service personnel, and number of vehicles should be provided for each solid-waste disposal method. These indicators provide users with information regarding total resources and a breakdown of resources between labor and capital.

Output Indicators

Reporting the number of tons of solid waste processed (average daily and yearly) by a landfill in a period will provide the user with significant information regarding workload. This indicator is also relatively easy to compute and compare. When combined with information regarding the remaining capacity (in tons) of the landfill, this indicator allows users to assess the remaining useful life of the landfill. When comparing number of tons of solid waste processed from year to year or between disposal providers, the interpretation of the comparisons should take into consideration explanatory factors such as the availability of alternative disposal facilities and programs, as well as the constraints on operations of the particular facility being evaluated. For example, the location and environment surrounding the landfill, the type of solid waste disposed of in it, the required pollution controls, and the required landfill cover can have a significant impact on landfill operations and processing capacity.

The most easily computed and understood workload indicators for waste-to-energy facilities are the percentage of capacity utilized, the number of tons of solid waste processed (average daily and yearly), the percentage reduction in the weight and volume of the solid waste processed, and the number of tons of ash produced from processing.

For recycling, recommended output indicators include the number of tons of solid waste recycled, the percentage of recycling capacity utilized, and the number of customers participating in the recycling program. These indicators should be easy to calculate and will provide some indication of how the facility's capacity is being utilized.

Outcome Indicators

Regarding landfills, perhaps the most important outcome indicators are those that measure the impact of the landfill on the environment. These include the number of days that surface water, groundwater, and noxious gas standards have been violated by the operations of the landfill. An additional indicator concerning environmental impact is the amount of toxic material deposited in it. Although these indicators may appear costly, they should already be calculated in most cases. Another measure that indicates the impact of the landfill on the surrounding community is the percentage of independent inspections that detect odor, noise, or other problems regarding the operation of the landfill. Independent inspections may also be somewhat costly; however, they would likely be the most valid indicator of community problems created by the landfill. Other helpful indicators may include the number of vermin sightings, citizen complaints, and incidents of citizen injury or property damage (requiring expenditures) that arise from the landfill's operation. An additional outcome indicator that should be reported is the amount of revenue received from landfill customers.

Outcome indicators for waste-to-energy facilities should also concentrate on evaluating the environmental impact of the facility. They should include a measure of air-quality violations caused by the facility, a measure of the amount of toxic residue in the ash, and a measure of problems caused by smoke, dust, or ash generated by the facility. These measures could be ascertained from citizen complaints, independent inspections (done in conjunction with government environmental agencies), or both. These outcome measures are likely to be more costly than the workload indicators; however, they probably have already been computed or could easily be computed from existing collected data. An additional relevant outcome indicator is the amount of revenue generated by the waste-to-energy facility from both tipping fees (fees paid in order for a collection vehicle to dispose of its load) and sales of energy.

Outcome indicators for recycling should include the percentage of total waste recycled (disaggregated by type of material), the percentage of recyclable waste recycled, the percentage of eligible customers participating in the recycling program, and the revenue from recycled products. These indicators will provide information about the overall success of the program. Comparisons made among the programs of different jurisdictions should again consider the differences in inputs and the constraints on collecting, processing, and disposing of the material.

Efficiency

Landfills, waste-to-energy facilities, and recycling facilities should each calculate and report the average cost of processing each ton of waste. This indicator is useful for making cost-per-unit comparisons over time within the same jurisdiction and cost-per-unit comparisons among jurisdictions. The information used to calculate these indicators will already have been collected and reported as input and output indicators.

Explanatory Information

In order to better interpret SEA indicators, as well as to compare solid-waste services over time and among jurisdictions, there are a number of attributes surrounding the provision of the services that

Exhibit 12-2
Recommended SEA Indicators for Solid-Waste Disposal: Landfills*

	Indicator	Rationale for Selecting Indicator

Inputs:	Expenditures
	  Current dollar
	  Constant dollar
		Provides information on total resources input

	Number of personnel Number of vehicles	Provides a breakdown of resources by labor and capital
Outputs:	Actual tons processed during period Average daily tons processed Cubic yards of landfill used	Indicators of workload; useful for year-to-year comparisons; can be used to help assess remaining life of landfill
Outcomes:	Percentage of days that environmental standards are met (leachate, surface water, groundwater, noxious gas)	Assesses the impact the landfill has on the environment
	Tons of toxic material as percentage of total material deposited in landfill	Assesses damage to soil and surrounding environment
	Percentage of independent inspections detecting odor, debris, or noise problems	Provides information for evaluating the landfill's operations and how it affects the surrounding community

Number of citizen complaints

Dollar amount expended due to personal or property damage from landfill operations

Revenue received from landfill customers ⎫
⎬ Indicates economic contribution of landfill
Total operating revenue as a percentage of cost ⎭

Efficiency: Cost per ton of solid waste processed — Indicator of efficiency; useful for year-to-year comparisons

Explanatory Information:
Composition of disposed waste
Type of landfill liner
Type and amount of landfill cover
Type of pollution controls
Climatic conditions
Future use of landfill (number of capacity tons remaining)
Percentage of recyclable waste recycled
Capacity
    Daily processing (in tons)
    Number of years

---

*The recommended indicators presented in this exhibit are illustrative. They are intended to serve as a starting point for use in the development of a comprehensive set of SEA indicators for external reporting of an entity's results of operation.

This exhibit does not provide illustrations of indicator disaggregation or of comparison data such as trends, targets, or other comparable entities. Both disaggregation and comparison data are important aspects of SEA reporting. They are discussed in the chapter and in the Overview.

Exhibit 12-2 (continued)
Recommended SEA Indicators for Solid-Waste Disposal: Waste-to-Energy*

	Indicator	Rationale for Selecting Indicator

Inputs:	Expenditures
	  Current dollar
	  Constant dollar
		Provides information on total resources input

	Number of personnel Number of vehicles	Provides a breakdown of resources by labor and capital
Outputs:	Percentage of capacity utilized Actual tons processed during period	Measures the amount of work performed
	Average daily tons processed	Easily calculated and understood; information is normally available
	Percentage reduction in weight Percentage reduction in volume Tons of ash produced per year	Indication of byproduct produced
Outcomes:	Percentage of days that environmental standards concerning air quality are met	Measures impact on air quality
	Percentage of independent inspections detecting smoke, dust, or ash problems	Measures effect on air quality and environment
	Tons of toxic residue in ash	Measures impact on environment and level of concern for facility's byproduct

Revenue from customers (tippings) — Measures economic impact

Revenue from energy sales — Indicates waste-to-energy disposal services; and revenue from sales of energy produced by facility

Efficiency:

Cost per ton of solid waste processed
Percentage of operating costs recovered
} Indicator of efficiency; useful for year-to-year comparisons

Explanatory Information:
Method of ash disposal
Description of applicable environmental standards
Type of pollution controls
Climatic conditions
Water and fuel consumption
Percentage of recyclable waste recycled
Capacity
  Daily processing (in tons)
  Percentage of plant capacity used

---

*The recommended indicators presented in this exhibit are illustrative. They are intended to serve as a starting point for use in the development of a comprehensive set of SEA indicators for external reporting of an entity's results of operation.

This exhibit does not provide illustrations of indicator disaggregation or of comparison data such as trends, targets, or other comparable entities. Both disaggregation and comparison data are important aspects of SEA reporting. They are discussed in the chapter and in the Overview.

Exhibit 12-2 (continued)
Recommended SEA Indicators for Solid-Waste Disposal: Recycling*

	Indicator	Rationale for Selecting Indicator

Inputs:	Expenditures
	  Current dollar
	  Constant dollar
		Provides information on total resources input

	Number of personnel Number of vehicles	Provides a breakdown of resources by labor and capital
Outputs:	Tons of solid waste recycled[a] Percentage of recycling capacity utilized[a]	Indicators of workload; aid in determining how much of capacity is being utilized
	Number of program participants[a]	
Outcomes:	Percentage of total waste recycled[a] Percentage of recyclable waste recycled[a] Percentage of eligible customers participating[a] Revenue from recycled products	Provide information on how well the program is accomplishing its disposal objectives
Efficiency:	Cost per ton of solid waste recycled Cost per participant[a]	Indicators of efficiency; provide composite information on cost of output

Explanatory Information:
    Capacity
    Daily processing (in tons)
    Nature of recycling program
    Types of material recycled
    Waste composition[a]
    Separating techniques
    Service area population (in thousands)

*The recommended indicators presented in this exhibit are illustrative. They are intended to serve as a starting point for use in the development of a comprehensive set of SEA indicators for external reporting of an entity's results of operation.

This exhibit does not provide illustrations of indicator disaggregation or of comparison data such as trends, targets, or other comparable entities. Both disaggregation and comparison data are important aspects of SEA reporting. They are discussed in the chapter and in the Overview.

[a] Designates an indicator that should be disaggregated by district.

need to be disclosed. Again, these attributes can affect an indicator and, if not disclosed, can cause it to be misunderstood. These explanatory factors should be divided into those that can be controlled by the government (for example, pollution controls) and those over which the government has no control (for example, climate).

Landfills can vary significantly in construction, surrounding environment, and pollution controls. Thus, explanations about the important operating characteristics of the landfill should accompany the reported SEA indicators. These characteristics include the type of construction of the landfill (including liner and type of covering), the type of pollution controls installed in it, climatic conditions affecting the operation of the landfill, and future use once it has reached capacity. Another very significant piece of explanatory information is the capacity of the landfill (daily processing capacity expressed as number of tons per day as well as total remaining capacity in terms of years). Capacity is one of the most important issues relating to landfills since the lead time to construct a new landfill facility is substantial. Further, acceptable sites for landfills are becoming more difficult to locate. Users of SEA indicators will need to look to explanatory information to better understand the costs associated with the landfill operation, its overall performance, comparisons among different landfills, and the future uses of the landfill.

Governments with waste-to-energy facilities should provide explanatory information regarding the facilities' daily processing capacity. Incineration units will often vary substantially, and, given their relatively small numbers, comparisons among these units will be difficult. Thus, considering input information will help distinguish the capacity and level of use of the unit being evaluated.

Explanatory information for waste-to-energy facilities should also include the method of ash disposal. Ash, along with air quality, is the most significant environmental issue related to incineration. Additional explanatory information should be provided regarding environmental standards applicable to the facility and its recycling practices. Climatic conditions may need to be disclosed since they may have an effect on air pollution. Explanatory information regarding the water and fuel consumption of the facility may also be useful.

Specific explanatory data regarding recycling should include the capacity of the recycling facilities operated by the government (number of tons per day) and the separation techniques used for recycling. The explanatory section should also include details regarding the nature of the recycling program, including whether it is mandatory or voluntary and the types of material that are being recycled. Information on waste composition is also helpful, since it is reflected in the results of the recycling program.

Street Sweeping

Exhibit 12-3 contains recommended SEA indicators related to street cleaning.

Input Indicators

In addition to actual expenditures (current and constant dollar), reported input information should include the number of street-cleaning vehicles and operating personnel (including first-line supervisors) assigned to street-cleaning duties. These indicators provide information on the capacity of the department to provide the service.

Output Indicators

The recommended workload indicators for street sweeping are the percentage of street-miles that receive regular sweeping and the number of street-miles cleaned. Another useful indicator is the amount of refuse collected.

Outcome Indicators

An indicator measuring whether the streets are satisfactorily clean should be provided. Either a customer survey or an independent evaluation of street cleanliness would meet this objective. Both types of indicators are previously discussed in the solid-waste collection and disposal section of this chapter. Another outcome indicator used to evaluate street-cleaning services is the number or percentage of scheduled cleanings not completed.

Efficiency

The indicator most likely to be useful in assessing efficiency is the cost per mile of street cleaned. Another indicator that may be of interest is the cost per ton of refuse collected from street cleaning. These indicators, as do others already described, provide information on input-to-output ratios and cannot alone indicate the success of the street-cleaning service.

Exhibit 12-3
Recommended SEA Indicators for Street Sweeping*

	Indicator	Rationale for Selecting Indicator

Inputs:	Expenditures
	  Current dollar
	  Constant dollar
		Provide information on total resources input

	Number of personnel Number of vehicles	Provide a breakdown of resources by labor and capital
Outputs:	Number of street-miles cleaned[a]	Provides information on workload
	Percentage of street-miles receiving regular street sweeping[a] Tons of refuse collected[a]	
Outcomes:	Percentage of street sweepings not completed on schedule[a]	Provides information on the timeliness of cleanings
	Average customer satisfaction rating[a]	Indicates customer perception of the service
	Percentage of streets rated acceptably clean	Provides assessment of service objectives
Efficiency:	Cost per mile of street cleaned Cost per ton of refuse collected	Indicates efficiency; provides composite information relating input to output

Explanatory Information:

    Frequency of street cleanings per month[a]
    Miles of street requiring street cleaning
    Terrain
    Climatic conditions
    Vehicle traffic
    Pedestrian traffic
    Parking conditions
    Building density
    Use of sand during winter

*The recommended indicators presented in this exhibit are illustrative. They are intended to serve as a starting point for use in the development of a comprehensive set of SEA indicators for external reporting of an entity's results of operation.

This exhibit does not provide illustrations of indicator disaggregation or of comparison data such as trends, targets, or other comparable entities. Both disaggregation and comparison data are important aspects of SEA reporting. They are discussed in the chapter and in the Overview.

[a]Designates an indicator that should be disaggregated by district.

Explanatory Information

Environmental characteristics that may affect the amount of trash found on the streets as well as the ability to clean the streets should be disclosed. These include the terrain, climate, vehicle and pedestrian traffic conditions, parking regulations or restrictions along routes, types and density of buildings along streets, and the use of sand in streets for traction in the winter. Additional useful information regarding street cleaning includes the frequency of cleanings and the reliability of street-cleaning equipment (measured by vehicle downtime or a similar measure).

DISAGGREGATION

The informational value of many of the solid-waste collection and disposal indicators will be enhanced if they are presented both in aggregate for the whole city and by geographical district. This will be particularly helpful in large cities or cities with diverse neighborhoods. In addition, if a city offers collection services to single-family, multifamily, and commercial buildings, then disaggregation by customer type will also be informative.

COMPARISON INFORMATION

The most widely used and least expensive comparisons are those over time within the same jurisdiction. If data are collected and indicators calculated in a similar fashion from one time period to the next, users will be able to discern trends. If any changes are made in the way data are collected or indicators calculated, disclosures should be made and prior-period indicators should be recalculated and presented, if possible, using the current methods. Explanations for significant year-to-year changes in indicators will give users additional insights for assessing SEA.

For governments that disaggregate information by geographical district, useful comparisons are those made between districts. In addition, if a government uses more than one type of sanitation collection method or organization (for example, sanitation collection is provided by the public works department for specified locations in a city and by privately contracted companies for different, specified locations in the city), indicator comparisons among the different types of providers may be useful.

Another indicator comparison, already instituted by a number of governments, is the comparison of actual SEA to a predetermined objective. In some cases, such as the PAR Index used by New York City,[4] the predetermined objective is integrated into the indicator. Many cities— for example, Winston-Salem, North Carolina—disclose predetermined indicator objectives along with the actual indicator calculation for the period. The notion of a predetermined objective for the indicator appears to have considerable merit.

A final type of indicator comparison is between jurisdictions. The type of service provider used for comparative purposes will in most cases be another governmental unit. In some instances, a government may want to compare itself to private-sector service providers if the information is available and relevant. As mentioned previously, intergovernmental comparisons (as well as comparisons between governments and private-sector service providers) are currently limited, and many public officials have expressed concern over comparing indicators from different governments or service providers. The concern is based on the notion that the conditions under which the service is provided may vary considerably. In addition, the current situation, where data collection and indicator calculations are not standardized, may make comparisons difficult. Since comparisons among jurisdictions and service providers can be beneficial to users, the standardization of data collection and indicator preparation should be of high priority. Once indicators are prepared in a similar fashion, the problem of considering the differences in conditions under which the services are provided can be addressed. In order to make comparisons among jurisdictions, explanatory information (such as climate, terrain, and waste composition) will play an important role in interpreting the indicators and making proper conclusions. Also, indicators are likely to be only meaningful as a set, since no single indicator is likely to tell the whole story regarding service provision.

---

[4]PAR stands for Productivity Analysis Reporting system. In New York, PAR compares hours worked and tons of garbage collected against predetermined standards.

CONCLUSIONS

Elected and administrative city, county, and state officials; media; citizen groups; and businesses can derive significant benefit from an SEA report regarding solid-waste services. SEA reports will be helpful for assessing the efficiency and effectiveness of the agency providing the service. In addition, they may bring attention to deficiencies in service inputs or the process of providing solid-waste services. This latter point may be particularly crucial for solid-waste disposal given recent revelations regarding the dwindling capacity of landfills and the need for alternative solid-waste disposal facilities. Indicators also can aid government officials in setting service targets and can be used for assessing personnel productivity.

The recommended SEA measures, although experimental in nature, are believed to provide the type of information needed to assess the efficiency and effectiveness of solid-waste collection and disposal. Also, for effective comparisons among cities and among districts within a city, we encourage governments to use the recommended SEA measures and provide the necessary explanatory information for their interpretation.

Most experts in solid-waste disposal suggest that a coordinated effort utilizing landfills, waste-to-energy, and recycling is necessary to meet the solid-waste disposal problem. Therefore, SEA indicators relating to the provision of these services will be necessary to ascertain the effectiveness and efficiency of these services and aid in resource allocation decisions.

13. Water and Wastewater Treatment

Priscilla A. Burnaby, Bentley College

Susan H. Herhold, University of New Hampshire

	Page
Introduction	288
Background	289
Scope	290
Methodology	290
Goals and Objectives of Service Area	290
Current Practice	291
Indicators Considered and Recommended	292
Recommended SEA Drinking Water Indicators	292
Recommended SEA Wastewater Treatment Indicators	293
Recommended SEA Storm Drainage Indicators	301
Disaggregation	304
Comparison Information	304
Explanatory Data	305
Conclusions	307

INTRODUCTION

The water of this nation is one of its most important natural resources. The maintenance of the drinking water and wastewater infrastructure is imperative for Americans to continue the lifestyle to which they are accustomed. In fiscal year 1985–86, total state and local direct expenditures for water supply exceeded $16 billion and wastewater treatment expenditures surpassed $13 billion. Together, the two services constituted over 4 percent of total state and local direct expenditures.[1] As costs increase due to compliance with federal and state regulations, such as the 1986 Amendments to the Safe Drinking Water Act, measurement of service efforts and accomplishments (SEA) becomes increasingly important to help ensure that resources are used economically, efficiently, and effectively. Drinking water and wastewater treatment authorities have recognized this need for better monitoring through SEA measures due to increasing public awareness of drinking water management issues; defending ever-rising usage rates; and controlling maintenance costs of more complex systems.

When considering the reporting of SEA measures, it is important to examine the needs of information users. Groups that could use the data for evaluating SEA are: the general public, industry, management, governmental legislative and oversight bodies, and the financial community. This chapter considers SEA measurement for drinking water, wastewater treatment, and storm drainage services. One objective of this chapter is to examine the present state of the art of nonfinancial reporting for the three services. Another is to recommend nonfinancial indicators to be considered for reporting in financial statements and other external reports.

For a more-comprehensive report covering the three areas, please see the separately published full report on water and wastewater. That report has an extensive bibliography, details of the information gathered, and an example report for each area.

---

[1] U.S. Department of Commerce, Bureau of the Census, *Government Finances in 1985–86,* GF86, no. 5 (Washington, DC: U.S. GPO, November 1987).

BACKGROUND

Unlike some public services, drinking water and wastewater treatment operating functions are often supported only partially or not at all through general taxes. Frequently they are financed by user fees. Although the drinking water and wastewater treatment functions bear some resemblance to a business, they differ from a profit-seeking enterprise in a number of ways. Wastewater treatment facilities are partially financed through federal subsidies (construction grants), and in some cases cost recoveries are guaranteed. Both drinking water and wastewater treatment organizations are usually in a monopoly position. Utility rates are normally set to meet costs and bond covenant requirements. Although break-even efficiency may be a factor, profit-maximizing efficiency motivations through competition do not exist. Financial and nonfinancial SEA measures are essential to enable customers, voters, and taxpayers to evaluate levels of productivity, the quality of service, and the appropriateness of established rates.

Both drinking water and wastewater treatment services are subject to federal and state regulation. Drinking water is regulated by the Federal Safe Drinking Water Act. While the federal government sets requirements for drinking water quality, the job of enforcing the law is delegated to the states. The Environmental Protection Agency (EPA) requires that drinking water be tested for health related concerns (primary testing) and for aesthetic concerns such as color and odor (secondary testing).

Wastewater is subject to the stipulations of the Federal Water Pollution Control Act. States that meet various requirements are allowed to enforce federal pollution regulations. If a state does not regulate pollution, the federal government does. Wastewater treatment plants are characterized by their size and type of treatment, which in turn are affected by the requirements of the Federal Water Control Act. Size is determined by the treatment capacity in millions of gallons per day (mgd). The amount of waste removed from the effluent depends on the processes employed to treat the wastewater. The treatment categories are: primary treatment (40 percent to 50 percent removal of pollutants prior to discharge); secondary treatment (85 percent removal); and tertiary (advanced) treatment (greater than 85 percent removal).

SCOPE

The nation receives 71 percent of its drinking water from publicly owned drinking water systems, 16 percent from private wells, and 13 percent from privately owned companies. This study surveys predominately publicly owned drinking water systems. Similarly, as publicly owned wastewater treatment facilities account for 92 percent of the total national wastewater flow capacity, this study covers only publicly owned wastewater and storm drainage facilities.[2]

The work performed by the three services (drinking water, wastewater, and storm drainage) encompasses a wide range of tasks. For drinking water this research study covers supply, distribution, and treatment; for wastewater and storm drainage it covers wastewater collection and treatment.

METHODOLOGY

Annual reports, budgets, special reports of drinking water and wastewater treatment departments, and other sources of information were gathered and reviewed. Several city and town officials were interviewed about their reporting and information systems. In addition, questionnaires were mailed to users and providers of the three services asking for suggested indicators.

GOALS AND OBJECTIVES OF SERVICE AREA

While all providers of the three services share the same primary goals, different utilities or municipal departments will have varying specific objectives depending on their situations and needs. The main goals of a public drinking water supply system are to provide customers with an adequate supply of safe drinking water at appropriate pressures and minimum cost. The drinking water supply should at least meet the quality standards mandated by federal and state laws and be acceptable to the consumers (i.e., homeowners, companies, agricul-

---

[2]Apogee Research, Inc., draft report: "A Consolidated Performance Report on the Nation's Public Works" (Bethesda, MD, August 11, 1987), pp. 214–223.

ture, or industry). These broad goals encompass secondary goals such as the ability to provide water in the future, the maintenance and/or replacement of the current infrastructure, and the provision of adequate customer service.

The main goal of the wastewater treatment service is the protection of human health by the elimination of public nuisances in the most cost-effective manner. This goal implies conformance to quality standards mandated by state and federal laws. Other goals are the maintenance and improvement of the nation's environment and the aesthetic characteristics of a community's waterways. Secondary goals include preparing for future demands on the system due to growth, maintaining the quality of the current pipelines and facilities, and providing adequate service to customers.

The main goals of storm drainage services are to provide rapid removal of storm water from public streets and to service the system regularly to ensure that changes in paving or blocked inlets will not cause the system to be overloaded by light storms. The goals should be pursued in the most cost-effective manner.

CURRENT PRACTICE

This investigation found that much SEA information is available, although often not provided. The amount of information presented in cities' annual reports on the activities of the three services varies greatly, ranging from nothing to several pages. Information provided includes a description of the department, its objectives, and a detailed listing of performance and workload measures. It appears that more outcome workload indicators are presented than efficiency indicators. Larger cities, usually those with separate water and wastewater treatment boards or commissions, have separate annual reports for drinking water and wastewater treatment. Some reports contain only financial statements; others provide a considerable amount of detail such as a listing of repairs by job number, a discussion of plans for the future, and several pages of nonfinancial indicators.

Although the number of nonfinancial indicators presented varies greatly in budgets as well, there are many more listed in most budgets than in the annual reports. In some budgets the work to be performed is broken down by job and service area. In the more detailed budgets there are maps of the city streets by block with a listing of repairs, mains, and plans for the future.

SEA data is also found in investor-targeted publications prepared by securities firms. The following are examples of information items included in two such publications: geographic area served; source of water supply; number of employees; number of customers; breakdown of revenues by client type (residential, commercial, etc.); miles of mains; gallons of water produced; treatment capacity; storage capacity; utilization (average consumption); description of facilities; description of capital programs; and economic indicators for community served.[3]

INDICATORS CONSIDERED AND RECOMMENDED

The recommendations for specific indicators for the three services are in Exhibits 13-1, 13-2, and 13-3. These include both the indicators and the rationale for their inclusion in annual reports. Among the criteria used to select the indicators were usefulness, feasibility and cost, and verifiability.

Recommended SEA Drinking Water Indicators

The SEA indicators and explanatory data recommended for drinking water are listed in Exhibit 13-1. Not all indicators are discussed below.

Input indicators selected provide information about total cost of operations, cost per household or other unit served, miles of pipeline, and number of employee hours. These indicators will allow comparison of cost and employee hours with similar size communities. When evaluating the number of employees, it should be kept in mind that many utilities subcontract significant portions of their work.

The maintenance of the current infrastructure (pipeline, etc.) is an important aspect of providing an adequate supply of water. Output indicators include: number of miles of water lines maintained, repaired, and inspected; number of breaks and leaks repaired; and total gallons pumped. The effectiveness of the maintenance program can be measured in terms of indicators such as percentage of unaccounted-for-water. If the pipes are leaking, there will be a differential between the amount of water pumped and the amount metered.

---

[3]Edward D. Jones & Co., *1986 Water Utility Industry Review* (St. Louis, 1987); and Merrill Lynch, *Water & Sewer Revenue Bonds: A Survey of the Major Issuers,* Perspective #46 (New York, December 1987).

Indicators of outcomes of the effectiveness of the maintenance program include number of leaks, breaks, and customer complaints. The safety and quality of drinking water would be disclosed through the outcome indicator for the number of days federal and/or state regulations were not met. Although it might seem that cities should disclose the number of incidents of water-related illnesses, this indicator was not selected. Many water-related illnesses are never properly diagnosed and/or reported to public health officials, and these statistics are viewed as highly unreliable.[4] The outcome indicator, percentage of service interruptions cleared within a goal period of time, provides information on promptness of response to customer complaints. The goal time would be determined by the reporting government.

The efficiency indicators, cost per million gallons treated and pumped, would indicate the cost of providing the service and would allow for comparisons of similar communities.

Recommended SEA Wastewater Treatment Indicators

The SEA indicators and explanatory data recommended for wastewater treatment are listed in Exhibit 13-2. Not all indicators are discussed below.

Input indicators selected include total cost of operations, cost per capita of wastewater treated, miles of infrastructure (pipeline), and number of employee hours. These indicators should provide information about the costs of the system and allow comparisons with similar size systems.

Several of the output indicators considered are the number of miles of sewer pipe maintained, repaired, and inspected; miles of new sewer constructed; and number of new services connected. These indicators would provide information about what is being done to meet current and future needs.

The condition and safety of the infrastructure and the success of the maintenance program can be measured with outcome indicators, such as the number of main stoppages per 100 miles of sewer main, the number of complaints, number of days effluent exceeded federal and/or state standards, and infiltration and inflow ratio (called the I & I ratio). "Infiltration" is groundwater that gets into the wastewater treatment

---

[4]M. Goldfield, "Epidemiological Indicators for Transmission of Viruses by Water," in G. Berg et al. (eds.), *Viruses in Water* (Washington, DC: American Public Health Association, Inc., 1976).

Exhibit 13-1
Recommended SEA Indicators for Drinking Water*

Indicator	Rationale for Selecting Indicator
Inputs:	
Total cost of operations	To allow comparison of cost with other departments and water entities
Cost per household or type of service	
Miles of pipeline	To indicate the size of the operations for which the entity is responsible
Number and capacity of treatment plants	
Number of employee hours	To indicate time spent on providing the service
Outputs:	
Miles of water lines maintained, repaired, and inspected (by geographic area)	To indicate amount of infrastructure maintained
Feet of new line constructed	To indicate the increase in the infrastructure to meet the needs of industry and the community in general
Number of new services connected, by customer type	
Number of breaks, leaks, etc., repaired (by geographic area)	To indicate the level of work performed on existing system beyond general maintenance
Total gallons pumped, metered, and treated	To disclose how many gallons were pumped, metered, and treated

Percentage of total gallons pumped by user category:
- Residential
- Commercial
- Industrial
- Used by department
- Free to schools, etc.
- Unaccounted-for

} To disclose the client mix and the amount of unaccounted-for-water

Outcomes:

Percentage of total gallons pumped that were metered — To indicate how many of the gallons pumped were metered

Number of calls about interrupted service — To determine how well the infrastructure is maintained

Number of main breaks
Number of breaks, leaks, etc., per 100 miles of pipeline per year (by geographic area, by severity, and type of pipeline)

} To indicate the condition of the infrastructure water lines

Percentage of service interruptions cleared in goal period of time
Percentage of breaks, leaks, and so forth, repaired within x hours of notification

} To indicate the ability of the service group to clear service calls within goal time

*The recommended indicators presented in this exhibit are illustrative. They are intended to serve as a starting point for use in the development of a comprehensive set of SEA indicators for external reporting of an entity's results of operation.

This exhibit does not provide illustrations of indicator disaggregation or of comparison data such as trends, targets, or other comparable entities. Both disaggregation and comparison data are important aspects of SEA reporting. They are discussed in the chapter and in the Overview.

Exhibit 13-1 (continued)

Indicator	Rationale for Selecting Indicator
Outcomes (continued):	

Number of complaints:
   Water pressure
   Water taste
   Water odor
   Water color
   Other (by geographic area)
	To indicate the quality of the water and the service delivery from the customers' perspective

Number of days did not meet federal and/or state standards (Include reason for noncompliance.)
   Primary—health related
   Secondary—aesthetic
	Indication of quality of water

Efficiency:	

Cost per million gallons pumped:
   Treatment
   Distribution
   Containment
   Other
	To indicate the cost of providing the service and the breakdown of the cost

Explanatory:	
Type of source of water supply and distance to source	The cost of water is affected by the type (above or below ground) and distance to the source and the difficulty in obtaining and bringing the water to the treatment facility
Quality of water at intake and treatments	The quality of source water is an important determinant of treatment cost

Average daily demand (by month)	To indicate the current demands on the system and to show how demand has changed over time
Billing rates: 　Residential 　Commercial 　Industrial	To determine the different billing rates
Total revenue from customer billing/total cost	To determine how much the city is subsidizing the department
Population served Square miles served	To allow the reader to understand the size and demographics of the system
Maximum daily demand/system capacity	To indicate the level of excess capacity in the system
Treatment-plant capacity (by treatment plant)	To indicate the general flow capacity
Holding-tank capacity	To indicate storage capacity in the system
Debt service coverage ratio	To show ability to pay debt
Projected water demand in 5 years/current capacity	To indicate the need for future expansion and funding

Exhibit 13-2
Recommended SEA Indicators for Wastewater Treatment*

Indicator	Rationale for Selecting Indicator
Inputs:	
Total cost of operations Cost per capita of wastewater treated	To allow comparison of costs to other departments and other wastewater entities
Number and treatment capacity of plants and level of treatment provided by each Miles of infrastructure (pipeline)	To provide a picture of the size of operations for which the entity is responsible
Number of employee hours	To indicate time spent on providing the service
Outputs:	
Miles of sewer pipe maintained, repaired, and inspected (by geographic area) Percentage of miles maintained requiring repair Percentage of above repaired this year	To indicate amount of infrastructure maintained, repaired, and inspected
Miles of new sewer constructed Number of new services connected	To indicate the increase in the infrastructure to meet the needs of industry and the community in general
Number of service calls completed (by geographic area)	To indicate the level of work performed on existing system beyond general maintenance

Amount of wastewater treated (by treatment type) (BG):
 Primary treatment
 Secondary treatment
 Tertiary treatment
} To indicate the flow through the system and the relative volumes requiring various treatments

Dry tons of sludge produced — To indicate the volume of dry sludge produced

Outcomes:

Number of main stoppages per 100 miles of sewer main (by geographic area)
Average service response time (in hours)
} To determine how well the infrastructure is maintained

Number of complaints (by geographic area) — To indicate the quality of service, particularly from the customer's perspective

Number of days effluent exceeded federal and/or state standards—number of violations of discharge permit (Include reasons for noncompliance.)
Number of days influent exceeded treatment plant capacity
Number of gallons effluent that did not meet federal standards/total number of gallons processed through system
Quality of water in receiving body downstream from discharge
} To indicate the ability of treatment process to remove pollution adequately

---

*The recommended indicators presented in this exhibit are illustrative. They are intended to serve as a starting point for use in the development of a comprehensive set of SEA indicators for external reporting of an entity's results of operation.
This exhibit does not provide illustrations of indicator disaggregation or of comparison data such as trends, targets, or other comparable entities. Both disaggregation and comparison data are important aspects of SEA reporting. They are discussed in the chapter and in the Overview.

Exhibit 13-2 (continued)

Indicator	Rationale for Selecting Indicator
Outcomes (continued):	
Infiltration and inflow ratio	To indicate the condition of the infrastructure and the effectiveness of the maintenance program
Efficiency:	
Percentage of repairs completed within goal time	To indicate ability of the service group to clear calls within goal time
Wastewater treatment cost per 1,000 gallons treated (by treatment type): Primary treatment Secondary treatment Tertiary treatment Sludge disposal or use cost/ dry ton Revenue from sales of by-products less costs	To indicate the cost of providing the service and for comparison with other wastewater entities
Explanatory:	
Description of what the receiving body is used for	To provide information on the system's impact on the environment
Population served Square miles served	To allow the reader to understand the size and demographics of the system
Average daily flow/maximum daily treatment capacity (by treatment plant)	To indicate the extent of excess capacity
Debt service coverage ratio	To show ability to pay debt
Projected needed capacity in 5 years/current capacity	To indicate the need for future expansion and funding
Total revenues from customer billings/total operating costs and debt service	To determine how much the city is subsidizing the department

system through cracks and "inflow" is stormwater that gets into the system through manholes and cracks. Because it is expensive to perform wastewater treatment on stormwater and groundwater that does not need it, high levels of inflow and infiltration indicate inefficiency. The I & I ratio is constructed as the relationship between wet weather flow through the system and dry weather flow. Due to weather changes, four I & I ratios could be disclosed, one for each season. Also, trend data are important for proper analysis; an increasing ratio indicates that the pipes are deteriorating.

Efficiency measures include wastewater treatment cost per 1,000 gallons (by treatment), sludge disposal cost per dry ton, and the amount of revenues from sales of sludge by-products less related costs. This will provide information on how successfully management is dealing with the sludge disposal problem. Another element of efficiency is customer service. An indicator that could point to a prompt response for customers' complaints is percentage of repairs completed within a goal period of time.

Recommended SEA Storm Drainage Indicators

The SEA indicators and explanatory data selected for storm drainage are listed in Exhibit 13-3. Not all indicators are discussed below.

Information on total cost is needed to evaluate cost-effectiveness. This set of input indicators includes total cost of operations, maintenance costs, and number of employee hours. These could be disclosed in terms of both actual and budget costs for the current year and actual costs for the two previous years.

To report the work performed the following output indicators are suggested: number of miles of storm drains maintained, repaired, and inspected; feet of ditches and number of catch basins cleaned; feet of drainpipe installed; and number of emergency calls responded to.

To assess the level of performance in the area of storm water removal, the following three outcome indicators were selected: number of complaints received, reported incidents of flooding, and percentage of complaints resolved within a prespecified period of time. These indicators emphasize customer perceptions of the quality of service. To the average resident, inconvenience caused by standing water may be the most visible aspect of storm drainage. This would again be measured in terms of the volume of citizen complaints. The above three indicators should be provided for three years so that short-term trends could be

Exhibit 13-3
Recommended SEA Indicators for Storm Drainage*

Indicator	Rationale for Selecting Indicator
Inputs:	
Total cost of operations } Maintenance costs }	To indicate level of cost for comparisons to other years and other storm drainage entities
Number of employee hours	To indicate time spent on providing the service
Outputs:	
Miles of storm drains maintained, repaired, and inspected (by geographic area) } Miles of ditches and creeks cleaned as percentage of total ditches and creeks } Catch basins cleaned as percentage of total catch basins }	To indicate amount of storm drainage infrastructure maintained, repaired, and inspected
Miles of drainpipe installed	To indicate the increase in the infrastructure to meet the needs of the community
Number of emergency calls responded to (by geographic area)	To indicate the level of work performed on existing system beyond general maintenance
Outcomes:	
Number of complaints received (by geographic area) } Percentage of miles of storm drains scheduled for maintenance, repair, and inspection that was actually completed }	To indicate the quality of the service received, particularly from the customer's perspective

Indicator	Purpose
Number of incidents of reported flooding (by geographic area)	To indicate the adequacy of the system
Percentage of complaints resolved within goal time	To indicate the level of response to citizen complaints

Efficiency:

Storm drainage cost per capita }	To indicate the cost of providing the service
Cost per mile of storm drains maintained, repaired, and inspected }	

Explanatory:

Statement of whether the sanitary system is separate from the storm drainage system	To provide general information on the system
Square miles of service area	To indicate the size of the system
Inches of rainfall this year by month (comparison of long-term flow to average) }	To indicate the demands placed on the drainage system and the average excess on the wastewater system
Storms exceeding a "5-year storm" }	
Days that rain exceeded storm drainage treatment capacity }	

---

*The recommended indicators presented in this exhibit are illustrative. They are intended to serve as a starting point for use in the development of a comprehensive set of SEA indicators for external reporting of an entity's results of operation.

This exhibit does not provide illustrations of indicator disaggregation or of comparison data such as trends, targets, or other comparable entities. Both disaggregation and comparison data are important aspects of SEA reporting. They are discussed in the chapter and in the Overview.

discerned. More direct efficiency indicators are storm drainage cost per capita and cost per mile of storm drains maintained, repaired, and inspected.

DISAGGREGATION

Several SEA indicators for drinking water, wastewater treatment, and storm drainage can be meaningfully disaggregated. The disaggregation can be by facility, geographic location, and client type. Disaggregation by facility will be used with capacity indicators such as maximum daily treatment capacity/average daily flow. This will allow the reader to understand more clearly which facilities in the total system may be having capacity problems.

Geographic location is important because different areas served may have various conditions that affect service quality. For example, hilly areas often have more problems with water pressure than flat areas. Some parts of a city may have an older, less efficient infrastructure than other parts, which could lead to increased incidences of interrupted services and unaccounted-for water. SEA indicators disaggregated by neighborhood would be very useful in analyzing the relative service levels in different parts of a jurisdiction. Several indicators from each of the three service areas are recommended for disaggregation by geographic area. These are SEA indicators for level of maintenance of the system and indicators of customer satisfaction (such as number of complaints).

The most common form of disaggregation disclosure is by client type (i.e., residential, commercial, industrial, or governmental). Client mix is important since it has implications for types of services required and costs. For example, industrial customers typically use large volumes of drinking water, which may lead to lower costs per gallon. On the other hand, industrial use may result in higher wastewater treatment costs. It is recommended that two indicators, percentage of total gallons pumped and billing rates, be disaggregated by client type.

COMPARISON INFORMATION

A utility can compare its SEA to an internally developed norm (i.e., workload standard), an externally developed norm, or other utilities. The consensus of managers and users interviewed was that internally developed standards and trend analyses are often more valid than comparisons to other cities. Intercity comparisons are often difficult due to the great variation among cities. However, there is one set of national norms that clearly should be employed for comparisons and effectiveness evaluations: state and federal quality standards for drinking water and wastewater treatment. Another possible national norm would be unaccounted-for-water. It appears that 15 percent is considered to be an acceptable limit for loss of drinking water.[5]

Disclosure of other norms at this time is on an experimental basis. There is a considerable amount of distrust of norms, because local conditions, which often cannot be controlled, affect costs and performance measures. Typical uncontrollable conditions include proximity of the water source, natural composition of the soil, and amount and intensity of rainfall. Also, valid intercity comparisons and comparisons to external norms require that the SEA indicators be prepared using uniform methods and assumptions such as cost allocation techniques. Standard methods of determining most SEA indicators currently do not exist, at least not at the national level. Perhaps experimentation in this area will eventually yield standardized measures.

Although the disclosure of norms is currently in the experimental phase, it appears reasonable and feasible for all municipalities to disclose actual results versus internal standards and trend data.

EXPLANATORY DATA

To help the reader understand the special aspects of the systems, additional explanatory information is suggested. The information chosen for presentation in the explanatory data sections for the three services is listed with the reasons for selection in Exhibits 13-1, 13-2, and 13-3.

To evaluate cost-effectiveness, one needs to know about the system itself. The cost of drinking water varies depending on its source, the initial water quality, and the distance the water must be transported from the source.

---

[5]P. F. Kosak, "Let's Standardize the Accounting of Unaccounted-for-Water," presented at the ASCE Conference on Critical Water Issues and Computer Applications (Norfolk, VA, June 2, 1988).

Explanatory information such as population served, square miles served, and average daily demand (by month) can be used to determine size and population density. High population density tends to reduce per capita costs due to a reduction in the amount of pipeline needed per capita.

The adequacy of water supply can be evaluated by looking at demand and capacity data. Explanatory data such as maximum daily demand/system capacity and treatment and holding tank capacity are suggested. In localities that are experiencing growth, the ability to provide water in the future is an important issue. The explanatory information item, projected water demand in five years/current capacity, will help address this aspect of a water utility's SEA.

If future needs are substantial and will require construction of new facilities, the utility's ability to borrow is important. The level of debt service coverage and the rates charged are indicators of an entity's ability to pay for new construction with debt and future rate revenue. Debt service coverage is defined as net revenues divided by this year's principal and interest requirements. Here net revenues refers to gross revenues and income minus maintenance and operating expenses.[6] Current billing rates are viewed as an indicator of a utility's ability to raise rates in the future. If current rates are comparatively high, investors are concerned that future rate increases may be very difficult to obtain politically.

When considering the general area of costs and rates, it is important that the user understand what portion of the costs, if any, are paid for by general tax revenues. The decision to use general revenues or user charges is political, and has an impact on citizens and taxpayers. The percentage indicator, total revenue from customer billing/total operating costs, is intended to provide information on the level of general government subsidization.

To analyze the SEA of a wastewater treatment organization properly, it is necessary to understand the local conditions and the characteristics of the system. Some wastewater treatment collection systems are integrated with the storm drainage system. During periods of heavy rainfall, this arrangement reduces the ability of the utility to treat wastewater properly. When there is an unusually heavy rainfall, the system

---

[6]Moody's Public Finance Department, *1988 Medians: Selected Indicators of Municipal Performance* (New York: Moody's Investors Service, Inc., 1988).

can become overloaded and raw sewage will bypass the treatment plant and be discharged directly into the receiving body of water. Therefore, explanatory information should include a statement regarding the separation or lack of separation of the two systems.

If effluent is discharged into a body of water, information should be provided concerning the quality of the water in the receiving body of water and what the receiving water is used for (e.g., swimming, fishing). This information is necessary to assess the impact on the environment.

Utilities should disclose information on the capacity of their treatment plants and the relationship of maximum daily treatment capacity to average daily flow. In regions with high growth rates, it is important that utilities plan for future demands. Several of the indicators relate to future needs, such as projected needed capacity in five years/current capacity.

When evaluating a city's SEA in storm drainage for any particular year, it should be noted that many indicators will be affected by that year's weather conditions. In particular, the intensity of rainfall and the volume of snowmelt vary from year to year. The National Weather Service provides data on the frequency of storms of different levels of intensity for specific locations. For example, a "five-year storm" would be a storm of such intensity that it occurs on average only every five years in a certain location. Typically, a storm drainage system will be built to successfully handle a certain level of storm water. Although standing water and flooding may result after storms that exceed the system capacity, in many cases it is not cost-effective to enhance the system.

Indicators included as explanatory information are the number of inches of rainfall this year by month and the number of days the rainfall exceeded the storm drainage treatment capacity. The indicators would also include storms that exceed "five-year storms" as defined by the National Weather Service.

CONCLUSIONS

In deciding which indicators to recommend for presentation in financial statements, the results of the questionnaires, interviews, and an assessment of current practice were considered. Many of the budgets and financial statements reviewed already contain some of the SEA indicators and explanatory information being recommended for reporting.

For those entities that are not currently reporting the recommended SEA indicators and explanatory information, a reliable system would have to be developed to capture the data. For explanatory information about the system and future plans, the engineering department would have to be involved in the development of the disclosures.

In order to include information in the annual report, the cost versus benefit and feasibility of providing that information should be explored. As most providers of drinking water, wastewater treatment, and storm drainage services already maintain extensive workload and financial records, it does not appear that inclusion of the selected indicators will be too costly.